The Government of Scotland

There is nothing more difficult to execute, nor more dubious of success, nor more dangerous to administer than to introduce a new system of things; for he who introduces it has all those who profit from the old system as his enemies, and has only lukewarm allies in those who might profit from the new system.

Niccolò Machiavelli, The Prince, Chapter VI

'I dinna ken muckle about the law,' answered Mrs Howden; 'but I ken, when we had a king, and a chancellor, and parliament-men o' our ain, we could aye peeble them wi' stanes when they were na gude bairns. But naebody's nails can reach the length o' Lunnon.'

Sir Walter Scott, The Heart of Mid-Lothian

The Government of Scotland

Public Policy Making after Devolution

Michael Keating

Edinburgh University Press

© Michael Keating, 2005

Edinburgh University Press Ltd
22 George Square, Edinburgh

Typeset in Sabon by
Servis Filmsetting Ltd, Manchester and
printed and bound in Spain by
GraphyCems

A CIP record for this book is available from the British Library

ISBN 0 7486 1822 8 (paperback)

Contents

Expanded Contents List

Tables and Figures

Figures

Preface and Acknowledgements

In one sense, Scottish devolution is an old project, advancing a programme launched by William Ewart Gladstone in the 1880s to convert the United Kingdom into a union of self-governing nations. In another sense, it is quite new, part of a movement across Europe that is transforming the geography of power and changing the scale of government, below the state, above it and across it. There is a large literature on these transformations, in law, public administration, politics, sociology and geography, but there is as yet surprisingly little on what difference the devolution of power makes to public policy. Scottish devolution is still in its early stages and many aspects of the settlement have still to be tested, but we can already discern some distinct patterns of public policy. This book is a first attempt to identify these and to explore the patterns of public demand, interest-group politics, party politics and institutional factors that explain them.

The research was supported by Economic and Social Research Council (ESRC) grant number L219 25 2020 under the Devolution and Constitutional Change programme, in which it forms part of a larger project on devolution and public policy in the United Kingdom, in collaboration with Sean Loughlin. It also draws on a project, also with Sean Loughlin, on territorial policy communities and devolution, itself part of the Constitution Unit project on Nation and Region in the United Kingdom directed by Robert Hazel and funded by the Leverhulme Trust. The European University Institute helped with travel funding to return regularly to Scotland to undertake interviews and attend meetings.

Linda Stevenson assisted with the research in the first phase of the project and Paul Cairney in the second, both based in the Department of Politics and International Relations at the University of Aberdeen. Craig Robertson assisted in the study of finance, while David Heald and Alastair McLeod advised me on how to disentangle this complex issue. Nearly a hundred people in the public and private sectors were interviewed, most of them twice, in 2000–1 and in 2003–4, and although academic convention and political discretion prevent their being named, their contribution is acknowledged. I have benefited from numerous conversations with, and help from, colleagues and, at the risk of missing someone out, should mention John Adams, David Arter, Charlie Jeffery, Michael Dyer, Robina Goodlad, Gerry Hassan, Mark McAteer, Jim McCormick, David McCrone, Nicola McEwen, Grant Jordan, Neil McGarvey, John McLaren, Duncan Maclennan, David Newlands, Arthur Midwinter, James Mitchell, Richard Parry, Lindsay Paterson, Richard Rose, Mark Shucksmith, Fiona Spencer, Ivan Turok, Neil Walker and Alex Wright. Eve Hepburn corrected the proofs and compiled the index. Further inspiration was gained from seminars and meetings organised by the Institute for Public Policy Research, the ESRC, the Scottish Council Foundation, the Political Studies Association Territorial Politics Group, the Constitution Unit and the British Council.

Michael Keating
Florence, June 2004

CHAPTER ONE

Devolution, Politics and Policy Making

Scotland in the United Kingdom

It has always been difficult to explain Scotland to foreigners. Having protested that it is not part of England, we have to explain that it is a nation but without its own state, it fields its own international football team but has no seat at the United Nations or the European Union, and has its own Parliament but sends members to the UK Parliament. Then we need to say that the United Kingdom is not a federation, since there is no English Parliament, but that it is not a unitary state either. The UK's 'union-state' (Rokkan and Urwin 1983) is indeed an unusual constitutional animal, which is difficult to fit into the standard categories of political and legal analysis. It is the product of a haphazard evolution, lacking a codified written constitution or a founding moment such as other countries experienced as a result of revolution or independence. More than the typical nineteenth-century 'nation-state' found across much of Europe, the United Kingdom resembles an *ancien régime*, the sort of untidy mixed constitution that prevailed more widely before the rise of the consolidated, rational state whose archetype is France. The UK's most recent changes, in 1999, are part of this gradual mutation. Until recently, it was common in progressive circles to lament this ancient and unmodernised constitution and to blame it for the secular decline of the United Kingdom as an economic and political power. There may still be force in this critique, but ironically it may be precisely the failure of the UK to convert itself into a modern, uniform nation-state that gives it the flexibility to respond to the radically changed circumstances of governing in the twenty-first century. With only a little exaggeration, one might argue that the UK has gone straight from being a pre-modern to being a post-modern state without passing through the usual stage of constitutional modernity. So the United Kingdom, and Scotland in particular, have been attracting much international attention as the site of a fascinating experiment in new ways of governing in a complex and changing world.

Scotland's union with England was a gradual process initiated with the 1603 Union of the Crowns, by which the two nations shared a monarch but retained their own separate states. The Parliamentary Union of 1707 has been subject to much historical controversy, notably over the means used to achieve it, as have its implications. In form, both the English and Scottish parliaments were dissolved in favour of a new Parliament of Great Britain. In practice, the English members carried on as members of an expanded House of Commons (with a similar provision in the Lords), with all the prerogatives of the old English Parliament, including the claim to absolute sovereignty. This has long rankled with many Scots, who insist that the old Scottish Parliament made no such claims but was based on ideas of limited sovereignty that have recently had a strong revival in the context of European integration. The Union did, however, incorporate some guarantees for the independent institutions of Scottish civil society, including the established Church, the royal burghs and the law. A rather confusing clause stipulated, 'that the laws which concern public right, policy, and civil government may be made the same throughout the whole United Kingdom, but that no alteration be made in laws which concern private right, except for evident utility of the subjects within Scotland' (Article 18 of Treaty of Union). Together with the distinctive education system, these became the pillars of a distinct Scottish public sphere over the next two centuries. It might have been logical to secure this sphere through a federal system, providing a degree of Scottish legislative autonomy within the state. This was rejected at the time, but claims for the restoration of a Scottish Parliament within the United Kingdom have re-emerged periodically ever since.

Eighteenth-century Scotland was governed through a brokerage system in which London allowed local elites to distribute patronage in return for supplying a body of reliable MPs for the government of the day in a system of managed dependency (Fry 1987). In other European countries, these old arrangements were often swept away in the name of national unity and equality during the eighteenth and nineteenth centuries. Modern ideas of government required a reformed bureaucracy, the elimination of corruption and a working system of taxation, and these were usually national in scope. Mass education, military service and an expanding bureaucracy were instruments for national assimilation and integration.[1]

In the United Kingdom, however, such assimilationist phases were interspersed with assertions of territorial distinctiveness, so that each part of the Union came to have a slightly different relationship with the whole. The first modern challenge to assimilation came in the 1870s when a threat to include Scotland in a single British Education Act was repulsed and the Scotch (later Scottish) Education Department was established. In 1885, after complaints about the quality of administration in Scotland and insensitivity in London to Scottish concerns, a Secretary (later Secretary of State) for Scotland was appointed. Gradually the Scottish Office expanded in scope and responsibilities and in the 1930s the various boards that administered Scotland were folded into it, and it was moved from London to Edinburgh (Mitchell 2003). The Secretary of State grew in status and came to assume a general responsibility for looking after Scottish interests. Although national insurance was lost in 1948 (Parry 2003), additional responsibilities were acquired in local and regional planning and the National Health Service. In 1962 an additional department, the Scottish Development Department, reflected the commitment to planning and urban renewal. During the 1970s, new tasks were acquired in economic development, with the Scottish Economic Planning Department (1973) and the Scottish Development Agency (1975). During the 1980s and 1990s, further transfers included regional assistance and universities, so that the Scottish Office was in charge of most domestic administration for Scotland, with the notable exceptions of macro-economic policy, taxation and social security.

Around the Scottish Office there developed an array of interest groups, some of which were purely Scottish and others branches of wider UK groups. A distinct civil society was preserved around the professions of law and education, the Church and other social institutions. Scottish local government developed on its own lines, supervised by the Scottish Office with few links to Whitehall. Much domestic legislation was given a separate Scottish version, to fit into Scotland's institutional and legal frame. A Scottish Grand Committee, in permanent existence since 1907, debated Scottish matters and from 1948 was responsible for the second readings of Scottish bills, with the committee stage taken in one of two Scottish Standing Committees. Scottish MPs tended to concentrate on Scottish matters, including their own legislation and committees, with only a minority deciding to operate at the UK level, usually by a conscious career choice (Keating 1975a). Scotland's court system remained distinct, with no appeals beyond Scotland except for some civil cases, which could go to the House of Lords. Observers could easily conclude that Scotland possessed the classic elements of a political system, an executive (the Scottish Office), a judiciary, and even elements of a legislature (the Scottish committees of Parliament).

Indeed, James Kellas (1973, 1989) characterised twentieth-century Scotland as a political system along Eastonian lines, charged with the 'authoritative allocation of values'. He credited Scottish institutions with a high degree of autonomy, arguing that if we look at the practices of policy making, 'what is noteworthy is not the lack of autonomy for Scotland, but how much independence there is within a so-called "unitary" and homogeneous British constitutional framework' (Kellas 1989: 212). Lindsay Paterson (1994) argued in a slightly different way that Scotland, compared with other small European nations, enjoyed a fair degree of effective autonomy. Emphasising Scotland's distinct civil society, policy networks and organisations rather than the formal institutions of parliamentary government, he argued that Scotland's elites, in union with a powerful neighbour, played a weak hand with skill and succeeded in retaining within Scotland the most important domestic functions of the evolving state. Education was an area of particular autonomy, focused on the teaching profession and the bureaucracy of the Scottish Education Department. Expansion of the size and scope of government in the twentieth century occurred within a Scottish frame so that 'the UK welfare state which emerged between 1910 and 1950 took a distinctive form in Scotland to such an extent that Scotland can be described as having had a welfare state of its own' (Paterson 1994: 102). The key features of policy making were consensus and consultation, although Paterson and his Edinburgh colleagues discern an increasing centralisation in the 1980s and 1990s, as the Thatcher government broke the old union conventions of informal self-government and encroached on Scotland's autonomous civil society (Brown et al. 1996; Hearn 2000). Moore and Booth (1989) also credited the Scottish Office with a high degree of autonomy, and even discerned a Scottish pattern of corporatism whereby government and Scottish interest groups could make binding deals on policy matters.

Other observers take a different view and emphasise the centralised nature of the British state despite the existence of Scottish institutions. Mackintosh (1973) and Midwinter, Keating and Mitchell (1991) criticised Kellas's idea that there is a Scottish political system on the grounds that these were all institutions of the central state, albeit organised territorially rather than by function. The Secretary of State was an MP of the ruling party nominated to the Cabinet and removable by the Prime Minister, with no accountability in Scotland. Party control and parliamentary/Cabinet authority meant that it was Westminster that framed the political system, requiring all decisions to conform to UK policy. They recognise a strong Scottish dimension to politics but, in contrast to Kellas and Paterson, emphasise the centralising thrust of UK public policies well before the arrival of Thatcher in power. Scotland in the welfare state era continued to be a managed dependency, in which Scottish politicians recognised a trade-off between autonomy and access. Scotland could press for autonomy to run its own affairs, or it could seek a distinct niche within the British centralised state with easy access to the centre; it could not have both (Keating 1975a). Following the First World War, the Scottish left, which had strongly supported Scottish autonomy, joined in the access game, abandoning home rule in favour of a strong Scottish presence at Westminster and material benefits for their constituents (Keating and Bleiman 1979). Within the Scottish Office bureaucracy there was strong defence of Scottish particularism in education and some pioneering work in regional planning and development, but the civil service remained a British institution and ambitious officials usually spent a spell in a Whitehall department, especially the Treasury (Scott 2003). The main economic interest groups were organised on a UK-wide basis, so that the preconditions for corporatism – a strong and autonomous government and strong interest groups – were absent. Most political questions were decided at the UK level. At the Scottish level, government was as far as possible depoliticised and consensus organised around the themes of planning (understood as a rather technical exercise) and of lobbying for Scotland. This was a marked feature of the celebrated tenure of Tom Johnston as Secretary of State during the Second World War, and inherited by his successors. All the main actors in public life understood the rule, which is that they must come together in a common lobby where

Scottish material interests were at stake, but without sacrificing partisan loyalties shaped by the British political system. So, while there was definitely a Scottish political arena, with its own roles and expectations, it was not a political system, with an ability to decide on the main lines of policy.

The Secretary of State for Scotland and the Scottish Office had three roles (Keating 1976; Ross 1981; Keating and Midwinter 1983; Midwinter et al. 1991). The first was to manage those administrative matters which, for historic reasons, were organised separately in Scotland; the second was to try to make policy autonomously in Scotland; the third was to lobby for Scotland at the centre. Policy was made in one of two modes: policy autonomy, where the Scottish Office, after clearing matters in Cabinet (or, in practice, Cabinet committee) was allowed to proceed on its own; and policy leadership, where policy was made jointly between the Scottish Office and the relevant Whitehall departments. In this latter case, the Scottish Office maximised its impact where it could contribute to the policy as a whole, rather than simply arguing a Scottish line, and it brought some considerable knowledge in areas like planning and regional policy, but the overall thrust of policy was still common to Britain and often, by imitation, extended to Northern Ireland as well. Policy autonomy was confined to limited fields and circumstances (discussed below). For the most part, the Scottish Office's task was to put a Scottish face on UK policy, adapting it to Scottish law and institutions.

Scottish MPs also played a distinct role, most tending to keep within the Scottish political arena, except where matters of material interest to Scotland were at stake in the UK arena (Keating 1975a). This did not mean that they exercised power, merely that they jealously guarded their role as intermediaries. Richard Crossman captured the spirit in his diaries. As Secretary of State for Social Services, he was about to go into the debate on the Social Work (Scotland) Bill 1968 but:

> just as we were going in we realised that the Scots would suspect some poisonous English conspiracy . . . I quote this to show how deep is the separation which already exists between Scotland and England. Willie Ross (Secretary of State for Scotland) and his friends accuse the Scot Nats of separatism but what Willie Ross himself actually likes is to keep Scottish business entirely privy from English business. I am not sure that this system isn't one that gets the worst of both worlds, which is why I'm in favour of a Scottish Parliament. (Crossman 1977: 48)

A. L. Lowell, an American observer, wrote equally provocatively in the early twentieth century:

> Every Scotchman is an Englishman, but an Englishman is not a Scotchman. The Scotch regard themselves as an elect race, who are entitled to all the privileges of Englishmen and their own privileges besides. All English offices ought to be open to them, but Scotch posts are the natural heritage of the Scots. They take part freely in the debate on legislation affecting England alone, but in their opinion acts confined to Scotland ought to be, and in fact they are in the main, governed by the opinion of the Scotch members. (Lowell 1908: 138)

What Crossman and Lowell were observing was the Scots' preference to keep their political theatre to themselves, even when performing the same play as on the English stage (although the Social Work Act was a rare example of Scottish policy innovation). All Scottish bills were voted on the floor of the House of Commons by the government majority and even Scottish parliamentary committees had a built-in government majority, drafting in English members when necessary to achieve this. The exception was the Scottish Grand Committee, where the added English members were dropped in 1980. This was less a concession than it seemed since the Conservatives would have lacked a majority even without the maximum allowed number of added members, and following the change the Committee abandoned the practice of voting. Second Reading votes reverted instead to the whole House. When the Conservatives found themselves with too few MPs to provide a majority on the Scottish Standing Committee, they drafted back in the English members who had been dropped in the 1970s.

The twentieth century saw a tendency to consolidation of interest groups, notably of capital and labour, at the UK level, where the real power lay. The tripartite bargaining of the 1960s and 1970s, in which government, business and unions came together to agree on priorities, was essentially a UK process, with only a weak reflection at the Scottish level, and that within the framework of UK priorities and plans. Scotland suffered a loss of middle-class leadership, failing to retain its own bourgeoisie such as existed in other stateless nations and regions or was being created in Quebec (Maxwell 1990). Political parties were another centralising force, operating across Great Britain and taking much the same line everywhere. Party government meant much the same thing in Scotland as in England, and it was the majority party at Westminster that laid down the line, with the Opposition seeking less to limit the government than to take its place.

Policy, in consequence, was progressively centralised during the twentieth century. The welfare state, especially under the Labour Government of 1945, was a force for uniformity, all the main measures of which were applied across the United Kingdom, although some were administratively devolved to the Scottish Office (the National Health Service) while others were recentralised (national insurance). Nationalisation brought further London control and even allowed the Conservatives in the 1940s to play the Scottish card against centralising socialism (Hutchison 2001), with Churchill quipping that, for Scotland, nationalisation meant denationalisation. Keynesian economic management was also centralising, and regional policy from the 1960s was explicitly a matter of central direction and planning of the spatial economy. Treasury control of public expenditure often meant detailed control of policy. In a study of Cumbernauld new town in the 1950s, when the Scottish Office sought permission to go against government policy of not having any more new towns, the role of the Treasury was central and intrusive (Keating and Carter 1987). Indeed, the relevant Treasury file has been annotated in hand by the Chancellor (Rab Butler) himself.

The ethos of consensus and consultation, which Paterson (2000) sees as a distinctly Scottish feature, was the hallmark of British policy making in the 1950s and 1960s (Kavanagh 1987). This was also a period in which Scottish and English electoral results showed a degree of convergence (albeit short-lived). In these circumstances, the question of Scotland's ability to go its own way was hardly relevant. It is only meaningful when Scotland and England produce different political majorities or policy demands. It is notable that such periods (the late nineteenth century, 1922–4, 1970–4 and 1979–97) have always produced campaigns for home rule. The first such test in modern times was the Heath government of 1970, whose programme made little concession to Scottish majority opinion. All of its main measures, notably the Industrial Relations Act, were applied to Scotland. Another controversial policy, on housing finance, was brought in through separate Scottish and England/Wales acts, but the policy was Britain-wide and the stated intention was to move by 1974–5 to a standard system based on the English 'fair rents' principle (Keating 1975a). The Thatcher/Major governments in the 1980s and 1990s saw the same pattern of imposing a UK party line, despite the occasional signal coming out of

St Andrew's House that Scottish ministers were saving the nation from the worst excesses of neo-liberalism. Notwithstanding the rule that the Scottish Secretary now had complete discretion in distributing the block allocation generated by the Barnett formula (see Chapter 6), there were no big differences between England and Scotland. Indeed, an examination of the spending plans for 1985 showed that, not only did the Scottish Office follow the English functional allocations exactly, but it even used exactly the same form of words to justify them (Keating 1985). Local government finance controls were introduced in parallel across the United Kingdom, although occasionally Scotland was used to pioneer things. The poll tax, although it originated in Scotland, was always conceived as a UK-wide measure. Privatisation was applied in Scotland as in England, the only serious exception being water, where the Scottish lobby was able to mobilise massively, although not to get its own preferred option. Urban bus deregulation, a brain wave of Nicholas Ridley in England, was extended to Scotland apparently with no consultation with Scottish opinion at all. Council house sales were a UK policy, although the impact was different in the various parts of the realm, as was contracting out of public services. Urban policy followed very similar lines, albeit using Scottish instruments (Keating and Boyle 1986). The Scottish Development Agency represented a distinct Scottish institution, but the thrust of its policies, away from industrial investment, away from social objectives and towards area regeneration, followed the overall UK line as reflected in the English and Welsh urban development corporations. Its transformation into Scottish Enterprise was not the result of a considered debate in Scotland, but of a Thatcherite businessman catching the Prime Minister's ear.

Certainly, there was more Scottish autonomy in some fields than in others. In education there is a distinct policy community resting on a long tradition; there has never been a single UK or British department of education and Scottish education has some distinct structural features (McPherson and Raab 1988). Yet even here, where ideology or party policy was at stake, uniformity prevailed. Comprehensive education under the Labour governments of the 1960s and 1970s, and Conservative provisions allowing schools to opt out of local authority control in the 1990s, were UK-wide policies. They made less impact in Scotland because the social conditions were different, not because government did not pursue them. One distinct policy developed entirely within Scotland was the pioneering Social Work (Scotland) Act 1968, although the fact that thirty years later people were still citing it as evidence for Scottish autonomy suggests that not much worth noting had happened since. More important, perhaps, was the Scottish ability to mould its own institutional structures, albeit in pursuit of UK-wide policies. Local government has always been organised differently, and Scotland has its own range of ad hoc agencies in economic development, training and other fields. Thus, while the policy might be the same in Scotland and England, the mechanisms for delivery were different.

Issues of social conscience, traditionally decided by free votes in the House of Commons rather than on party lines, were sometimes treated separately in Scotland. In 1965, Leo Abse's attempt to legalise homosexual relations between consenting adults failed in the House of Commons, with Scottish MPs leaning two to one against while English and Welsh MPs were evenly divided. The message was not lost on the sponsors of reform and subsequent bills, from Humphrey Berkeley and again from Abse, applied only to England and Wales. With most Scottish MPs staying away, the reform passed and the Scottish law was not reformed until ten years later when a Labour government concluded that the discrepancy was an anomaly. The failure of Scottish divorce legislation to match the English reform in the 1960s and early 1970s was less a matter of Scottish autonomy than of the shortcomings of the Scottish legislative system. With only seventy-one Scottish MPs in the House, there were never enough to overcome filibustering and force closure, so allowing successive bills to be talked out. The fact that one of the filibusterers was a Scottish Conservative MP who had got his own divorce under the reformed English law by virtue of his London domicile was just one oddity. Another was the staunchly anti-home rule Labour MP who argued that the vote should be confined to Scottish members (Keating 1975a). Reform of the abortion law, on the other hand, was sponsored by a Scottish MP, David Steel, and applied on both sides of the border.

While we must be cautious about attributing much autonomy to Scotland before 1979, the advent of the Thatcher government did mark a difference. Government paid less respect to the autonomy of institutions of civil society, whether in Scotland, England or Wales. So the trades unions, the universities, the local government system and some of the professions were brought under tighter state regulation and control. It was to a large extent the existence of this independent civil society that made the unitary and centralised British constitution workable. Parliament may have insisted on its sovereign right to control everything, but there was an understanding that it would not actually try to do so. Nor did the efforts to roll back the state lead to an increase in Scottish autonomy. Privatisation in the 1980s and 1990s was not used to rebuild an indigenous Scottish business class on the lines undertaken by Quebec during the Quiet Revolution, but rather produced British and multinational conglomerates responding to the stock market. In the second place, Thatcherism broke the old pattern of political consensus and negotiation in favour of a partisan and unilateral approach to policy making. This produced across England, Scotland and Wales a new movement for constitutional reform, for a formal division of powers to replace the old understandings. The fact that no government between 1979 and 1997 had actually won the election in Scotland added another element of grievance and revived demands for home rule, which had been steadily rising since the 1960s.

To talk of Scotland's autonomy from Westminster before 1999 thus risks confusing administrative decentralisation with political devolution. It also risks confusing the autonomy that some elites may have exercised due to their position within Scottish civil society with the autonomy of the nation as a whole. One effect, indeed, of the guarantees to various Scottish institutions under the Union settlement, together with the growth of the bureaucratic state, was to privilege certain actors within Scotland. So certain Scottish elites, where they had carved out their own niche, or could get the go-ahead from London, could often act autonomously from Scottish society as a whole. This may have been normal in pre-democratic eras such as the oligarchical polity of the eighteenth and nineteenth centuries. As Bulpitt (1983) has demonstrated, the British state generally was content to limit itself to the 'high politics' of diplomacy, empire and taxation, leaving day-to-day management of 'low politics' in the hands of local worthies. This kind of elite autonomy, however, came under challenge from rising democracy from the late nineteenth century. Territorial autonomy in a democratic society implies local democratic control and accountability, but in Scotland ultimate accountability was to the Westminster Parliament, where Scotland held less than 12 per cent of the seats. Administrative devolution from the 1880s, and especially from the 1930s, left Scotland in the hands of a more enlightened elite than the old one, but an elite nevertheless. Tom Johnston's celebrated wartime administration, often cited as the high point of the Scottish Office, illustrates the point well, since Johnston had moved from his early home-rule radicalism to a belief in consensus and government by experts. Governments in Scotland have had a remarkably free hand, unconstrained even by the weak form of parliamentary control that exists in English matters.

Scottish civil servants were subject to less ministerial control, since the ministers had such broad spans of responsibility and were in London for much of the week. This explains, for example, the ease, unparalleled in Europe, with which the Scottish Office was able to redraw the local government map twice in the space of just over twenty years. The Wheatley reforms, themselves inspired by civil servants in the Scottish Development Department, were put through with remarkably little change, in stark contrast to the contemporary reforms in England (Keating 1975b). The result was perhaps a more rational system than that which prevailed south of the border, but was the result of a more depoliticised process. In 1996, inspired this time by partisan considerations, the Scottish Office was able to scrap the regions and design a system giving Scotland the largest average population per basic unit of local government of any developed country. Again it was the very weakness of local political input to the process that permitted this. Scottish policy and professional communities in law and, arguably, in education, enjoyed a degree of autonomy within the limits of overall UK policy from broader social and political influences. This autonomy of Scottish elites was such that many of those who enjoyed a privileged position within the Scottish arena were opposed to home rule in the 1970s; the teachers' unions were unusual in being both part of a Scottish policy community and supporting home rule. Those Scottish MPs who were most absorbed in Scottish matters also tended to be most opposed to home rule (Keating 1975a).

Governments did not, then, have to respond to Scottish public opinion and, paradoxically, the less support they had in Scotland the freer the hand they had in making policy for it, as was shown in the early 1970s and between 1979 and 1997. The House of Commons, weak though it is, does provide some constraint on governments, especially where the government's own backbenchers are restive. The Heath, Thatcher and Major governments had too few Scottish backbenchers to worry about this, and there was little danger of English MPs risking the displeasure of the Whips for a mere Scottish matter. Nor has the House of Lords shown much interest in curtailing the application of UK measures in Scotland. The Conservative presence in Scottish local government, which first appeared only in the 1960s, had almost faded away thirty years later, removing another restraining influence. As a result, governments had such a free hand that we might even say that on some matters Scotland conformed more closely to the 'UK line' than did England. The poll tax was tried out first in Scotland and, despite the mass protests it aroused there, it was opposition in England that forced its abandonment.

By the late 1990s, the disjuncture between Scottish political demands and government policy was so great as to power the biggest and most sustained of the many home rule movements since the 1880s. The Campaign for a Scottish Parliament (originally Assembly), launched in the wake of the failed devolution proposals of 1979, gradually gained support and in the late 1980s launched a new Scottish Constitutional Convention. Supported by the Labour and Liberal Democrat parties, the Convention mobilised a broad swathe of Scottish civil society, including local government, trades unions, churches, small businesses and the voluntary sector behind a demand for reforms in the government of Scotland. This had two linked dimensions, one internal and the other external. Power was to be shifted within Scotland, away from the old elites who had a secure niche in the centralised state. Scottish government was to be democratised and made more accountable and participative as part of a 'new politics'. At the same time, power was to move from London to Scotland. The meaning of new politics, however, was not always clearly spelt out.

Doing it Differently: New Politics in Scotland

Home rule for Scotland had been promoted for over a century as a means of decentralising the British state and making policy responsive to Scottish interests. By the 1990s, however, there was a widespread disillusionment with politics and politicians going well beyond the issue of London government; indeed, it is a worldwide phenomenon. There was a fear that if devolution simply reproduced the old Westminster system at a more intimate level it would do little to assuage these democratic discontents.

Westminster government is based on the principle of parliamentary sovereignty and supremacy, with no restraint on the powers of Parliament. Since the electoral system normally gives a single party an absolute majority of seats, this translates into strong single-party government. The counterbalance is provided by an officially recognised Opposition, or alternative government. Parties compete for the favour of the electors and alternate in power. Once in power they carry out their programmes so that governments govern and oppositions oppose. Adversary politics is epitomised by the design of the parliamentary chamber, with the two sides confronting each other across the gangway, and party discipline is strictly applied to front and backbenchers alike. Reformers have criticised this as unduly adversarial and partisan, with all questions reduced to simplified opposition between parties based on outdated social divisions. At times it may seem that, as the parties themselves become less distinguishable for their policies, they have to exaggerate their partisan differences. Another feature of the Westminster system is the existence of a permanent civil service, responsible for advising ministers and for carrying out policy. While a politically neutral civil service is an important foundation for democracy, critics claim that its very permanence gives it undue influence, allowing civil servants to steer successive governments back to the same policy lines.

Of course, this does not tell us all there is to know about policy making in Britain. Since at least the 1960s, students of the policy process have emphasised the importance of interest groups and outside pressures on governments of whatever persuasion. Pluralists play down the role of party politics and stress the competition among groups to bend the ear of government or to subject it to economic or political pressure. In some versions of pluralism, government almost disappears altogether or becomes a mere arena in which interest groups fight it out. For some, this is healthy since there is competition and if any one group gets too powerful the others will team up to bring it back to size. Others point out that not all groups are even potentially equal and that a pluralistic system will always benefit the rich and the strong. Government is needed to look after the weak and to impose some overall coherence on public policy.

During the 1970s it was observed that relations between governments and interest groups were changing again, in response to the problems of governing complex modern social and economic systems. Rather than being buffeted by competing interest groups, governments were incorporating them into the policy process on a selective basis, to the mutual benefit of both. This is the basis for the 'corporatist' view of the policy process. While the Westminster model implies strong government and weak groups, and the pluralists the reverse, corporatism sees strong government and strong groups working together. In 1970s Britain this often took the form of 'tripartitism', with government, organised business and the trades unions negotiating over major items of economic and social policy, bypassing parties and Parliament. By the late 1980s this form of policy making had become more difficult, given the internationalisation of business and the weakness of trades unions, together with an ideological shift to neo-liberalism. In the 1990s, however, corporatism made a rather surprising comeback, albeit in modified form, as concerted action, by which the social partners could act together to adapt the national economy to global conditions. This was especially noticeable in some of the smaller European states, including Ireland. Devolved and regional governments have looked at these examples and explored their own scope for such strategies, to adapt the regional economy to global and European challenges (Keating et al. 2003).

In the run-up to devolution, much was made of the opportunity for a 'new politics', breaking with the old British policy process, although the term was never clearly defined, except perhaps negatively: as the opposite of the Westminster model, interest-group politics and closed corporatism (Jordan and Stevenson 2000; McGarvey 2001; Mitchell 2001). It can be traced to the roots of the home rule campaign of the 1980s and 1990s in civil society, embodied notably in the Scottish Constitutional Convention. Although this included the Labour and Liberal Democrat parties and could approve nothing without their agreement, it also encompassed a wide range of groups including the trades unions, the churches, local government, voluntary groups and part of the small-business community. In the absence of a Scottish Parliament and given the weakness of Scottish representation at Westminster, the role of 'civic Scotland', as this network of groups and interests came to be known, was enhanced and its members increasingly politicised. This resonated in a society in which, as in other western countries, there was an increasing disillusionment with, and cynicism about, politicians and political parties. There was a new vogue for more participative types of policy making and a new relationship between governors and governed. Academic analysts were charting new modes of policy making and representation, including the idea of 'governance', in which policy is not made by government but negotiated within society; of social capital, referring to the denseness and activity of citizen organisations; and civil society, seen as a self-regulating public domain somehow apart from the state. These fed into the debate in Scotland as elsewhere. Many of these ideas were consistent with New Labour ideology, the search for a middle ground and a break with the class politics of the past (Mitchell 2000).

The result was a demand that home rule should not merely substitute a Scottish Parliament for the Westminster one, but should provide a framework for a broader and more radical reform of government (Brown 2000). This ferment of ideas can be distilled into four key elements. First, politics should be non-partisan, with cooperation across party lines. Second, politics should be consensual in substance, guided by a search for agreement rather than highlighting differences; and should be non-confrontational in style. Third, politics should be more participative, open to the representatives of Scottish civil society and not just the political class. Fourth, politics should be more inclusive, bringing in previously unheard voices. These were laudable aims, but they embody a number of confusions and even contradictions. Advocates of non-partisanship and consensus were often impressed by the cross-party work of the Constitutional Convention during the 1997 referendum campaign and assumed that this could be carried over into day-to-day politics.

In fact, there is a big difference between agreeing on the mechanisms by which we are governed, which is important in any society, and agreeing on the substance of policy, which is often neither possible nor desirable. There was something of an illusory consensus in Scottish politics in the 1990s, given the overwhelming opposition to the Conservative government. With it out of the way, other political divisions would certainly emerge. It was inevitable that, once the Parliament was established, the parties and professional political class would move in, and the representatives of civil society would take a different role. Parties, indeed, are one of the main mechanisms by which parliamentary democracy works, providing choices, debate and accountability. Consensus politics may be a fine ideal for some issues, but it may also stifle pluralism, dissensus and debate. The term civil society has a positive ring to it, conjuring up images of responsible citizenship and serious debate about the public interest. Yet if we call this by another name and talk about interest groups or, even more pejoratively, special interests, a different image of selfishness and struggle for advantage emerges. Nor does more participation necessarily entail greater inclusiveness. It is well known that some groups have more skills and resources and are better able to take advantage of new opportunities. It may be the role of government to restrain them in the interests of the poor and disadvantaged. Paterson (2002a), for example, contrasts the civic Scotland of middle-class people belonging to established groups and who trust institutions, with a politically disadvantaged group who favour more radical change and look to political means, including a stronger Scottish Parliament, to achieve it. Further confusion is added when advocates of new politics, consensus and participation call at the same time for radical policy initiatives. If radicalism is anything more than a rhetorical flourish, this calls for strong leadership, such as is provided by political parties, and a willingness to face down opposition and interests.

So any assessment of the degree to which Scottish policy making incorporates the principles of the new politics must recognise the distinct and even incompatible elements within the slogan (Mitchell 2000). Several of the features of the new politics were incorporated into the settlement, and will be discussed in subsequent chapters. Diversity was increased in the Parliament and the role of the big parties limited by proportional representation. This ensures that government in Scotland will nearly always be by coalition and that the Executive will not always be able to prevail. The main parties agreed to promote gender balance, although only Labour has a firm commitment to equal numbers of men and women members. The shape of the Parliament is a hemicycle, on continental lines, rather than the Westminster model in which government and opposition face each other across the gangway. There is a commitment to more consultation on policy development. The Consultative Steering Group (1999), appointed to consider the procedures of the Parliament, emphasised the principles of sharing of power between the people of Scotland, the legislators and the Executive; accountability of the executive to the Parliament and of the Parliament to the people; access and participation; and equal opportunities. Committees in the Parliament were to be more powerful than at Westminster and less partisan. A Civic Forum was set up to represent the interests of civil society. Like much of the preparatory work on devolution, these innovations focused on the Parliament and mechanisms for representation. Rather less attention was given to the role of the civil service or the political parties, although these have proved to be key elements in the working of the new system. So we have a combination of old and new elements, whose effects need to be examined through the workings of the policy process.

Multilevel Policy Making

The second dimension of change concerns the relationship of Scotland to the UK. Although a Scottish level of politics existed before 1999, the elected Scottish Parliament, with a responsible Executive in place of the Scottish Office, introduces a previously absent level of political power. Some matters remain the exclusive competence of the central government in London, while others are devolved to an autonomous Scottish level. Although the Scottish model is unusual in several respects, there are valuable insights to be gained from other systems of government where two or more levels share policy-making powers. An obvious point of comparison is federal systems, even if the United Kingdom is not yet a full federation. One classical version of federalism is the 'layer-cake' model. Here there are two levels of government, each with clearly defined powers and making policy independently within its own field. Perhaps the early days of the United States approximated to this ideal, when government was simple and its tasks limited. In a modern state, however, government's role has grown in size and complexity and the functions of the two levels always seem to impinge on each other. The lower level may be responsible for education, but the federal government, responsible for national economic growth, will have a strong interest here. Transport systems need to be planned and managed over the whole territory. Law and order and criminal justice must be enforced in a comparable manner, to prevent criminals fleeing across internal borders. Business regulations cannot be radically different, lest firms simply relocate or play off one jurisdiction against another to get the best deal. Newer policy areas are particularly difficult to fit into the old categories. Environmental problems know no boundaries and need to be addressed at higher levels, be this by central state control, cooperation among governments, or international regulation. The rise of the welfare state has led to greater uniformity in policy making in federal systems, given the existence of a national labour market and the mobility of labour. Citizens in a modern democracy are able to make comparisons between one part of the state and another and will not tolerate lower levels of provision than their neighbours. Interest groups and professional associations and networks tend to operate across the whole of the federation, influencing governments at all levels.

So the old layer-cake model of federalism has long given way to more complex visions in which levels are not so much independent as interdependent. In cooperative federalism the powers of the two levels are complementary and exercised together. Germany does not divide functions between the two levels but shares them. The federal government concentrates on broad policy making and legislation, while the Länder are responsible for implementation. Even in systems with a clearer division of functions, there are large areas of policy where both levels of government are involved, putting a premium on negotiation and agreement. Policy 'communities' or 'networks' of experts, professionals and interest groups form within the various policy fields, often sharing the same ideas and values but ignoring jurisdictional boundaries. The horizontal division of policy making by territory thus gives way to a vertical division by function. This gives us the metaphor of the 'picket-fence', which portrays functional policy communities, operating across the whole of the federation, as more important than the territorial divisions within it. So educational administrators, or health policy makers, or social workers, together with the related interest groups, have more in common with their professional counterparts at other levels of government than with other professionals at their own level. This is an important insight, and we will find that there are such vertical policy communities in the United Kingdom, operating across the Westminster and devolved levels. Yet even this model has been criticised as too simple and has given way to new metaphors including the exotic culinary image of the 'marble cake', an American delicacy in which the various layers, instead of being separated horizontally, are swirled together in random patterns. The trick then is to discern who is making policy where and in what circumstances, a task that requires a great deal more than merely reading off a list of formal competences assigned to each level of government.

Devolution, a distinctly British term coined in the nineteenth century, bears some resemblance to federalism and to systems of regional government in other European countries, but with three distinct features. First, powers and authority are transferred to the nations and regions, but without affecting the sovereignty of the Westminster Parliament. Westminster retains the constituent power and could even suspend or abolish the devolved institutions (as happened in Northern Ireland in 1972, 2000 and 2002). As in federal systems, there are broadly three blocks of competences: those devolved to Scotland, those reserved to the centre and those shared between the two. Yet, unlike in a true federation, the constitutional

limits apply only to Scotland and not to Westminster, which retains the right to legislate even within devolved spheres, although
under the Sewel convention (see Chapter 4) this should happen only
with the consent of the Scottish Parliament. Second, the UK settlement is highly asymmetrical. Westminster continues to rule directly
in England and proposals for regional government there fall far
short of creating units comparable with Scotland. This creates a
structural imbalance since Westminster, doubling as the UK and
English government, will be the predominant partner. Third, devolution builds on an existing system of administrative decentralisation and traces of the old system are apparent in institutions, in the
practice of politics, especially in the political parties, and in the
mind-set of the bureaucracy.

The Scotland Act of 1998 provides for a Scottish Parliament with
general competence over all matters not expressly reserved to
Westminster. This is in contrast to the failed Scotland Act of 1978,
which sought to spell out in great detail the powers to be devolved,
but it is consistent with the form adopted for the Parliament of
Northern Ireland between 1921 and 1972. Matters reserved to
Westminster can be grouped under four headings. Defence, foreign
affairs and national security are classic state functions, which even in
federal systems are reserved to the centre. Second is a series of economic provisions designed to protect the freedom of trade and the
single UK market and provide a level playing field for business
through the United Kingdom. These include reservations on company
law, copyright and intellectual property, competition policy and
industrial relations. Third, there are provisions to secure the national
welfare state, especially where cash payments are concerned. These
are intended to maintain equal standards of social justice, spread the
burden of welfare payments, and prevent people moving around in
search of better benefits. Finally, there is a residual category of competences that might have been devolved but, as a result of political
and bureaucratic bargaining, were not. These include broadcasting
regulation, regulation of certain professions traditionally managed at
the British or UK level, railways (since partially devolved) and the law
on abortion and embryology.

A notable feature of the Scottish settlement is the reservation of
nearly all taxes. The Scottish Parliament can raise or lower the basic
rate of income tax up to three pence in the pound, but this would
yield a very small amount. It also has control over local government
taxation, including the rules for council tax, and itself sets and col-

lects the Unified Business Rate (UBR), which is then distributed to local government. It is clear, however, that any attempt to use local taxation or the UBR to raise money for the Scottish Parliament or Executive themselves, as opposed to local councils, would run foul of the law.

The devolved powers are not enumerated in the Act, but in practice come under the following broad headings: health; education and training; local government; social work; housing; planning; economic development; home affairs, justice and most criminal law; the environment; agriculture, fisheries and forestry; sport and the arts. Some of these areas, like education, are fully devolved, while in others, like economic development, parts are reserved.

Several important functions, notably in agriculture and fisheries and environmental policy, are also shared with the European Union, creating further complexity. So we have, as in most federal and devolved systems, a reserved area, a devolved area and one in which powers are shared. In addition, the interdependence among areas that are apparently clearly placed at one level or another creates further instances of effectively shared authority. This is particularly noticeable in welfare state matters where, generally speaking, Westminster has reserved cash payments while personal social services, training and housing are devolved. This has caused some problems in the treatment of housing benefit, and in the Scottish proposals for financing long-term care for the elderly when the Scottish Executive tried to claim back from the Department of Work and Pensions funds that would be saved by its new scheme. There are interdependencies between the unemployment benefits scheme (reserved) and labour market policy (partly devolved), which have been highlighted by the New Deal programme. These might produce policy distortions or perverse incentives – a cynic might argue that there is no incentive for the devolved governments to spend money getting people into work since that would serve to reduce total welfare payments into their territories. There are also functional overlaps in energy matters, with Whitehall responsible for policy but the Scottish Executive retaining power to approve the construction of new power stations on planning and environmental grounds. This could cause tensions in the event of a decision to develop more nuclear power in Scotland. Transport is divided, with roads devolved but railways and air transport reserved, but adjustments have been made to transfer rail subsidies to Scotland and in practice the Scottish Executive has been involved in decisions on rail priorities

Table 1.1   Devolved and Reserved matters

Reserved matters

The Crown, the Union of the Kingdoms of Scotland and England, the Parliament
  of the United Kingdom;

International relations, including foreign trade, except for:
  observing and implementing EU and European Convention on Human Rights
  matters;

Defence and national security; treason; provisions for dealing with terrorism;

Fiscal and monetary policy, currency, coinage and legal tender;

Immigration and nationality, extradition;

The criminal law in relation to drugs and firearms, and the regulation of drugs of
  misuse;

Elections, except local elections;

Official Secrets, national security;

Law on companies and business associations, insurance, corporate insolvency
  and intellectual property, regulation of financial institutions and financial
  services;

Competition, monopolies and mergers;

Employment legislation, including industrial relations, equal opportunities,
  health and safety;

Most consumer protection; data protection;

Post Office, postal and telegraphy services;

Most energy matters;

Railways and air transport; road safety;

Social Security;

Regulation of certain professions, including medical, dental, nursing and other
  health professions, veterinary surgeons, architects, auditors, estate agents,
  insolvency practitioners and insurance intermediaries;

Transport safety and regulation;

Research Councils;

Designation of assisted areas;

Nuclear safety, control and safety of medicines, reciprocal health agreements;

Broadcasting and film classification, licensing of theatres and cinemas,
  gambling;

Weights and measures; time zones;

Abortion, human fertilisation and embryology, genetics, xenotransplantation;

Equality legislation;

Regulation of activities in outer space.

Main Functions Devolved to the Scottish Parliament

Health;

Education and training;

Local government, social work, housing and planning;

Economic development and transport; the administration of the European
  Structural Funds;

Table 1.1 *continued opposite*

Table 1.1 *continued*

The law and home affairs, including most civil and criminal law and the criminal
    justice and prosecution system; police and prisons;
The environment;
Agriculture, fisheries and forestry;
Sport and the arts;
Research and statistics in relation to devolved matters.

and air links. Politically sensitive overlaps have also arisen in the treatment of asylum seekers. There is also scope for devolved administrations to expand the application of their competences by invoking the aims of policy rather than the means. In its first term the Scottish Executive launched a strategy on broad band although telecommunications are clearly a reserved matter.

These examples illustrate that Scottish policy making falls into two categories: matters on which Scotland can go its own way; and matters in which intergovernmental cooperation is necessary. In developing its own policy line, the Scottish Executive has faced the challenge of transformation from a government department applying central policy to a government in its own right, and this has been gradual. There was a lack of policy capacity in the old Scottish Office and of an ability to give strategic leadership, which was carried into the new institutions but has gradually been addressed (see Chapter 4). Innovative groupings of functions, such as the combination of industry with further and higher education in Scotland, or the replacement of ministries of agriculture with departments of rural affairs, have been a force for change. There was a lack of research capacity over large areas of policy, and of an integration of research into policy development. Political leadership was often weak, as most functions were the responsibility of junior ministers without their own authority.

In intergovernmental policy making there are also challenges of adaptation. Before devolution, the Scottish Office was tied into the Whitehall policy network through a dense network of ministerial and official committees and regular working contacts among ministers and civil servants. Papers were exchanged, each level knew what the other was doing and care was taken not to get too far out of line. Yet while the Whitehall departments generally took the lead in joint policy making, there was no formal hierarchy and indeed no UK department at all in large areas of policy including education,

housing, local government and social services. The devolution settlement builds on this administrative heritage with the effect that,
over large areas of public policy, there is now no 'centre' at all. This
contrasts with Germany, where the division of powers (legislation to
the Bund, execution to the Länder) means that both levels have parallel ministries, or Spain, where the central ministries have shown
little inclination to retreat in the face of the autonomous administrations. There was an attempt in Italy to solve the problem by abol-
ishing ministries but these managed to pop up again in new forms.
Even Canada and the United States have federal departments for
health, and the US (but not Canada) has one for education. This lack
of federal departments, combined with the end of the old interministerial committees and contacts, could have centrifugal effects. It is
partly to combat this tendency that the Joint Ministerial Committees
have been set up but, while these appear to be a means of exchanging ideas and innovations, they are a far cry from the interdepart-
mental committees that prepared policies in the pre-devolution age
and there would obviously be great political sensitivity about their
being seen as a top-down measure to impose policy from the centre.

Another mechanism for coordination are the concordats: non-
statutory frameworks for agreement on areas of functional interdependence. These provide for policy variation to be limited and for a
negotiation of differences, but it is clear that London will have the
last word in the event of disagreement. It is by no means clear how
they would fare were different political parties in control at the two
levels. There are also legal mechanisms for pulling devolved administrations and assemblies into line should they exceed their powers
but these, too, are untested given the consonance of political alignments between London and Edinburgh and Cardiff. This makes a
big contrast with Spain, where political antagonisms produced a
spate of court references in the 1980s, which served to set the
bounds for devolved government.

Under the Labour government, many policy initiatives have come
out of the Prime Minister's office and the Treasury rather than functional departments, and devolved administrations have sometimes
been involved in these. The Treasury's scheme for evidence-based
policy, for example, provides funding for research and innovation,
and draws in both Whitehall and devolved departments. The
absence of UK departments across many policy fields, together with
the weight of English departments, has meant that these have often
taken the policy lead, dragging devolved administrations along.

The devolution settlement provides for block grants for the devolved assemblies, calculated on a share of increases or decreases in corresponding English programmes (the Barnett formula). While these sums are freely disposable, in practice they may constrain policy innovation. Scotland can only reallocate resources within its block and cannot take the key decision on how much of the national produce should be devoted to public spending as against private consumption. Should the government in England move towards charging for services rather than financing them from taxation, Scotland will need to follow suit, or make compensating cuts elsewhere. This issue has arisen over free personal care for the elderly and the abolition of up-front university tuition fees in Scotland, and proposals to charge top-up fees in English universities.

Provisions for capital spending might also be a force for uniformity. Technically it is for the devolved administrations to determine whether they will use Public–Private Partnerships (PPP) (formerly the Private Finance Initiative). Yet they do not have borrowing powers like other sub-state administrations and should they wish to finance projects publicly they would presumably have to do so from current revenue. So even if public financing were to be cheaper in the long run, as many people believe it is, devolved administrations might be steered into private finance in order to get projects going quickly. The detailed rules for PPPs in turn are controlled by the Treasury. Proposals to allow hospitals in England to gain 'foundation' status and borrow money in the market – a policy rejected in Scotland – pose the same question.

The financing system also tempts groups to look constantly across the border to see whether their service has got a smaller increase than its counterpart in England. During the early years these potential conflicts were contained. There was plenty of money to go around following the public expenditure review, the main difficulty being in spending it all; and the government presented the accounts in such a way as to make comparisons of increases in individual functions very difficult. In the future, tensions may increase.

Many devolved functions are subject to European Union law, notably in agriculture, fisheries, environment and industrial policy. This has become a major issue of contention in Germany and Belgium, where regions complain that it entails a loss of power not only to Europe but to central government, since it is the state as a whole that determines European policy. The response in Germany and Belgium has been to use the clause in the Treaty on European

Union allowing the Länder, regions and communities to participate in the Council of Ministers and even to represent the member state where regional matters are involved. Yet while this may enhance regional influence, it does not permit policy divergence, since regions must represent the state as a whole and agree a common line. There is provision in the United Kingdom for devolved governments to participate in the Council of Ministers, but they must support a common line and the relevant concordats make it clear that Whitehall will have the last word on the line to be followed. The UK government is also responsible for the implementation of EU policies and has override powers in case devolved administrations do not fulfil their obligations.

The context for UK devolution is a modern, integrated welfare state and there are questions about how much divergence is possible in practice in these conditions. Three important sets of constraints arise from the existence of a UK common security area, a common market and the welfare state. While criminal justice is largely devolved, the lack of barriers among the parts of the UK, the need for common standards and a concern not to create conditions that could be exploited by wrongdoers, lead to a lot of cooperation. Concern to maintain the common market is responsible for many of the limitations on devolved bodies, especially in Scotland and Wales. There are no powers to tax business, except through the Unified Business Rate, and development grants are kept in line through the concordats to prevent market distortions or bidding wars. Competition among the territories for mobile investment is also a pressure for uniformity, since all will want to maintain a friendly business environment. Of course, this does not imply uniform policies, since there are many different models of local and regional development, but it will impose limits on the range of policies adopted and may produce convergence in regulatory, planning and environmental policies. The common labour market similarly imposes limits on the ability of devolved administrations to establish their own model of industrial relations, even within the limits of their competences. While there is a lot of support for devolving active labour market policies, neither side of industry has ever shown support for devolving labour law or regulation. The common market and travel area also influences responses to issues like foot-and-mouth disease or meat exports, where a separate Scottish line was not taken even where it was legally possible.

The common welfare state poses practical and political limitations.

Fears that differences in welfare provision will trigger migration have found only limited support in the experiences of other countries, since other factors such as employment and family networks have proved more powerful, but there may be some distortions. More important perhaps are the shared assumptions of the postwar welfare settlement for broadly equivalent basic services, free at the point of use. 'Social citizenship' in the United Kingdom has been linked to a British identity and indeed many have credited the welfare state with forging a sense of British, if not UK, unity during the twentieth century. Scotland's decisions to abolish up-front student fees and to fund long-term care for the elderly have tested these limits, provoking politicians and the media into discovering all manner of 'anomalies'. Although the Scottish block grant is freely disposable, if finance raised on a common tax base is used to fund substantively different entitlements in the various parts of the United Kingdom, this is going to cause major political opposition. This is not to say that convergence will always be to the English line; it may be that pressure within England will lead to the adoption of Scottish or Welsh innovations there. So marginal differences in welfare state provision are possible under devolution, but radical changes could destabilise the settlement.

Yet while these contextual factors make radical policy divergence more difficult in the modern state than might have been the case in simpler times, other contextual changes open up possibilities for innovation. The tasks of government are shifting away from laying down binding norms through legislation, towards the pursuit of social and economic goals through selective promotion and regulation. In these circumstances, it is less useful to think of the distribution of power as a zero sum game in which a gain for one side entails an equivalent loss for another. If instead of talking of power we look at governing capacity – that is, the ability to address social and economic problems and to make and implement policy in a complex society – then it is quite possible for two or more levels to gain at the same time. Formally weak governments may exercise a lot of influence by being at the centre of functional and transnational networks, or mobilising political support and resources.

Stateless nations like Scotland or Catalonia, and regions across many parts of Europe, are at the centre of these transformations. Government in Britain, as elsewhere in Europe, is changing in scale. The nation-state is no longer the container for all functional systems in the economy, civil society or government, to the extent that it ever was. Economies are increasingly internationalised and global-ised, while at the same time economic change and the adaptation to global trends is becoming a local and regional phenomenon (Keating 1998). Culture is undergoing a parallel change, simultane-ously globalising and localising at the expense of the nation-state. Political institutions follow the same trend, with the rise of 'meso' or intermediate government and a strengthening of the European Union (Sharpe 1993; Balme 1996). For much of the postwar period, nation-states sought to integrate their diverse regions and localities into the national economy and polity through a variety of instru-ments including regional policies, encouraging industry to move to needy areas, national and regional plans and a host of special initia-tives. Scotland was the site of many such initiatives, including stra-tegic plans, new towns, regional development grants and efforts to locate strategic industries including modern steel plants and car fac-tories. Since the 1980s, however, this sort of centralised top-down model of regional policy, in which the various regions are allocated their place in a national system of production, has given way to a new, bottom-up model in which territories must find their own place in the spatial division of labour. Rather than occupying com-plementary roles in a national economy, territories must compete for advantage in a European and global economy. Now it may be that much of this new regionalist literature is exaggerated, espe-cially when it portrays nations and regions as condemned to dog-eat-dog competition for survival (Lovering 1999), but there is no doubt that it has affected politics at the meso level, as we can see from the repetition of the theme of competitiveness in Scottish Executive policy pronouncements in almost every policy field. A whole literature has now developed on how such regions and nations can mount successful projects in conditions of increasing internationalisation and globalisation.

Federal systems have experienced the same effect, so that the old model of cooperative federalism has to some degree given way to one of competitive federalism in a national and global context. Competitive federalism has several dimensions. The federated units compete for economic growth through attracting capital and tech-nology and improving their business climate. Their governments compete to impress their own citizens with the virtues of their poli-cies and administrative competence. They also compete in policy innovation, imitating the best from other governments, avoiding the worst and seeking better solutions to policy problems. Dente (1997) has shown how the evolution of types of federalism has followed the development of complexity in social and economic problems. In a stable world, where both problems and solutions are known, traditional layer-cake federalism, in which each tier looks after its own responsibilities, will work quite well. In times of transition, when problems are known but the solutions are not, then cooperative federalism, in which the powers and resources of different tiers are pooled, may be more effective, as was the case between the 1930s and the 1970s. In a turbulent world, policy problems and issues are constantly being redefined, so that neither the problem nor the solution is known. In these circumstances, competitive federalism, in which governments at different levels experiment and innovate, regardless of the formal division of functions, may be appropriate. Policy might diverge at a number of levels and in more or less fundamental ways. The most radical would result from the identification of different issues, producing a distinct policy agenda in Scotland. Less radically, the same issues might be identified but defined and framed differently. Then issues might be defined the same way, but different policies adopted. Least radically, the same policies might be adopted, but delivered using different instruments, which might give scope for differential implementation or to benefit different client groups.

The remaining chapters in this book analyse policy making under devolution, starting with the policy environment, moving through institutions and processes and finishing with some case studies.

A fundamental issue is whether Scottish people do indeed want to go their own way. Evidence on this is mixed, as is shown in Chapter 2. Scottish electors in general seem committed to the same blend of economic and welfare policies as those in the remainder of the United Kingdom, and share much the same outlook on questions of social tolerance and order. Yet there is a certain egalitarian ethos which has dominated public debate and framed political discussion. Party politics is another key factor. Scotland in the first two parliamentary terms has been controlled by Labour–Liberal Democrat coalitions not far removed politically from the government in Whitehall, and the Labour Party has sought to present a united front on both sides of the border. In the first parliamentary session, coalition politics produced two highly salient shifts in Scotland, on student fees and long-term care for the elderly, and a more liberal line on law and order. In the event of differences in control at the two levels of government, there would obviously be more pressure for divergence, which might put strain on the system of accommodation put in place at a time of consistent political alignments.

Scotland has always had its own interest groups, which fall into three types. There are purely Scottish groups, Scottish groups affiliated to British or UK federations, and Scottish branches of British groups. Since devolution, UK federations have tended to strengthen their Scottish level and give it more autonomy, but the pattern of change is very varied, as we will see in Chapter 3. There has also been some difficult adaptation, as Scottish interest groups have shifted from the politics of lobbying for a larger Scottish share of UK resources to contributing to policy formation within a self-governing Scotland. Gradually, however, networks have adapted to the new circumstances and policy communities are reconfiguring.

The Scottish Executive has evolved from the Scottish Office and is gradually being transformed into a government in its own right, as traced in Chapter 4. The Scottish Parliament is altogether newer and has brought a degree of politicisation and scrutiny to policy making that was often absent before.

Chapter 5 examines intergovernmental policy making, including both UK and European dimensions.

Getting and spending money is at the heart of policy choice and this is covered in Chapter 6.

Finally, a number of policy areas are examined, including public service delivery, health, higher education, social inclusion, economic development and rural policy, to chart the direction of policy making since 1999 and the degree to which devolution has made a difference.

Notes

1. This is not to say that territorial politics disappeared; there were still complex systems for intermediating between centres and peripheries. France had its *notables*, Italy its *notabili* and Spain its *caciques*, politicians who supported the national government in Parliament in return for patronage back home. Even agents of the central state, like the French prefects, could do their job only by bending central policies to local interests.

CHAPTER TWO

Parties and Elections

Public Opinion and Political Culture

One of the main impulses behind devolution was the belief that the Scottish public had been frustrated over many years by the imposition of policies designed with the larger English electorate in mind. This implies that the Scottish Parliament would face a distinct range of electoral demands and pressures for policy divergence. Advocates of the 'new politics' might add that there is an underlying consensus within Scotland that had been denied expression by the UK parties, with their insistence on polarising issues on irrelevant lines. Others have suggested that Scotland is naturally politically to the left of England. This interest in diversity contrasts with the 1960s, when the received wisdom was that Britain was a homogeneous polity, in which the principal socio-economic cleavages were the same everywhere (Blondel 1974; Finer 1974). It is a difficult issue to resolve. The demand for policies on the part of the electorate is not independent of the supply of policies by the parties, which respond to public opinion but also shape it. Patterns of party competition shape the political agenda, opening up new political spaces and closing off others. This is not merely a matter of advocating specific policies. It is also to do with image, ethos and adapting to the prevailing views of the community that they are addressing.

Political myths play a role here, as parties seek to create and then reflect a favourable image in tune with the dominant community spirit. The recurrent myth of Scotland as a naturally progressive country, held back by a conservative England, can be traced back to the late nineteenth century, through the legends of Red Clydeside during the First World War, to resistance to Thatcherism in the 1980s. Margaret Thatcher, for her part, sought to valorise another myth, of Scotland as the birthplace of free-market capitalism, an individualist society in which people were judged on their competitive merit. A myth does not depend for its power on its truth or falsehood, but on whether it taps into contemporary sentiments. Red Clydeside, according to revisionist historians, was a defensive action on the part of privileged sectors of the male, Protestant working class, and Thatcher's invocation of Adam Smith ignores the profoundly social content of the Scottish Renaissance, but both serve a purpose. Another myth is that of egalitarianism, a society in which everyone can get on. This may be at odds with the reality of a socially stratified Scotland, but this does not stop it being used by the left in the promotion of socialism, and by the right in the pursuit of a meritocracy. Scotland's religious heritage left it with an image of social conservatism, which hindered the liberalising reforms of the 1960s, but this coexists with a more recent image of progressivism derived from the electoral dominance of the left during the 1980s and 1990s. The clash of these two images was dramatically illustrated in the debate over the repeal of Section 28/2A (the clause banning the 'promotion' of homosexuality in schools and local government) in the early days of the Scottish Parliament. A more recent myth is of Scotland as a naturally pro-European country, in contrast with the prevailing Euroscepticism further south. Like the other myths, this is given a historical basis by tracing Scotland's connections with the continent over the ages.

Political attitudes are thus complex and multilayered, a set of keys on which leaders and parties can play. We cannot simply extrapolate from public opinion data to the structure of policy demands within Scotland. It is, nonetheless, useful to see what these data tell us. There is now a wealth of information available from the regular British and Scottish Election Studies and the British and Scottish Social Attitudes Surveys. These show the Scots as sharing the same broad vision of the modern welfare state and mixed economy as citizens in other parts of the United Kingdom; indeed there has been convergence of attitudes more broadly across Europe. The most common way to characterise political attitudes is on the left–right scale. Yet we know that right and left are rather crude categories and that some positions might be difficult to classify. Old alignments are becoming less relevant while new issues,

Table 2.1   Attitudes in Scotland, England and Wales, 2000–1:
percentage agreeing or strongly agreeing

	Scotland	England	Wales
Economic policy			
* Private enterprise is the best way to solve Britain's economic problems	23.7	31.1	25.7
* There is no need for strong trades unions to protect employees' working conditions and wages	14.4	13.4	13.6
Social equality			
+ State benefits for unemployed people are too low and cause hardship	43	40	
* Ordinary working people get their fair share of the nation's wealth	11.7	16.2	14.9
Social liberalism			
* People who break the law should be given longer prison sentences	66.9	61.1	65.0
+ Homosexual sex is always wrong	39	36	
* Censorship of films and magazines is necessary to uphold public morals	64.4	61.3	67.0
Race and immigration			
* Immigrants increase crime rates	27.3	41.9	31.9
* Most asylum seekers who come to Britain should be sent home immediately	37.0	51.1	51.3
+ Describe themselves as a little or very racially prejudiced	17	25	
Environment			
* We worry too much about the environment today and not enough about people's jobs	32.0	25.2	26.8
Europe			
+ Approve or strongly approve of British membership of the European Union	43.5	41.0	
+ Would vote to join the Euro	30.4	30.1	

Source: * British Election Survey, 2001 + British/Scottish Social Attitudes Surveys, 2000, 2001 (no separate figures for Wales)

such as social tolerance or the environment, have come onto the agenda. In Table 2.1, attitudes in Scotland, England and Wales are analysed under six principal headings.

The first has to do with views on the management of the economy and the preference for private enterprise versus state planning. Here the Scots show slightly more suspicion of private enterprise than the English, perhaps reflecting the greater dependence of Scotland (and Wales) on state aid and regional policies in recent decades. Scots are also slightly less trusting of big international companies, but there is no significant difference in Scottish and English attitudes to trades unions, which are still broadly supported in both countries.

The second set of issues has to do with economic and social equality, and the questions help to test the proposition that Scots are naturally more egalitarian. Here the most impressive finding is that British people in all three nations harbour a certain sense of social injustice, with most thinking that ordinary working people do not get a fair share of the wealth, although again Scots are slightly more likely than others to think so. A question asking whether there is one law for the rich and one for the poor elicited the same balance of answers. One issue on which Scots have diverged markedly from English views is on education, where they have continued to support comprehensive schools, even as support for selection grew in England during the 1980s and 1990s. This may reflect more egalitarian social attitudes, as well as different Scottish traditions in a field that has always been rather autonomous.

The third set of issues concerns social liberalism and authoritarianism, which can be tapped in a number of ways. Table 2.1 suggests that Scots are slightly more favourable to censorship and take a somewhat harder line on law and order, a finding confirmed by other questions in the same survey. This suggests that the Scottish Executive's shift towards a tougher populist stance on law and order after 2003 may have brought it into line with public opinion, after the relatively liberal phase between 1999 and 2003, when the Justice portfolio was held by the Liberal Democrats. Attitudes to homosexual relations, an issue raised by the controversy over Section 28/2A in the early days of the Parliament, and over proposals for same-sex couples in the second session, show little difference between Scotland and England. This does appear to be a case of convergence, since in 1983 Scots appeared significantly less tolerant in this area than the English (Park 2002).

Next come questions of race and immigration, where Scotland comes out as holding a less negative view of immigrants and a less hostile view of asylum seekers. This might reflect the low level of immigrants and asylum seekers in Scotland as compared with some regions of England, but it is a finding that is consistent across various surveys. When asked if they themselves were at all racially prejudiced, Scots are slightly less likely to agree than the English, a finding sustained by other measures of prejudice (Park 2002).

On environmental matters, there is a small difference, with Scots putting more emphasis on economic development and jobs. This, too, may reflect conditions, since Scotland has not in general felt the development pressures found in the south of England, but has suffered from industrial decline and loss of jobs.

There is a widespread view that Scots are more favourable to European integration than the English. Here again we need to distinguish between the attitudes of the parties and those of the voters. In 1975 Labour in Scotland and the SNP were opposed to membership of the then European Community, but by the mid-1980s both had changed their view, along with the trades unions (Keating and Jones 1985). The switch is partly reflected in public opinion. In the referendum in 1975 Scots voted Yes, but in smaller numbers than England and Wales. Since the 1990s, they have consistently come out as slightly more favourable to Europe or, perhaps more accurately, slightly less hostile. Attitudes towards joining the Euro have fluctuated along with those in England, with generally slightly less hostility but sometimes also less enthusiastic support. There was a point in the mid-1990s when Scottish opinion was close enough to supporting the Euro to make a referendum victory on the issue possible, but thereafter support fell away along with that in England. Interestingly, despite the SNP's support for Euro membership as an integral part of their independence strategy, it is not SNP voters but Labour voters who are more inclined to the Euro. In the British Social Attitudes Survey of 2001, voters were asked to place themselves on a scale of support or opposition to the Euro. Labour voters were the only group with a majority in the top half of the scale, although English Labour voters were even more pro-Euro. Scottish Liberal Democrats were less keen on the Euro than their English counterparts, although Scottish Conservatives were less hostile than English Conservatives. This all suggests that the elite consensus in Scotland in favour of Europe does not stem automatically from public opinion, and that public opinion itself responds to a complex of partisan, national and other signals.

The final issue dimension concerns attitudes to Scottish independence or further home rule. Since 1999 support for a return to centralised government, with the abolition of the Scottish Parliament, has been very slight: about half the proportion of the population that voted against devolution in the referendum of 1997 (Paterson

2002b). This suggests that devolution is accepted as part of the constitutional scenery. Support for independence also fell off after 1999, with people opting for devolution within the UK, but there has been consistent support for giving the Scottish Parliament more powers, notably in matters of taxation. These questions are always susceptible to the precise wording and context of the question. For example, when asked in a series of surveys around 1998–9 about the three options of devolution, independence and no Scottish Parliament, the great bulk of respondents opted for devolution and only about a quarter for independence. Yet in the very same surveys, when asked how they would vote in an independence referendum, around half responded Yes. This apparently contradictory result is found across other stateless nations (Keating 2001) and suggests that Scots do not make a clear distinction among the categories but see them as a continuum of more or less autonomy. They might not support independence immediately, but many Scots are open to the possibility in principle. This ensures that the independence question will remain one of the structuring features of Scottish politics, taking on more or less importance according to the circumstances at any given time.

Summing up, there is a small but persistent Scottish bias to positions that might be considered in some respects more left wing; the centre ground in Scottish politics is somewhat to the left of that in England (Paterson 2001a). This might be connected with the social class structure of Scotland, with more working-class people, and indeed surveys have shown that this is indeed the case. The Goldthorpe scale of social stratification, the most commonly used, has five categories and, as Table 2.2 shows, Scotland has more people in the working class and fewer in the salariat (white-collar occupations), although the figures in between are rather similar.

Table 2.2   Percentage of population by social class in Scotland and England

	Scotland	England
Salariat	28.3	37.9
Routine non-manual	20.8	20.2
Petty bourgeoisie	5.6	7.7
Foremen and technicians	8.2	8.3
Working class	37.0	25.9
Total	100	100

Source: British General Election Survey, 2001

This, however, does not explain greater support in Scotland for more redistributive policies and public spending, since the differences among the social classes within Scotland and England are actually rather small, but all social classes in Scotland are more redistributive than their counterparts in England (Surridge 2003). More revealing, perhaps, than people's objective social class as measured by occupation, is subjective self-identification. Scots are more likely than the English to describe themselves as working class, irrespective of their objective occupational class identity (Surridge 2003). Those identifying themselves as Scottish are also more likely to support redistributive economic policies (Paterson 2002b), and Scottish identity has been increasing over the years (McCrone 2001). It seems that in the course of the 1980s and 1990s, Scottish national identity was rebuilt around themes of resistance to neo-liberalism, including a substantial section of the middle classes. To some degree, Scottish identity fills the role in sustaining social solidarity previously played (if only partly) by class. The mixture of beliefs and values and their linkage to the theme of Scottishness is less a matter of precise views on public policy matters than a generalised 'moral economy' (Hearn 2000), summed up in the critique of neo-liberal excess, 'it's no' fair'. So providing free personal care for the elderly, or not charging up-front student fees, might be considered left-wing, since they are based on universal provision, or right-wing, as they benefit better-off families most and are supported by the Conservative Party. Both policies, however, tap a sense of shared responsibility and community ethos that challenges the neo-liberal and market-driven assumptions of much public policy under successive British governments. There is thus a certain syndrome of national identity, class identity and values, suggesting again a sense of common or collective identity and a real, if rather vague, sense of the common weal, providing some resistance to neo-liberalism. Again this should not be exaggerated, but it does provide a set of themes on which politicians can play, adapting their policies and rhetoric to shared assumptions and norms.

The Party System

Parties are important relays between public opinion and policy makers. Under the Westminster model, they compete to win elections on the basis of policy programmes and governing competence, and answer at the polls for any failures. Yet they also shape public opinion and the dynamic of party competition helps set the policy agenda. While, on most issues, Scottish public opinion diverges only slightly from that of the rest of the UK, the party system and patterns of competition are now quite distinct and this explains much of the dynamic of Scottish politics. In recent years, commentators have emphasised the declining influence of class and ideology everywhere, with parties seeking the safe centre ground. Yet this centre ground may not be the same everywhere, and parties need to adapt to prevailing local norms and expectations, so that territory may be regaining in importance. This was not always the case. Scotland participated fully in the consolidation of the British two-party system in the 1950s; at the General Election of 1955 the Conservatives and Labour gained almost identical proportions of the vote in England and Scotland (although Wales was heavily inclined to Labour), taking 97 per cent of the total. Closer analysis, however, shows that part of the explanation was that the parties were adapting themselves to local environments rather than the other way around, and that the main parties in Scotland represented distinct electoral coalitions, adapted to their competitive needs. This was particularly so for the Conservatives, who put together a broad anti-Labour coalition in Scotland in the 1950s but proved unable to adapt to changing conditions from the 1970s. Labour, while pressing a uniform policy line across Great Britain, was also attentive to the distinct needs of its Scottish electorate and trimmed its appeal accordingly.

From the late 1950s, the Scottish Conservatives started a long decline that was to persist for over forty years and reduce them to a minor party. Labour was the initial beneficiary of this, peaking at 49.9 per cent of the vote in 1966, but thereafter it was the smaller parties who gained. As the Scottish Liberals detached themselves from the Conservatives from the late 1950s, they were able to repenetrate their historic areas of strength and in the 1980s and 1990s, allied with the Social Democrats and then as the Liberal Democrats, gain a large number of seats in relation to their vote. The rise of the Scottish National Party (SNP) can be traced back to the early 1960s, but their real breakthrough came in October 1974 when they took 30 per cent of the vote and eleven parliamentary seats. After falling away, their support picked up again from the late 1980s and by the end of the 1990s they had established their place as the second party of Scotland. These trends tended to be masked by the first-past-the-post electoral system for Westminster elections, which gave Labour

Figure 2.1   Percentage vote in UK elections, Scotland, 1945–2001

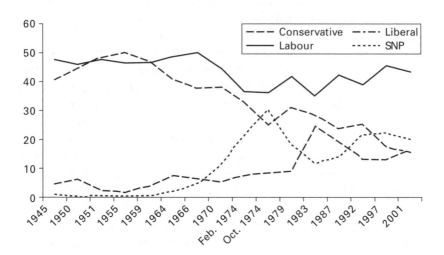

a dominating position, helped the Liberals in their successive forms (as their support is concentrated) and penalised first the SNP and then the Conservatives, who lost all their parliamentary seats in 1997.

The mixed proportional electoral system for the Scottish Parliament allowed smaller parties to gain list seats and, indeed, the two-ballot system seems positively to encourage small parties by permitting electors to cast a vote for a large party in the constituency and at the same time indulge themselves by giving the second vote for a smaller one.[1] Two parties in particular have gained from this: the Scottish Socialists, carving out a place to the left of Labour; and the Greens, campaigning on a post-materialist agenda. In addition, a number of independents and a Pensioners' candidate won list seats in the 2003 elections. The result is that Scotland has gone in fifty years from a balanced two-party competitive system to a multi-party system, with one dominant (although not majority) party, an Opposition that is distinctly smaller, and a number of lesser parties.

Elections for local, regional and devolved assemblies have often been labelled as 'second-order' elections, in which voters use the opportunity to make a judgement on the ruling parties at the centre rather than on local issues. Second-order elections are characterised by low turnout, a setback for the party ruling in central government and increased support for minor parties. In this situation, devolved elections cease to be a means of debating policy for the devolved government and holding it to account. At first sight, there seems to be evidence that the Scottish elections are second-order. Turnout has been lower than at Westminster, although this is complicated by the fact that both have fallen since 1997, so that turnout in the UK election of 2001 was no higher than in the Scottish election of 1999, but it fell further in the Scottish election of 2003. The main parties do not help here. British election campaigns cover issues like health and education on a UK-wide basis, although they are at stake only in England. This perhaps explains why polls since 2001 have consistently shown a plurality of Scots believing that changes in these areas, for the better or the worse, are to be credited to Westminster rather than Holyrood. Only the Liberal Democrats have taken care to distinguish devolved and reserved matters in their electoral publicity, issuing a Scottish manifesto at the UK elections that avoids addressing devolved issues. The SNP manages to get devolved issues into the UK election campaign by promising that, with independence, it will be able to manage all these questions better. Labour and the Conservatives, however, tend to confuse the levels of responsibility and have taken care that their party branches at the two levels are not giving out different messages.

On the other hand, election results in Scotland do not merely mirror those in England. Pollsters now ask people separately how they would vote for Holyrood and Westminster, and there is always a gap between the two, with the SNP and the smaller parties doing better in the former. In the 1999 Scottish elections, one in five voters reported voting differently from the way in which they would have voted at a Westminster election, with Labour as the main loser (Paterson et al. 2001). Given the traditional strength of party attachment in Britain, this seems rather high. Nor can it be entirely explained as a protest vote against the incumbent UK Labour government, as the second-order theory would predict, since it was not closely correlated with attitudes to the UK government (Paterson et al. 2001). It does seem, then, that many electors are motivated by distinctly Scottish considerations when voting for Holyrood, if not always with matters devolved to the Scottish Parliament. These elections are an opportunity to debate the issues in a distinctly Scottish arena, unencumbered by a deafening UK campaign. They are deciding who is going to rule the devolved institutions but, in a wider sense, it is about who is going to speak for Scotland across the policy range and at all levels.

Table 2.3   Scottish Parliament results, 1999 and 2003

	Year	Constituency MSPs	Regional MSPs	Total MSPs	% of seats	% constituency votes	% list votes
Labour	2003	46	4	50	38.8	34.6	29.3
	1999	53	3	56	43.4	38.7	33.6
SNP	2003	9	18	27	20.9	23.8	20.9
	1999	7	28	35	27.1	28.7	27.3
Liberal	2003	13	4	17	13.2	15.4	11.8
Democrat	1999	12	5	17	13.2	14.2	12.4
Conservative	2003	3	15	18	14.0	16.6	15.5
	1999	0	18	18	14.0	15.5	15.4
Green	2003	0	7	7	5.4	0.0	6.9
	1999	0	1	1	0.8	0.0	3.6
Scottish Socialist	2003	0	6	6	4.7	6.2	6.7
Party	1999	0	1	1	0.8	1.0	2.0
Others	2003	2	2	4	3.1	3.4	8.9
	1999	0	1	1	0.8	1.9	5.7

Party competition in Scotland is dominated by Labour, which has won a plurality of votes in every election since 1964 and has been unchallenged for first place in recent decades, forcing the other parties to position themselves around it, both on socio-economic and on constitutional issues. On socio-economic issues, there are three parties on the centre-left, Labour, the Liberal Democrats and the SNP, and one party on the centre-right, the Conservatives. There is no extreme right or even seriously right-wing or neo-liberal party, but there is a far-left party, the Scottish Socialists, and a Green presence. This all tends to push the political debate towards the left, with the need to emphasise social inclusion and welfare themes. On the constitutional issue, there are two pro-home rule parties, Labour and the Liberal Democrats, while the Conservatives have reluctantly accepted devolution as a reality they must live with. Three parties are in favour of independence, the SNP, the Scottish Socialists and the Greens, ensuring that the issue of further steps towards self-government will remain on the agenda. The pattern of party competition also leans in a pro-Europe direction, with three of the four main parties adopting a pro-European stance (Labour, SNP and Liberal Democrats) and the Conservatives making less of Euro-scepticism than their counterparts south of the border. This pattern of competition differs markedly from England, where a centrist

Table 2.4 Percentage composition of Labour and SNP vote in Scotland, 2001

	Labour voters	SNP voters	All Scotland
Salariat	27	28	28
Routine non-manual	20	22	21
Petty bourgeoisie	3	10	6
Foremen and technicians	10	8	8
Working class	40	32	37
Total	100	100	100

Source: British Election Study

Labour Party faces its principal opposition on the right, and this in turn shapes a distinct policy agenda in Scotland.

Voting in British elections has traditionally been conditioned by social class and, to a certain degree, this continues to be the case. Labour is historically a working-class party and has its strongholds in the industrial areas of central Scotland. As the industrial working class declines, accounting now for a little over a third of the electorate, Labour might be expected to suffer, unless it can reach out to other social classes. In fact, Labour has always had a significant middle-class vote and has gained a lot of support among white-collar workers and professionals. The SNP before the 1980s was often seen as a petty bourgeois party, rooted in the small-business class and small-town Scotland, but since then has made a conscious effort to reach out to working-class voters, without which it cannot overtake Labour as Scotland's leading party. As Table 2.4 shows, both have to a significant degree succeeded in becoming 'catch-all' parties, drawing on all sections of society, so that the class profile of their vote is rather similar to that of Scotland as a whole, but with the SNP depending more on the middle classes and Labour more on the working class. This broad support potentially gives them some room for manoeuvre in shaping their policy appeal, but it also constrains them, since any move to right or left risks losing part of their social base. They can thus be expected to seek the centre ground, but with Labour more sensitive to working-class demands and the SNP concerned also with the needs of small business.

Tables 2.5 and 2.6 reverse the pattern, to show how members of each social class voted. Here, the even spread of the SNP vote, punctuated only by its strong presence among the petty bourgeoisie, again shows through. A comparison with England, however, shows

Table 2.5   Percentage vote by class, Scotland, 2001

	Labour	Conservative	SNP	Liberal Democrat	Other	Total
Salariat	45	18	19	16	2	100
Routine non-manual	48	15	19	17	1	100
Petty bourgeoisie	25	32	32	11	0	100
Foremen/technicians	60	12	19	7	2	100
Working class	62	10	19	7	2	100

Source: British Election Study

Table 2.6   Percentage vote by class, England, 2001

	Labour	Conservative	Liberal Democrat	Other	Total
Salariat	38	37	23	2	100
Routine non-manual	45	30	23	2	100
Petty bourgeoisie	34	46	17	3	100
Foremen/technicians	52	25	21	2	100
Working class	66	21	11	2	100

Source: British Election Study

that it is not just Scotland's larger working class that accounts for Labour's success. In 2001, Labour got a larger proportion of the vote in Scotland than in England within the salariat and non-manual occupations, but did slightly worse among the working class because of the presence of the SNP. It does seem, then, that Labour has a particular appeal to the professional and white-collar classes in Scotland. The Conservatives, by contrast, got a lower proportion of the Scottish than of the English vote in every social class, despite having no competitors on the centre-right of the political spectrum. Within Scotland, they were heavily defeated by Labour in every class except the petty bourgeoisie; the latter were the only group in which they managed to equal the SNP. Again, it appears that there is a Scottish effect, benefiting the parties of the centre-left and providing little room for expansion on the right.

Party competition in Scottish Parliament elections is also shaped by the electoral system, a mixed proportional one. There are seventy-three constituency seats elected on the first-past-the-post system used for Westminster, and a further fifty-six members elected by proportional representation from party lists in eight regional constituencies. Electors have two votes, for the constituency and for the list, and the list members are distributed within each region among the parties on the basis of the list vote, after subtracting the seats they have already won in the constituencies of the region. This is a version of the German electoral system, but since the number of list members is rather small, it does not achieve full proportionality. Yet it does make it almost impossible for a single party to win a majority of seats, so that governments will be minorities or coalitions. Given the relative sizes of the parties and the dimensions of political divisions, the Labour and Liberal Democrat parties have a large advantage. Labour is likely to be the largest party, given its hold on constituency seats in industrial Scotland, giving it the first move in coalition-making. Along with the Liberal Democrats, it holds a centrist position on both the socio-economic and the constitutional issues, making it possible for these two parties to form a fairly cohesive coalition and difficult for opponents to put together a rival one. A Conservative-led coalition looks out of the question for the foreseeable future. There has been speculation about an SNP-led coalition with the Liberal Democrats, but this has always foundered on the issue of an independence referendum, on which the SNP insist. Another possibility might be a 'rainbow coalition' of the SNP and the minor parties. In the first Holyrood election, however, there was little doubt that Labour would be the main governing party, almost certainly in coalition with the Liberal Democrats. The same was true in 2003, but this very factor encouraged support for the smaller parties, injecting an intensely competitive element into the elections.

The Labour Party

The Labour Party had distinct origins in Scotland in the nineteenth century but by the First World War had become an integral part of the British party. The main concession to Scottish sensibilities was the Scottish Advisory Council (later the Scottish Council of the Labour Party) established in 1915 and a Scottish Conference which could debate Scottish and, from the 1970s, British and international matters, but without any policy-making power. Neither became a major focus for political action, as attention was increasingly focused on London. Even in the 1970s, when the Labour government was trying to introduce devolution for Scotland, the party declined to give its Scottish arm the last say on party policy in devolved fields. Only in 1994 did Labour allow the Scottish Labour Party (as it was renamed) to make its own policy on Scottish matters, and its officials are still appointed and paid by the central party (Lynch and Birrell 2004). Trades unions were also focused on the UK level after the 1920s, and the Scottish Trades Union Congress was never particularly close to the Labour Party (see below). Party membership in Scotland has persistently been low, even as the party has prospered electorally, and its organisation was traditionally weak, leading to financial and administrative dependence on London (Donnachie et al. 1989). After the Second World War, Labour's parliamentary representation was dominated by former local councillors, who made little impact at Westminster, except for an ambitious minority who aimed for a UK career, giving Scottish matters a wide berth (Keating 1975a). Scotland made little impact on the party as a whole, with few Scots elected to the National Executive Committee and only one Scottish MP among the thirty-two elected to the Shadow Cabinet between 1951 and 1964. In the Labour governments of 1964–70 and 1974–9 the only Scots in the Cabinet, apart from the obligatory Secretary of State, were George Thompson, Tom Fraser, Judith Hart and John Smith, and none of them for more than a year and a half, despite the large Scottish presence in the parliamentary party.

The centre of gravity of Scottish Labour lay, rather, in municipal government. In the postwar years, Labour gained a dominant position in the cities of Glasgow, Aberdeen and Dundee and in the industrial towns and coalfields of central Scotland. Urban redevelopment and the expansion of the welfare state provided rising resources for local government, while control over council house allocation, jobs in direct-labour departments, and teaching and other positions, sustained political machines and patronage opportunities. Housing was the dominant local issue, and the centrepiece of Labour policy was sustaining low council house rents; by the 1970s Scotland had the highest level of public ownership of housing in western Europe. Around this there formed a strong subculture, linking the Labour Party, the Cooperative Movement and the trades unions (Hutchison, 2001). Powerful municipal leaders tended to stay at the local level, while the second tier opted for parliamentary obscurity. In the internecine party battles of the 1950s and 1960s, Labour's Scottish leadership tended to stay on the right, while promoting a municipal socialism based on low rents and expanding services. On the left, the legend of Red Clydeside provided a rallying point, in spite of the efforts of revisionist historians to debunk it, and such memories fed into actions like the Upper Clyde Shipbuilders work-in of 1971. Another counterpoint to the prevailing conservatism during the 1960s was nuclear disarmament. Given the presence of both British and American Polaris (later Trident) submarines based on the Clyde, this took on a particular salience in Scotland, as did the Campaign for Nuclear Disarmament (CND) in the 1960s and 1980s. Anti-war themes continued to mark the Scottish left and draw more activists into Labour politics in the succeeding years.

During the opposition years of the 1980s and 1990s, a new generation rose to prominence in Scottish Labour politics, breaking with the old pattern. In local government, new leaders sought to adapt municipal socialism to the times, abandoning the dogmatic defence of council housing and engaging in the new agenda of urban renewal and economic development. Some of them were to move into Parliament, joined by others without the traditional municipal apprenticeship. As Labour's fortunes collapsed in England, Scottish MPs became a more significant presence in the parliamentary party and, eventually, the leadership. As a result, the Labour Cabinets of 1997–2001 contained as many Scottish MPs as all previous Labour Cabinets put together (excluding the obligatory Secretary of State for Scotland). While Donald Dewar was the only Cabinet-ranking minister to transfer to the Scottish Parliament, the others have retained a political base in Scotland and provide an important link between Scottish and UK politics. Labour leaders in the Scottish Parliament have tended to come from a slightly younger group, who came to prominence in the 1990s and lack Westminster experience, creating an alternative centre of gravity. Backbench Westminster MPs have been the losers from devolution, deprived of most of their constituency work and their role in dealing with local authority matters, most of which now go through Holyrood. A municipal interest remains strong, which may explain the greater sensitivity shown in Scotland to local government, but the image of Labour machine politics has lingered to cause the party recurrent embarrassment. The decision of the Scottish Executive, as part of its 2003 coalition agreement with the Liberal Democrats, to introduce proportional representation in local government therefore has large repercussions on the balance of influence within the Scottish body politic, since it will destroy the one-party municipalities which are the power base of the Labour machine.

Labour has been organisationally weak in Scotland since its beginnings in the early twentieth century. Many of the branches after the First World War were in reality Independent Labour Party, and the disaffiliation of the ILP in 1932 dealt a severe blow. In the 1960s there were recurrent crises, including the disbandment of the Glasgow City Labour Party. At the crucial General Elections of 1974, Labour had less than half the number of agents in relation to seats in Scotland as in England (Hutchison 2001). Membership figures in the party were always somewhat fictitious, but were consistently lower in Scotland, especially in the party's electoral heartland around Glasgow. After an increase in the mid-1990s, Labour membership across Britain declined again and by 2003 only about 8 per cent of it was in Scotland (Lynch and Birrell 2004).

Since devolution, the Scottish Labour Party has the right to make its own policy on devolved issues through Policy Forums and the Annual Conference. In practice, like parties elsewhere, it has ceased to be an important source of new ideas. Under Tony Blair, the party moved to the centre ground in politics (a centre that itself has moved to the right since the 1970s) and rebranded itself as New Labour. The new members brought in during the 1990s were generally from the middle classes, allowing the party to position itself as a 'catch-all' party appealing to all sections of society. By the 2000s, it was generally regarded as being rather closer to business than to the trades unions. Despite a widespread view that Scottish Labour has been resistant to the New Labour message, the party membership in Scotland closely resembles that in the rest of Britain, both in social background and in their views (Hassan 2004; Surridge 2004).

Although no longer a significant source of policy initiative, the party remains an important mechanism for political recruitment and the leadership has exercised tight control on who can become a party candidate. In 1999 several high-profile figures, including sitting MPs, were excluded from the list of those eligible to become Scottish parliamentary candidates for not being sufficiently reliable supporters of the UK and Scottish leadership. One of them, Dennis Canavan, stood as an independent and was elected in 1999 and again in 2003. There are few independent-minded Labour back-benchers such as are still occasionally found at Westminster. Dissident ideas, in consequence, tend to come from the minor parties, whose presence in the Parliament owes something to voter rejection of the control tendencies of Labour. The Scottish Labour Party is notorious for infighting and division, but this nowadays tends to be about power and factionalism rather than competing visions of social democracy, further curtailing debate on policy.

Labour's attitude to Scottish devolution has always been ambivalent. In the early twentieth century it supported home rule as part of the radical agenda of the day, but relegated the issue after the First World War (Keating and Bleiman 1979) as it penetrated the British political system and turned its attention to Westminster. Labour governments in 1924 and 1931 sidestepped the issue, and during the Depression of the 1930s Scottish Labour was conscious of Scotland's dependence on UK assistance. Attlee's reforming government after 1945 brushed aside the Scottish Covenant and Convention movements, and in 1958 the party in Scotland formally dropped its commitment to a Scottish Parliament. It was committed by this stage to centralised planning and nationalisation, and based its electoral appeal on a class politics that recognised no boundaries within Britain. Its rhetoric was anti-nationalist, especially from the 1930s, as nationalism in Europe gained a bad name, and some of its more nationalist members abandoned it in favour of the various groupings that flowed into the SNP. Yet the Labour home rule tradition never quite died out, and there were voices speaking up for a Scottish assembly or parliament throughout the party's history. From the 1960s there was renewed interest in the question, and home rule's pedigree as an early socialist issue meant that it could be reintroduced into the policy portfolio if need be. It was the electoral threat from a resurgent SNP that forced the pace in 1974, and in that year the Scottish Council was pressed by London to concede an elected Scottish Assembly in advance of the October General Election. As the subsequent bills made their way through Parliament and through the referendum of 1979 the party remained divided, with senior figures campaigning for the No side and Labour voters left confused. Pushed back into opposition, however, Scottish Labour stuck to the commitment, and pressed it on an unenthusiastic Labour leadership. Like other European social democratic parties at the time, Labour was reconsidering its centralist ideology and opening up to local and regional demands, while the charge of centralisation could be used as a political weapon against the Thatcher government. Some left-wing and home rule enthusiasts went so far as to argue that the Conservatives had no 'mandate' in Scotland, having lost the election there and repealed the devolution act, which had gained a majority at the referendum. The Labour leadership trod more warily. The no mandate argument could play into the hands of the SNP, and raise questions about the legitimacy of future UK governments based on Scottish but not English votes, so it was an issue Labour chose to exploit without deploying the argument itself. There was a similarly detached attitude to cross-party organisations like the Campaign for a Scottish Assembly, a legacy of Labour's traditional suspicion of inter-party collaboration, with the leadership insisting that Scottish devolution would come from a UK Labour government and in no other way.

These attitudes began to change in the late 1980s, and Labour was persuaded to enter the Scottish Constitutional Convention along with the Liberal Democrats and smaller parties – the absence of the Conservatives and the SNP certainly facilitated Labour's participation. Over the next few years it was able to use its position in the Convention to ride the devolution issue, keep its links with Scottish civil society, and pose as the leading party in Scottish politics, committed to a moderate measure of constitutional change. Remaining anti-home rule elements were muted and the party's younger neo-nationalist element was reined in, while the promise of a referendum enabled the party to park the issue during the 1997 election campaign. During the referendum campaign, Labour took a leading role in a broad coalition for a Yes vote, with both the SNP and the Liberal Democrats. After 1999, the contours of the issue changed again as the depleted Conservative Party abandoned its opposition to devolution, but the SNP emerged as the main opposition in the Scottish Parliament. Labour then reverted to a strong unionist tone, attacking nationalist plans to break up the United Kingdom. Its unionist rhetoric, however, had changed from the earlier phase. References to class solidarity had disappeared, as had the arguments for state control and centralised planning. Emphasis was now placed on economic self-interest, pointing to Scotland's financial dependence on the United Kingdom. There were some efforts to mobilise a sense of British identity as an emotive weapon against nationalism, but the emotive underpinnings of Britishness are no longer as strong as before (see above) and even the use of the term 'divorce' was given an economic twist ('divorce is an expensive business'). Some people in the party have always remained sceptical about devolution, while a smaller neo-nationalist wing would like to go further. In the mainstream are those who see the 1999 settlement as striking the right balance and seek to hold the line there.

Labour in Scotland has perhaps remained closer to the trades unions than English Labour, as indicated by the concordat the

Scottish Executive signed with the Scottish Trades Union Congress. Public-sector trades unions have also influenced the decision to retain the traditional type of public service provision (see Chapter 7) against the emphasis in England on competition and differentiation. This is not so much a distinction between the Labour Party on both sides of the border, since British Labour Party Conferences have been unenthusiastic or hostile to things like foundation hospitals, but reflects a greater willingness on the part of the Westminster government to ignore party pressures. It may also owe something to Scottish Labour's support base among public-sector workers and professionals, compared with British Labour's efforts to make itself a party appealing to private-sector managers and business. Coalition with the Liberal Democrats in the Scottish Executive has pushed Labour still further from its counterparts in England, on free personal care, student fees, and proportional representation in local government, yet the party has sought to present a seamless image across Great Britain. Its manifesto for the 2001 General Election included a mix of domestic policy issues which were all Westminster responsibilities in England but some of which were devolved in Scotland. Under Henry McLeish there was some attempt to highlight decisions such as introducing free personal care for the elderly or signing the Flanders Declaration (see Chapter 5) on regional representation in Europe to show that Scotland could strike out on its own. Rhodri Morgan as First Minister in Wales made a great deal of political capital out of departures from New Labour orthodoxy. Donald Dewar and Jack McConnell, on the other hand, were reluctant to do anything that could give the SNP a political opening, tending to play down policy differences and emphasise the continuity between Westminster and Holyrood policies.

The Conservative Party

Modern Scottish Conservatism can be traced back to the merger of the Conservative and Liberal Unionist parties in 1911. In England this produced the Conservative and Unionist Party, but in Scotland the predominance of the Liberal Unionists was such that the party became simply the Scottish Unionist Party.[2] For the next half century the party thrived as a coalition of social forces adapted to the contours of the Scottish political landscape. There was a rural element, based on the landowning classes, farmers and a strong tradition of social deference, especially in the Highlands and North-east. An urban bourgeoisie provided social and political leadership in the cities and financial support, and brought in a large section of the middle classes. Populism, often suffused with anti-Catholic and anti-Irish appeals, tapped a part of the urban working-class vote. Finally, Unionists were able to pick up the remains of the Liberal Party, including those left over from the National Government of 1931. 'Liberal Unionist' and 'Liberal and Conservative' were frequently used as labels, with little worry about copyright (Dyer 2001). Conservatism dominated the Scottish professions, including such distinctly Scottish ones as law and teaching, and was a strong presence in the Church of Scotland, making the Unionist Party an important part of the Scottish Establishment. A final element was a certain pragmatism that allowed them to adopt middle-of-the-road social and economic policies from the 1930s, combined with a willingness to use the Scottish Office to lobby for Scottish interests and for funding. They did not have a base in local government, preferring to back broad anti-socialist coalitions of progressives, moderates and independents.

Early signs of trouble appeared with the electoral setbacks of 1959 and 1964, heralding a long-term decline. A party reorganisation in 1965 involved setting up a single Scottish organisation, amalgamating the National Liberal associations into a renamed Scottish Conservative Party, and contesting local government elections. Another reorganisation in the 1970s brought more central control and, recognising the decline of independent Scottish business as a source of funds, partially merged the Scottish organisation with its English counterpart. Yet despite apparent recoveries in 1970 and again in 1979, the secular decline in Conservative fortunes continued as their previous support bases were undermined (Dyer 2001). Rural voters became less deferential, although Conservative MPs actually became more upper class and anglicised over the postwar years, creating a larger social and political gulf (Keating 1975a). Urban bourgeois leadership collapsed with the indigenous Scottish business class, and sectarian voting waned. Glasgow is a stark example. In 1955 the Conservatives held seven of its fifteen seats. In 1997 they held no seats and were fifth in the popular vote, behind Labour, SNP, Liberal Democrats and the Scottish Socialist Party. Edinburgh held out longer, but in 1997 the Conservatives lost their last seat there. This was not merely a case of middle-class flight, since the surrounding suburban seats showed the same trend. From the 1950s, the Liberals under Jo Grimond reasserted their independence and in the 1960s made some progress in their old strongholds around the rural periphery; by the 1990s they were dominant there. In other rural areas, the SNP edged out the Conservatives, partly by squeezing their vote, but also by uniting the anti-Conservative electorate.

During the 1980s and 1990s, Conservative Secretaries of State would sometimes give the impression that they were resisting the imposition of Thatcherite policies on Scotland, although in fact all the main measures were reproduced north of the border (Midwinter et al. 1991). Perhaps the main achievement of the Scottish Office during this time was to prevent the ever-threatened 'Barnett squeeze', the convergence of Scottish and English spending levels as provided for in the funding formula (see Chapter 6). At the same time, there were repeated efforts to convert Scotland to neo-liberal ideas. One of the intellectual centres of the new right had been in St Andrews University, and Conservatives, including Thatcher, would argue that capitalism, individualism and the market were rooted in Scottish history, particularly the Enlightenment (Mitchell 1990). Ministers insisted that the welfare state had created a 'dependency culture' in Scotland, bolstered by a 'left-wing' Establishment and even by Scottish Conservative ministers who, in being seen to defend Scottish interests, reinforced the assumption in favour of high public spending (Thatcher 1993). The policy conclusion was that voters needed to be weaned off the state, so that they could see their real interests. It was this sort of reasoning (more akin to Gramscian Marxism than traditional Conservatism) that led to the genesis of the poll tax in the 1980s and its introduction first into Scotland. Yet the effect appeared to be the alienation of even more of the Scottish middle classes. Some efforts were made to rebuild a Scottish bourgeoisie, with the conversion of the Scottish Development Agency to Scottish Enterprise, on the advice of Thatcherite businessman Bill Hughes, and the appointment of business leaders to quangos and agencies of various sorts. Yet the privatisation policies of the Conservative government failed to support this, with no effort to build up Scottish ownership and control. Governing Scotland with a diminishing support base and refusing to heed calls for devolution, the Conservatives ended up with an image of being 'anti-Scottish'.

Conservative attitudes to Scottish home rule derive from an ideology that stresses order, hierarchy, patriotism and parliamentary supremacy. Lacking the appeal to class solidarity or the attachment to central planning of Old Labour, their concept of the Union is rooted in older conceptions of the state as a form of constitutional balance within unity. Traditional Conservatives were not natural centralisers or statists, and believed in the need to manage diversity within the union, as long as the central principle of parliamentary sovereignty was untouched. It may be that the aristocrats who provided the party leadership until well into the twentieth century, as a UK-wide political class with stakes in all parts of the union, had an instinctive understanding of this denied to their successors. There is a Tory home rule tradition which, like its Labour counterpart, never quite died out but, for most Conservatives, a Scottish Parliament has been a step too far since, as the representative of a self-conscious nation, it would inevitably challenge the ultimate authority of Westminster. This attitude, forged in the debates over Irish home rule in the nineteenth century, and refined in the writings of A. V. Dicey (1912; Dicey and Rait 1920), was transposed to the arguments over Scottish home rule in the twentieth century. Occasionally, the Conservatives have played the Scottish card against Labour's centralisation. In 1950, Winston Churchill declared that 'if England became an absolute Socialist state . . . I personally cannot feel that Scotland would be bound to accept such a dispensation' (quoted in Turner 1952). In the 1960s, Edward Heath responded to the rise of Scottish nationalism in his Declaration of Perth, promising a Scottish Assembly. This was fleshed out in a report by a committee chaired by elder statesman Alex Douglas Home, proposing an elected Scottish Assembly to take the committee stages of Scottish bills, with the other stages taking place at Westminster. This idea, although rejected by the Conservatives' Scottish Conference at the first opportunity, lived on into the 1970s as official party policy. Heath's commitment to some form of Scottish devolution was linked to the philosophy of self-help that informed the early part of his government of 1970–4, but no attempt was made to legislate for it. Conservatives gave a wary reception to Labour's devolution plans in 1974 but, with the arrival of Margaret Thatcher as leader in 1975, turned sharply against, precipitating the resignation of most of the Scottish Conservative front bench. Conservative home rulers kept a very low profile during the 1980s and 1990s, some of them serving in government, and the party opposed devolution during the election and referendum campaign of 1997.

Scotland appears to have baffled Conservative leaders in these years, not least Margaret Thatcher (1993), who liked to think of the

Scottish Enlightenment as a form of proto-Thatcherism. John Major, who succeeded her in 1990, made defence of the Union a centrepiece of his election campaign in 1992, and engaged in a 'taking stock' exercise after it. Both were prepared to advance administrative devolution to the Scottish Office, covering economic development, regional aid, universities and expenditure priorities within the block grant, in an effort to assuage Scottish discontent. Such a strategy was probably politically counter-productive, as its main political effect was to focus attention on the Secretary of State for Scotland as the centre of Scottish demands, and on his non-accountability to the Scottish electorate. As the support base for an indigenous Scottish Conservatism declined, the Conservatives were increasingly seen as an 'anti-Scottish' party as opposition to Thatcherism was linked to themes of nationality and nationalism. A 1987 opinion poll found that 32 per cent of Scots believed that Thatcher as Prime Minister was good for the UK, but only 9 per cent thought she was good for Scotland (Midwinter et al. 1991). By 2001 the impression had not disappeared, with an ICM poll showing that 45 per cent of Scots thought that the Scottish (sic) Conservative Party was mainly an English party, with 26 per cent considering it British and only 20 per cent rating it as a Scottish party.

In 1997, the Scottish Conservatives lost all their remaining seats and were left leaderless. After calling for a No vote in the devolution referendum of that year, they accepted political realities and announced that they would recognise the Scottish Parliament as a permanent fact and work within it. This placed them alongside Labour as a party of the new constitutional status quo, opposing further moves to autonomy but protecting what exists. Some Conservatives, however, have sought to outflank Labour and correct what they see as an element of instability in the system by calling for fiscal autonomy, allowing Scotland to raise its own revenue as well as spend it. This, in their view, will allow a proper debate in Scotland about the size and role of government and the balance between the tax burden and public services.

Following their 1997 defeat, the Conservatives underwent an internal debate about their future, in the absence of their former leaders, most of whom left active politics. Some voices called for rebuilding the party on distinctly Scottish lines, in the image of the Bavarian Christian Social Union, an independent party in permanent alliance with the German Christian Democrats. Such ideas quickly foundered on the lack of financial and organisational resources for such a venture. Instead, the Scottish party was given the right to make its own policy on devolved matters.

Some have argued for a move to the right, as the only party in Scotland calling for deep tax cuts and expenditure retrenchment. Others called for a move to the centre and the renunciation of Thatcherite ideas. These issues provoked deep divisions in what remained of the party, and prevented it making much of a contribution to the policy debate in Scotland. Within the Scottish Parliament, however, the Conservatives, rescued by a proportional electoral system which they had opposed, regrouped as the second party of opposition. They have pursued a moderate Conservatism reminiscent of 1950s and 1960s Toryism, accepting the Scottish Parliament but alert to any failings of the Executive.

The Scottish National Party

The SNP was founded in 1934 from a merger of nationalist organisations that had emerged in the preceding years, but for the first thirty years of its life it was something of a fringe party. Signs of growth appeared in the early 1960s, but the first breakthrough came with the Hamilton by-election of 1967 when it overturned a large Labour majority. This was enough to shock the government of Harold Wilson into setting up a Royal Commission on the Constitution, which reported in 1973, coinciding with another SNP by-election win at Govan. At the General Elections of February and October 1974, the nationalists gained seven, then eleven seats, and some 30 per cent of the vote. They lost all but two of their seats in 1979, but a 1988 by-election victory, again at Govan, sparked another revival and since then the SNP has established itself as one of the major parties of Scotland, coming second to Labour in 1997, 1999, 2001 and 2003, and forming the official Opposition in the Scottish Parliament.

For many years the SNP was as much a social movement as a political party, with a loose organisation, fluctuating membership and a variety of views linked by a belief in more Scottish self-government (Brand 1978). Its support base in the early years was in the small towns of rural Scotland, and the party's image was one of rather dull respectability, with little of the revolutionary fervour one might expect in a nationalist party. Also lacking has been a strong cultural emphasis; the party has rather preferred to talk earnestly about economic matters. It has never, however, become the party of the Scottish

Establishment. Few prominent business leaders or trades unionists have supported it, nor does it have a large hold over Scottish intellectuals. SNP policies were rather vague during its early years, and until the 1970s its platform was still based on the Social Credit principles adopted in the 1930s (Hanham 1969; Brand 1978). As it has gained support and become a credible candidate for office, the party has had to formalise its organisation and refine its policy programme. This has caused some division within party ranks.

As the only explicitly nationalist party in Scotland, the SNP has accommodated a diversity of views, from home rulers who would be content with a Scottish Parliament within the United Kingdom, to those seeking a radical break with the British state. Although the contours of the argument have changed, this division has never gone away. During the 1970s and 1980s it took the form of 'gradualists' versus 'fundamentalists', the former believing that devolution under a Labour government would be a first step to independence, the latter that it was a trap that would deprive the movement of its momentum. There were even some who wanted to call for a No vote in the referendums of 1979 and 1997, insisting that independence would come all in one step or never. With the arrival of the Scottish Parliament in 1999, it was declared that 'we are all fundamentalists now', since all could agree that the next step was independence. Yet the arguments continued, over whether the party should make independence its main or only campaigning issue, or whether it should first win a Scottish election and show competence in governing before holding a referendum on independence. Others argued that European integration and the changed nature of sovereignty in the modern world made the whole question moot and that the SNP should imitate the Catalan nationalist party *Convergència i Unió*, which does not support independence as a principle, but seeks to advance Catalan self-government whenever and wherever it can. As we have seen above, this reflects Scottish public opinion, which sees self-government as a matter of degree rather than a clear choice between independence and union, but for the SNP independence is such a defining feature of its existence that it is difficult to see how it could abandon it altogether.

There have also been divisions on Europe. During the 1950s the party looked with favour on European integration as something that might help small nations, but by the 1970s had turned sharply against it and campaigned for a No vote on continued membership of the European Community in 1975. Yet a pro-European sector persisted within the party, and by the 1980s it was, like the Labour Party, moving back to a pro-European position as the governing Conservatives became ever more hostile. This was not unique to Scotland, as other European nationalist and regionalist parties were treading the same path (Lynch 1996). In 1988 the SNP adopted the slogan 'independence in Europe', arguing that Scotland should be a full member state of the European Union, and since the 1990s it has argued for Scottish membership of the European single currency, although it is sometimes hazy on the details. Beyond this there is still a certain ambivalence, as some of the fundamentalists of the party are still very unhappy with the surrender of sovereignty implied in the European project, and need to be reassured that the party supports an intergovernmental rather than a supranational conception of the Union.

Another recurring division is between left and right. The SNP has historically been strong among middle-class voters in the small towns, and its presence in the petty bourgeoisie has already been noted. Since the 1980s, it has added a substantial working-class vote but, although this is large, it does not translate into constituency seats given the dominance of Labour in the industrial areas. Strategists have long been aware that to make a real electoral breakthrough the SNP must win seats in Labour's heartland of the central industrial belt, but without frightening off its traditional voters.

A left-wing ginger group appeared after the 1979 election reverses, the '79 Group, seeking to push the party to the left and outflank Labour, causing a major rift. Leaders of the Group were expelled from the party, although most were soon readmitted and one, Alex Salmond, became party leader in 1990.

From the late 1980s, the party repositioned itself as a left-of-centre party, freely using the 'socialist' label which Labour was trying to shake off. By the 1990s it was 'social democratic', and in 2003 described itself as 'a democratic left-of-centre party committed to Scottish independence'. Like the Liberal Democrats, it had discovered a lot of space to the left of New Labour, into which it was able to stray without losing any of its traditional support. It has defended public services, opposed privatisation and Labour's Private Finance Initiative, and for a while advocated nationalisation of key industries. In the Scottish Election of 1999 it accepted a challenge put down by the Labour government, which had cut a penny from income tax, announcing that if it won the election it would put the penny back on for public services. With the accession of John

Swinney to the leadership in 2000, there was a move back towards the centre-right, with the promise of a low-tax Scotland, slashing corporation tax in particular to attract firms to invest in Scotland. Right wingers like Jim Mather and Fergus Ewing were appointed to key positions in the Shadow Cabinet. There has been a tendency since the 1990s for the left wing to be more fundamentalist on the independence issue; previously it was the other way round. John Swinney was faced with regular challenges on both fronts before allowing Alex Salmond to return in 2004.

Such recurrent divisions and changes in stance are manageable because the SNP membership is less engaged in details of social and economic policy than in the promise of independence and the way it can be achieved. In the 1970s and 1980s, the Scandinavian social democracies – prosperous, Euro-sceptic and with generous welfare states – were the model; by the end of the 1990s, the Irish economic miracle showed the way. There is also a fundamental belief that Scotland is a rich country, exploited and held back by the union with England so that, with independence, there will be more money for everyone. In the 1970s, North Sea oil provided the underpinning for this argument, but it is not the only one, since the argument preceded the oil and continued once the oil issue had lost its salience. Consequently, there is less concentration on the social and economic transformation that might be possible with independence, and which could be the precondition of prosperity. Nor, compared with other European nationalist movements, is there much concentration on nation-building within Scotland, or on the creation of new nationally minded elites in business, trades unions or the sciences who could lead the national revival.

Organisation in the SNP, reflecting its extra-parliamentary origins, is based on the branch, which does not correspond to the parliamentary constituency but to the presence of local activists. There are also constituency associations, responsible for candidate selection and campaigning. Supreme power is held by the Annual Conference, chosen from branches and constituencies, and this elects the National Executive Committee. Intermediary bodies are the National Council, which meets between Annual Conferences, and the National Assembly, a forum for policy development. In the 1970s, when the party first elected a significant number of MPs, there was tension between the parliamentary group and the party activists back home. This unwieldy structure has been widely criticised as ill-adapted to a modern political party interested in winning elections and developing consistent policy, but the power of the activists within the branches is such that it has proved very difficult to streamline it. This power was demonstrated rather starkly in the choice of candidates for the electoral lists at the 2003 elections, when some of the party's most prominent MSPs were demoted down the lists, apparently for straying from party orthodoxy or for becoming too prominent. Leadership is correspondingly weak. Until 1989 there was a party Chairman, regarded as first among equals and with none of the authority of Conservative or Labour leaders. Since then there has been a National Convenor, generally referred to as 'leader' and enjoying a high media profile. This individual does not need to be an elected politician, but the continuous institutional presence of the SNP at Westminster and in the Scottish Parliament since the late 1980s has encouraged the emergence of a parliamentary leadership as a new power base in the party, and since 1989 the National Convenor has been an MP, then an MSP. At the same time, the organisational basis of the party has been improved and professionalised, making the SNP more like the other major parties (Lynch 2002).

The Liberal Democrats

Liberalism was the dominant force in nineteenth-century Scotland, regularly winning an absolute majority of the vote up to the First World War. It was, however, badly damaged by the split over Irish home rule in 1886 and even more so by the divisions caused by the Lloyd George coalition after the First World War and the National Government in the 1930s. By the 1940s it had been reduced to isolated groups of notables prone to making deals with the Unionists to gain a share of power. Following the election of Jo Grimond against Conservative opposition in 1950 and his accession to the Liberal leadership in 1956, the party took a more independent line and during the Liberal revival of the 1960s regained a number of its historic seats in the North-east and the Borders. During the 1970s it had to compete with the SNP for the third-party vote and was reduced to three MPs. The formation of the Social Democratic Party by Labour dissidents in 1981 and its alliance with the Liberals gave them a chance at a time of poor SNP fortunes, and the Alliance, contrary to some predictions, did as well in Scotland as in England. During the 1980s and 1990s the Alliance parties (merged into the Liberal Democrats in 1987) gained a large number of Scottish seats in relation to their vote because of the concentration of their strength – in 1997 they came fourth in the popular vote but second in the number of seats. Since most of their seats were held against the Conservatives, they were able to cooperate with the Labour Party in the Scottish Constitutional Convention, regarded by Liberal Democratic circles in London as a useful precedent in Lib-Lab partnership, and were natural coalition allies for Labour in the first Scottish Executive in 1999.

Unlike the other British parties in Scotland, the Liberal Democrats, like the Liberals before them, are a separate party from their counterpart south of the border, with complete policy and organisational autonomy. The British Liberal Democratic Party is a federation of English, Scottish and Welsh parties although, rather like the devolution settlement, it is an asymmetrical one, with the Federal Conference also taking policy decisions on English matters. There is a Scottish party leader, now chosen from the MSPs, although four out of the seven British Liberal leaders since the 1930s have also been Scottish MPs. The Scottish Liberal Democrats also take some pains to emphasise that they practice devolution, being unembarrassed about policy divergences between Scotland and England, and ensuring that their Scottish manifesto for UK General Elections makes reference only to reserved matters. Yet links with the party in London are close and neither policies nor party strategy diverge markedly.

Historically, the Liberal Party supported Home Rule All Round from the late nineteenth century and, while some Social Democrats were less keen, Liberal Democrat policy favours a federal United Kingdom within a federal Europe. Details of this have often been hazy, particularly over the question of whether England should be a single unit, but in the meantime Liberal Democrats have supported Scottish and Welsh devolution and English regional government. This reforming spirit extends to other areas of the constitution, including the incorporation of the European Convention on Human Rights, reform of the House of Lords, freedom of information and proportional representation, and the party has tended to take a less authoritarian view than either Labour or the Conservatives on matters of civil liberties and law and order. During the first session of the Scottish Parliament, the Liberal Democrats held the Justice portfolio, resisting many of the populist and authoritarian law and order measures being promoted in England. This was not always to the liking of Labour, which has often regarded them as too 'soft' on these matters (McLeish 2004), and after the 2003 elections Labour took on this portfolio to press for a populist line, especially on youth disorder. The Liberal Democrats were, however, able to water down proposals to gaol parents of young delinquents which they had opposed during the election campaign.

On social and economic issues, the party is rather close to the European social democratic mainstream and for a while was able to outflank Labour on the left by advocating increased levels of public spending financed, if need be, by additional taxation. In England, the party pulled back from this after 2001, seeking votes from disillusioned Conservative voters in the south, but the lack of serious competition from the right made this less appealing in Scotland.

Generally, the Liberal Democrats' policies have been close enough to New Labour to allow them to govern in coalition in the Scottish Executive. In the first Scottish Parliament they forced Labour to drop up-front tuition fees and to introduce free personal care for the elderly, popular policies that could be presented as defending the universal welfare state but which benefited middle-class voters enough to attract the support of the Scottish Conservatives as well as the nationalists. They were also instrumental in getting a slightly more liberal Freedom of Information Act in Scotland. In the second session of the Parliament they insisted on a commitment not to introduce the new university 'top-up' fees proposed in England, as well as on the introduction of proportional representation in local government elections.

The Minor Parties

Unlike in England, Scottish Labour faces a serious challenge from the left in the form of the Scottish Socialist Party (SSP). This originated in the Militant Tendency, a dogmatic Trotskyist group that infiltrated the Labour Party and gained some influence in Glasgow, Liverpool, London and the English Midlands, before being expelled in the 1980s. Scottish Militant had a degree of support in alienated working-class communities that enabled it to launch into electoral politics on its own, capitalising on the anti-poll tax demonstrations of the late 1980s. Its leader, Tommy Sheridan, was elected to Glasgow City Council while serving a gaol sentence for civil disobedience, and gained a respectable share of the vote in the Pollok constituency at the General Election of 1992. Changing its name to Scottish Socialist Party and merging with the Scottish wing of the

Socialist Workers' Party, the group then entered serious electoral politics, contesting all but one of the seats in the Scottish elections of 2003.[3] In the process the SSP has shed some of its doctrinal Trotskyism and reinvented itself as a demotic leftist party reminiscent in some ways of the old ILP. It stands for traditional socialism, with the nationalisation of large firms and banks, an immediate and substantial rise in the minimum wage, and the replacement of council tax by a steeply progressive Scottish Service Tax, and its long-term aspiration is an independent Scottish socialist republic. This formula, together with the charismatic leadership of Sheridan, proved attractive enough to tempt many electors to give it their second vote in 2003, enabling the SSP to gain seven seats in the Scottish Parliament.

The Greens were the other beneficiaries of the proportional list vote, electing one MSP in 1999 and six in 2003. Separate from the Greens in England since 1990, they are in principle committed to Scottish independence, although not primarily a nationalist party. Their platform is based, not surprisingly, on environmental issues, including promoting public transport and renewable energy, but extends to issues of international development and peace.

Neither the SSP nor the Greens have been serious contenders for office, even in coalition, in the first two terms of the Scottish Parliament, but they may still be policy influentials. After 2003 the Labour–Liberal Democrat coalition enjoyed only a small majority in Parliament, and the programme of government made several gestures towards the environmental agenda, while the SSP could make alliances with individual Labour MSPs on key issues, as indeed it did in the first Parliament on warrant sales where it was able to force the Executive to back down. The small parties also present an electoral challenge, so that Labour cannot take either its core working-class vote or its appeal to left-of-centre, middle-class, postmaterialist voters for granted. This is another contrast with England, where the challenge to the three traditional parties has come rather from the right in the form of the UK Independence Party and the British National Party, neither of which made as much progress north of the border.

The Evolving Scottish Party System

Scottish politics has come a long way in the last forty years. The UK parties have progressively taken on a Scottish dimension and

Scottish names. Since the 1970s they have issued distinct Scottish manifestos, and their policy stance has evolved from defending Scottish interests to promoting distinct policy ideas for Scotland. The presence of the SNP has kept the constitutional issue to the fore-front and pushed the other parties towards devolution and adopting stronger Scottish campaigning themes. Since the late 1990s, the presence of a far-left party, albeit a small one, has exposed the left flank of both Labour and the SNP, while the Greens have brought the environmental issue to the fore. Party politics has gone from being the least competitive to the most competitive in Britain, so that, with the possible exception of Labour seats in industrial Clydeside, no seat in Scotland can be considered the natural posses-sion of any party. All this has broadened the political agenda in Scotland compared with England, where the parties since the late 1990s have tended to seek the same centre ground, and has moved political competition somewhat to the left. The European issue has been contained to a large extent, with all the main parties broadly in favour, another contrast with debate at the UK level. All of this reflects the distribution of Scottish public opinion, which is more inclined to traditional social democratic themes and slightly less anti-European than that down south, but in turn it helps to sustain and shape that opinion. On the other hand, the British parties must reconcile the needs of party competition in the Scottish environment with support for their parent bodies, which brings a certain amount of strain. They must also seek to respond to Scottish political demands in a context in which the scope for policy divergences is necessarily limited (see Chapter 1).

Notes

1. Tactical voting is certainly possible under the Scottish system, but elec-tors seeking to split their votes risk cancelling their two votes out, as seats won in the constituency section are deducted from the total to be distributed through the lists.
2. The Union in question is that between Britain and Ireland, not between Scotland and England.
3. They gave a free run to Labour left-winger John McAllion. Ironically, this allowed the SNP, which elsewhere lost votes to the SSP, to oust McAllion and take the seat.

CHAPTER THREE

The Policy Environment

The term policy community, in the academic literature, refers to organisations and individuals concerned with a given policy sector.[1] It may include government officials, business groups, trades unions, voluntary groups and perhaps the media and academics. Often these will be bound by common understandings of the issues at stake and shared norms, persisting under successive governments and helping to shape and reshape policy. Such policy communities are usually conceptualised as sectoral, confined to individual policy fields, but operating across the entire United Kingdom. If this is so, then Scottish policy makers will be faced with a uniform pattern of demands, pulling them back into UK policy networks. If, on the other hand, Scotland has its own policy communities, demands are likely to be distinct and may diverge from those in England. It may, further, be that social compromises and trade-offs among policy sectors, objectives and groups are struck at the Scottish level, producing a policy-making dynamic in Scotland and allowing the emergence of a specific Scottish model (Keating and Loughlin 2002).

Scotland has long possessed its own interest groups in some sectors, while in others it is incorporated into UK networks and organisations. Often, this seems the result of historic accident. So the Scottish Trades Union Congress was organised partly as a result of a decision by the British TUC in 1895 to exclude the local Trades Councils, and partly because of a need to address specific Scottish legal questions (Keating and Bleiman 1979). The Educational Institute of Scotland, now the biggest trade union for Scottish teachers, was founded by 1847 by royal charter. In other cases, separate groups have emerged as a response to administrative devolution and the need for an interlocutor with the Scottish Office and its agencies. More commonly, it has stimulated the establishment of Scottish branches of British or UK bodies. Such is the case in housing and social services. It is impossible to give a definitive list of all the interest groups in Scotland, but the Consultative Steering Group's list of 797 consultees gives us some idea; Table 3.1 shows them broken down into six categories.

Table 3.1   Types of groups in Scotland, 1998, percentage

Scottish organisations	22.3
Scottish branch of UK organisations	50.4
UK group without Scottish branch	5.4
Scottish regional groups	18.8
Multinational corporations	1.8
Private companies	1.3

Source: Consultative Steering Group

Devolution does not seem to have altered these proportions significantly so that the predominant pattern is the Scottish branch of a wider group. There is, however, evidence of internal devolution within some of these organisations, particularly those within the second category. Groups have needed to strengthen existing Scottish levels or establish new ones in order to provide an input to the policy process. The devolved Parliament and Executive have looked for interlocutors to represent key interests and provide a policy input, and this has strengthened Scottish peak-level bodies grouping industries, sectors or the interests of labour and the voluntary sector. So the territorial level of interest articulation has grown in comparison with the sectoral or vertical one, with new constellations of interests, alliances and competition for influence.

Devolution has also produced a rationalisation of group activity, with a clearer distinction between UK and Scottish matters, corresponding closely to the division of competences in the state, and an increase in policy capacity at the Scottish level. The Confederation of British Industry and the Institute of Directors, for example, have given their Scottish branches autonomy over devolved issues and enhanced their presence in Scotland. Other bodies, such as the

Scottish Trades Union Congress, have converged in the other direction, establishing a clearer division of roles and more co-operation with their UK opposite numbers. Some groups, which operated at the regional or local level within Scotland, have also strengthened the Scottish level. Less well-resourced bodies, like individual trades unions and social groups, have had more difficulty adapting to the new system.

Business Groups

Like other parts of the United Kingdom and Europe, Scotland at one time had its local business class, captains of industry who were also political and social leaders. The decline of this class started after the First World War, with the crisis in Scottish industry and the subsequent 'drift to the south' of capital and business opportunities. Nationalisation after 1945, and again in the 1960s and 1970s, meant a further loss of local control, while privatisation in the 1980s and 1990s was not used as an opportunity to rebuild Scottish business ownership. Instead, there was a further decline in local ownership and an expansion of inward foreign investment, so that by 1989 less than a third of Scottish manufacturing industry was Scottish-owned (Ashcroft and Love 1993). As Table 3.2 shows, most firms are Scottish-owned, but these tend to be small enterprises and account for a little over half of turnover. Foreign-owned firms, just 1 per cent of the total, account for 10 per cent of jobs and nearly a fifth of turnover.

Table 3.2   Ownership of firms in Scotland, 2002, percentage

	Firms	Jobs	Turnover
Scottish	96	69	54
Other UK	3	21	28
Foreign	1	10	18

Source: Scottish Executive

As early as the 1930s there was some business concern about the decline of the Scottish economy, and the Scottish Council was formed by the shipbuilder James Lithgow (Kellas 1989). After the war it merged with a similar government-sponsored body to form the Scottish Council (Development and Industry), including business, trades unions and local authorities. The organisation of business itself was largely confined to industry-specific bodies and local chambers of commerce until the 1960s, when the rise of tripartite concertation prompted the creation of the Confederation of British Industry (CBI). There was a regional dimension to all this, through the Regional (and Scottish) Economic Development Councils. While the English Councils were abolished in 1979, the Scottish one continued a low-profile existence as one place where the three sides (government, business and unions) could continue to meet, if not to make policy.

The loss of Scottish ownership and control has sporadically been a political issue. In the 1970s there were warnings that excessive reliance on inward investment could mean a loss of power and influence, and during the 1980s there was a series of political battles over takeovers of Scottish firms. Banking and finance is one sector in which Scotland has retained its own firms, and there was a mighty conflict in the 1980s over a proposed takeover of the Bank of Scotland, leading to an understanding that the Scottish banks should have some degree of political protection. Consolidation of the banking industry in the 1990s undermined this and, after the Royal Bank of Scotland had taken over English-based National Westminster in 1999, any remaining protection was swept aside. When the Bank of Scotland was subsequently taken over by the Halifax, even the Scottish Nationalists accepted that local ownership in a global economy was an unrealistic dream. Yet at the same time, government policy did make some effort at reinventing the local bourgeoisie, by encouraging prominent business leaders, entrusting them with important public policy responsibilities in urban development and filling the boards of quangos with them. Big business was consistently hostile to political devolution and operated on a UK and global level, while keeping close links with the main Whitehall economic departments and enjoying easy access to ministers (Lynch 1998). Yet at the same time business leaders increasingly recognised the importance of regional development policy, infrastructure and planning, and supported the extension of administrative devolution through the Scottish Office, with which they had rather privileged contacts. It is a pattern that recurs in many European countries, with big business stressing the need for a large common market and macro-economic policy, opposing political devolution or regulation but accepting the supply side help that can be provided by local and regional administrations.

This strategy, in which links with London are the major key and those with Edinburgh a minor complement, has to some extent persisted after devolution, but with some necessary change. Hostility to devolution abated during the late 1990s and, at least in public expression, has largely disappeared.[2] Instead, business has come to accept it, reorganised its representation and learned to play under the new rules. This, for a sector that has traditionally been rather fragmented, has presented something of a challenge (Raco 2003). The Confederation of British Industry, the main employers' organisation, has introduced an internal devolution, so that its Scottish branch (officially still a 'regional' branch of the UK body) has authority to decide on matters falling within the remit of the Scottish Parliament. There has been some enhancement of the policy-making capacity of its Scottish Office, based in Glasgow, and it maintains good links into the relevant departments of the Scottish Executive. Most of the members of CBI Scotland, however, are Britain-wide and multinational enterprises, and its main policy lines are firmly British. The Institute of Directors represents individuals rather than firms and has traditionally taken a more strictly free-market approach than the CBI. It, too, has introduced internal devolution, with a Scottish Council to decide on devolved matters but, as with the CBI, the policy lead comes from London. Scottish Financial Enterprise is a promotional body set up in 1986 and dedicated to the interests of the financial services sector in Scotland. Although its membership is based in Scotland, the industry is regulated at a UK and European level and these remain the key points of reference. Scottish Chambers of Commerce (SCC) is a federation of local chambers, of which Glasgow is the oldest in the United Kingdom. While chambers were somewhat moribund in the postwar years, there has been a certain revival recently, following initiatives at the UK level and an effort to match the continental experience of dynamic local business leaderships. Again most of the policy leadership comes from the British level, with an input from local chambers, but SCC does maintain links into the Scottish Executive and the parliamentary committees. Scottish Council (Development and Industry) is often seen as a business organisation, although its membership includes trades unions and local government. Its diverse membership made it impossible to take a line on devolution, although it has a history of criticising excessive centralisation and calling for more economic power in Scotland. It remains an important forum for the discussion of economic issues, but the role it previously held at the centre of debate has been eclipsed by the Scottish Parliament and the rise of other economic development forums.

Devolution highlighted the absence of a single coherent voice for Scottish business and these 'big five' business groups have formed a loose organisation to coordinate their efforts in order to enhance business input into post-devolution policy making. This produced one policy success in persuading the Executive to drop workplace parking charges, but otherwise is more useful as a focal point for putting pressure on politicians. Standing somewhat apart is the Scottish Federation of Small Business (SFSB), part of the British Federation of Small Business, but with autonomy to make policy on devolved matters. Unlike the other business groups, SFSB, with its local membership of Scottish firms, was pro-devolution and is pro-Europe. It is less well-connected within UK and Scottish government, and tends to be somewhat resentful of the privileged position of big business, which to some extent explains its support for constitutional change.

Agriculture is represented in Scotland through three bodies. The National Farmers Union of Scotland is not affiliated with the National Farmers Union based in England and presses for the distinct interests of Scottish agriculture. Devolution has not changed the expression of these interests radically, but rather reinforced the dual territorial and sectoral concerns. At the same time, there are common interests with English farmers, with whom it shares an office in Brussels to keep abreast of European matters. In the Highlands and Islands, farmers are organised by the Crofting Foundation, formerly the Crofters' Union. As agriculture is a devolved matter, both unions are closely linked to decision makers in the Scottish Executive, although less strongly to the Parliament, with its urban bias. At the same time, agricultural policy is highly Europeanised, so that they have been very concerned with Scottish representation in the European Union. The Scottish Rural Property and Business Association (SRPBA) (formerly the Scottish Landowners' Federation, SLF), representing the large estates, is the equivalent of the Country Land and Business Association (formerly Country Landowners' Association) in England, although it is a separate body, dealing with a distinct set of issues under Scottish law. At one time, the SLF might have been seen as the defender of the aristocracy and the lairds and of the old rural order, but in recent years many estates have passed into the hands of capitalist enterprises and are part of big business; SRPBA now favours foreign ownership of estates as a way to bring in investment. Landowners long enjoyed a rather protected status in Scotland, especially under Conservative governments, but the parties of the centre-left have historically favoured land reform and it was inevitable that this would become a priority issue for the Scottish Parliament. SRPBA has therefore had to adapt rather quickly to devolution and get into the Scottish political game, by changing its name, broadening its scope and becoming more active at the political level.

Scotland has its own representative organisations in the fisheries sector, although these have traditionally been rather fragmented, by locality and sector. Indeed, for many years it was the Scottish Office that sought a united lobby to defend Scottish fishing interests in the UK and in Europe. Now the dominant body is the Scottish Fishermen's Federation, which groups about 90 per cent of the Scottish fishermen and, given the relative size of the industry, is the main fishing body in the United Kingdom. The Fishermen's Association Limited, founded in 1995, is formally a UK body with membership extending to Northern Ireland, but is based in Aberdeen. Repeated crises in the fishing industry, and the need to present a united front in Europe, have forced these groups to cooperate more, despite the legacy of past divisions.

Although the allocation of powers in the Scotland Act seems reasonably clear, it was not obvious in 1999 which level of government would really be the centre of political power in Scotland or what would be the relationship among the local, Scottish, UK and European levels. There was a certain learning phase, in which producer groups felt out the new patterns of influence, while historic orientations continued to be important. The result is a complex pattern, with an emerging Scottish level everywhere but not always predominating. We can understand these patterns by reference to three sets of institutional factors. First is the ownership of the firms and the location of their production. Second is the market for their products. Third is the level at which the activity is regulated. Big firms doing business in Scotland are mostly externally owned, are regulated mainly at UK and European levels, and trade in UK and global markets. We find, accordingly, that the main focus of attention for their representative groups are UK government departments. They do, however, have to pay attention to the Scottish level more than in the past, because some matters affecting them, such as transport or planning policy, are devolved. Small businesses tend to be Scottish-owned and to operate in the Scottish market. Like large firms, they are generally regulated at the UK or European levels but, as elsewhere in Europe, are also dependent on locally produced public goods including grants, infrastructure and the services of Scotland's network of business support agencies. They have not been invited into the networks of big business and tend to look to the Scottish level for support and action.

Some groups are cross-pressured and need to operate at both levels. Scotland is a major centre for banking and finance and many of the firms are still Scottish-owned. Yet they operate in global markets and are regulated at UK and European levels. Scottish banking and financial interests are concerned to maintain the health of the sector locally and to retain headquarters functions in Scotland, but recognise that survival requires that they play a global game and engage in cross-border mergers and takeovers. Yet they need to play the Scottish card in their fight to maintain control functions and high-level managerial jobs in Scotland, and this means mobilising Scottish political opinion, the Executive and the Parliament, as was seen in the case of the Bank of Scotland. Political pressure ensured that, despite the predominance of the Halifax in the merged bank, its headquarters would be in Edinburgh.

The whisky industry is similarly cross-pressured. It is by definition a local industry since the marque can only be awarded to whisky produced in Scotland, but it is largely externally owned. Indeed, there were some spectacular takeover battles in the 1980s. The industry is regulated at the UK level, except for certain matters like water quality; taxation is a particularly critical issue. Whisky sells in global markets, with the vast bulk of production being exported. This means that the industry is largely oriented towards the UK level of policy making, although contact is maintained with the Scottish Executive and Parliament.

Agriculture and fisheries are sectors where businesses are locally owned and operated, while regulated at Scottish and European levels. Ironically, the joint effects of devolution and Europeanisation are to strengthen the networks at UK level, which is the nexus of the other networks. Scottish institutions are often used as allies and as channels of influence to UK and European levels, in much the way that the old Scottish Office was. There has also, however, been some pressure from these groups to extend the scope for Scottish discretion in modifying and applying European regulations.

Agricultural and fisheries interests are deeply involved in European affairs, as policies for these sectors are determined at the EU level. Business groups are less well-connected to Brussels, tending to leave European matters to their UK headquarters; and CBI Scotland did not join Scotland Europa (see Chapter 5). Scottish Council (Development and Industry), however, has taken an interest in European affairs and in 2003 called unequivocally for the UK to join the Euro. The membership survey on which this call was based was rather more ambiguous. Around half felt that Scotland was at a competitive disadvantage outside the Euro, but most favoured the government's cautious strategy of membership subject to the Treasury's five tests and a referendum. A majority had not heard of Scotland Europa or the network of Euro Info Centres in Scotland.

Allowing for these differences, all Scottish groups have been affected in some way by constitutional change. Business is now more politically exposed and must defend its place and interests in the Scottish political arena in a way that was not necessary before. This has led it into some corporate philanthropy, to an acceptance of the social-inclusion agenda, and to the need to keep an eye on proceedings in the Scottish Parliament. The increase in consultation by both Executive and Parliament has placed new demands on the Scottish groups, further drawing them into the Scottish networks and encouraging them to abandon their earlier suspicion of devolution. From about 2002 onwards, the increased emphasis by the Executive on economic development (see Chapter 7) also made for a closer involvement of business groups. On the other hand, Scotland does not yet have the self-confident business community found, for example, in Quebec and has still to find a coherent voice in the new system.

Trades Unions

Trade unionism in Scotland, as in other parts of the United Kingdom, had local origins and most of the early trades unions were Scottish rather than British. After the First World War, however, unions followed industry in consolidating with their counterparts in the south, citing lack of resources, the need to negotiate with UK firms, and the importance of dialogue with government in London. Another factor was a loss of faith in the ability of the Scottish economy to generate resources or pay wages at the same level as England, and the conversion of the unions, along with the Labour Party, to centralised planning and state intervention. Mergers with

British unions continued, with the last major Scottish industrial union, the Scottish Horse and Motormen's Association, joining the Transport and General Workers' Union in the 1960s. By 2000 only four of the forty-six unions affiliated to the STUC were Scottish, and three of these were teaching unions. From the 1980s, Scottish trade unionism shared the general trend to decline, so that by 2001 trade union membership accounted for just 35 per cent of the workforce, slightly higher than the UK average of 29 per cent, but lower than in Wales, Northern Ireland or northern England. Trade unionism is now more likely to be found in the public sector, where 66 per cent of employees are unionised (59 per cent in the UK as a whole), than in the private sector, where only 21 per cent are (19 per cent for the UK as a whole) (Brook 2002).

The Scottish Trades Union Congress (STUC) was founded in 1897 and is quite separate from the Trades Union Congress (TUC) in London, with both UK and Scottish unions affiliating to both organisations. STUC provides a focus for trade unionism in Scotland, although its influence has waxed and waned, as have its relations with the TUC. There was a lot of rivalry in the early years, and between the 1940s and the 1980s relations both with the TUC and with the Labour Party were often soured by the more left-wing stance of the STUC, due to the larger presence of shop-floor workers and trades councils and the influence of the Communist Party. The STUC's status was enhanced when it played a role in the regional development initiatives of the 1960s and 1970s, although the main tripartite issues like prices and incomes policy were negotiated through the TUC. In the 1980s, the STUC became, in the absence of other forums, a focus for opposition to the economic policies of the UK Conservative government. It established a Standing Commission on the Scottish Economy, a Manufacturing Steering Group, and a series of conferences to discuss Scotland's economic plight, and played a key role in the campaigns against the closure of the Ravenscraig steelworks. Yet at the same time, it did not break off relations with government to the degree that happened at UK level, and continued to participate in the tripartite Scottish Economic Council after its counterparts in England had been abolished. This gave it a rather broad role, as a tribune for Scottish interests and a forum for social and political mobilisation on a range of issues.

STUC was an early and enthusiastic supporter of home rule for Scotland although, like Labour, it effectively abandoned the cause after the 1920s (Keating and Bleiman 1979). A residual sympathy remained, however, and it reaffirmed its support for devolution to the Royal Commission on the Constitution in 1969, some years before the Labour Party did. The commitment was firmed up in the 1980s and 1990s, when STUC provided much political and logistical support for the Scottish Constitutional Convention. Trade union support for devolution, however, has always been ambivalent. They favour a Scottish Parliament and increasingly emphasise the need to give it powers to develop the Scottish economy, but at the same time support rather centralised economic management and strongly resist the decentralisation of labour regulation or wage bargaining. This puts trades unions a step ahead of the business community, which has tended to favour functional decentralisation of regional development functions but not political devolution, but a long way from the nationalists, who want full control of economic policy making, and their position more or less corresponds to the current list of powers of the Scottish Parliament.

Since devolution, the STUC, like other groups, has had to reorganise its work so as to make an input to policy rather than simply lobby or oppose. Its five standing committees have been replaced by short-term working groups to respond to current issues. A clearer division has been established between devolved matters, on which STUC takes the lead, and reserved matters, which are generally left to the TUC. This has required closer cooperation between the two congresses, itself facilitated by the lessening of the old political antagonisms. Relations with the Scottish Executive were certainly facilitated in the first two sessions of the Scottish Parliament by the dominance of the Labour Party, which has been rather more accepting of the broader role of trades unions than has New Labour in London. In 2002, a concordat was signed between the STUC and the Scottish Executive providing for regular consultation, including meetings with civil servants.

Individual unions have adapted according to whether they are primarily concerned with reserved or devolved matters. In primary and secondary education, the main union is the Educational Institute of Scotland (EIS). Its presence has both enhanced the role of the profession in Scottish policy making and maintained a distinct policy community from the rest of the United Kingdom. Other public-sector trades unions need to concern themselves with the Scottish level, which directly affects their members' employment and conditions, but the fact that most wages are still negotiated at a British or UK level means that there is a strong focus on London. Normally this takes the form of joint negotiating machinery involving Whitehall and the devolved administrations, although there is no obligation to proceed this way. If government is successful in decentralising wage bargaining, this will no doubt change. In 2002, a new contract and terms for medical consultants was approved by British Medical Association members in Scotland but not in England, reflecting the different conditions there and the lack of emphasis on private practice in Scotland. The Scottish Executive then concluded a separate deal in Scotland, encouraged by the Department of Health in London, which saw this as a contribution to breaking up UK-wide bargaining. Schoolteachers' pay and conditions were negotiated separately even before devolution, and this has remained the case, maintaining the independence of the Scottish teaching unions; but university pay is negotiated on a UK basis and in 2004 this was even extended to take in the old Scottish colleges which became universities in the 1990s.

Private-sector unions tend to look to the UK level, which regulates employment law, but are engaged at the Scottish level in strategies for jobs and economic development. Yet, like many other bodies, trades unions have had difficulty contributing to the Scottish policy agenda because of a shortage of policy-making and research capacity, a deficiency they are only now struggling to remedy. Unions also link into government through the Labour Party, which tends also to bridge the Scottish and UK levels. Were unions in Scotland faced with a hostile government in London, there might be more of a tendency to play the Scottish card to mobilise opposition. Even under New Labour there have been tensions, as the RMT (railway) union allowed some of its Scottish branches to finance the Scottish Socialist Party, although the parent union was affiliated with Labour. Scottish unions have also been active at the European level, which they embraced in the 1980s as a way of bypassing an unsympathetic central government. The STUC General Secretary was a member of the European Economic and Social Committee and the organisation has been active in Scotland Europa. Since 1999, however, it has tended to leave European matters to the TUC in London.

The Professions

There is a long tradition in Britain of professional self-regulation, whereby formally private bodies determine qualifications and admission to occupations demanding a high level of skill and ethical integrity. As these bodies also represent their members, it is not always easy to distinguish between them and trades unions, especially as in some professions the term trade union is disdained. There has, however, been a growing tendency to separate the roles. Professions in Scotland, like other groups, may be organised on a Scottish, a British or a UK basis, depending on historic circumstances and the level of government at which they are regulated. The Scotland Act 1998, which reserves certain professions and devolves others, was largely based on existing practice under the Scottish Office system, so that in some cases a function is devolved but regulation of the corresponding profession is not.

Primary and secondary teaching is entirely devolved as part of the integrated Scottish education system. Since 1965, professional regulation has been the responsibility of the General Teaching Council, based on the principle of professional self-regulation and with which Scottish teachers must be registered. University education was brought under the Scottish Office only in 1992 and, although devolved, universities are part of a UK policy community as well as a Scottish one. Universities Scotland, the representative body, is part of the wider Universities UK, but has also developed extensive links with the Scottish Executive, which have deepened over the years. Law is a historically separate matter, regulated by the Law Society of Scotland and the Faculty of Advocates. These have close relations with the Scottish Executive on matters of law reform, criminal justice and civil law. As traditional insider groups, they have not had to adapt radically in their relationship with government, but have become much more active at the parliamentary level.

The medical profession, by contrast, is much more integrated at a UK level. The British Medical Association represents doctors and mainly fulfils the role of a trade union, operating across the United Kingdom and preferring uniformity of pay and conditions. Professional self-regulation is the responsibility of the General Medical Council, whose approval is valid throughout the UK. There are several Royal Colleges for surgeons, physicians and general practitioners in the British Isles, with important responsibility for setting examinations and regulating entry into the professions. For historic reasons, Scotland has more than its share. The Royal College of Surgeons of Edinburgh, established in 1505 by royal charter, has some 15,000 fellows, only half of whom are based in the United Kingdom and only a quarter of these in Scotland. The

Royal College of Physicians and Surgeons of Glasgow registers about a third of the physicians in the UK. The Royal College of Surgeons of England, on the other hand, is largely confined to England but must share the market with the Scottish-based colleges and the Dublin college, established when Ireland was still part of the United Kingdom. There are also strong international links, as many overseas surgeons and physicians take their qualifications with the Scottish-based colleges. As regulation of the medical professions is a reserved matter, qualifications and training standards are UK-wide and the colleges are part of a single policy community. Since devolution there has been a certain tendency for the Royal College of Surgeons in England to see itself as the predominant English body, but this has been resisted by Glasgow and Edinburgh, who do not want to be confined to their local markets. On the other hand, the colleges are consulted regularly by the Scottish Executive on policy matters and are part of the Scottish health policy network.

Professional organisations in social work, housing and town planning are organised on a UK-wide basis, but there have been long-standing differences in the way these issues are organised in Scotland. Social work provided one of the few examples of policy divergence under the Scottish Office – the Social Work (Scotland) Act of 1968 – and housing and planning policies have differed in priorities and instruments, reflecting the distinct conditions of Scotland. Devolution has strengthened the Scottish dimension and increased the workload of the relevant professional bodies.

While many professional bodies straddle the United Kingdom, adopting the same attitudes on both sides of the border, there is a certain public-sector ethos in Scotland and a willingness to accept a larger role for the state and for public provision. Evidence for this is perhaps scanty, but it is consistent. Few doctors availed themselves of the provisions to become fund-holders under the Conservative government (see Chapter 7); Scottish consultants in 2003 accepted a contract turned down by their English colleagues because it would interfere with their private practice; Scottish academics show a greater civic commitment and are less likely than their Oxbridge counterparts to see the university apart from society (Paterson 2003). This in turn is reflected in the closer relationship between government and the professions in Scotland, with important effects on public policy (see Chapter 7).

The Voluntary Sector

This is a broad term for a wide range of bodies (some 25,000 on the database of the Scottish Council of Voluntary Organisations) concerned with social, environmental, cultural and other matters, relying on the work of citizen volunteers with some professional help. It has two roles: lobbying for resources and policy goals; and providing services themselves as a 'third sector' between government and private business. The voluntary sector has a strong Scottish focus, consisting overwhelmingly of Scottish groups or autonomous branches of UK bodies, able to take their own policy line. An umbrella is provided by the Scottish Council of Voluntary Organisations (SCVO), founded in 1936, which groups about 1200 organisations and local Councils for Voluntary Service. The voluntary sector has been supported by governments of all political persuasions, the Conservatives seeing it as an alternative to state – and especially municipal – provision, with Labour and the Liberals seeing it as a form of citizen participation and democracy, while New Labour has identified it as a third way between state and market. Consequently, it has seen its funding grow, with 40 per cent of it coming from government sources, including the Scottish Executive, local government and Communities Scotland. The sector was overwhelmingly in favour of home rule, as the SCVO found when it tested opinion in 1997, since devolution held the promise of more access, more resources and more responsibilities for citizen groups. More generally, SCVO has pursued the 'new politics', being sceptical towards political parties, professional politicians, local government and the civil service.

Before devolution, the Labour government launched a Scottish Compact with the voluntary sector, promising consultation, dialogue and an encouragement of volunteering; it was renewed in 2004. The Civic Forum was seen as another important means of access, as were the committees of the Scottish Parliament. There is no doubt that, as a result, the voluntary sector has increased its role in the consultation process and during the first term (1999–2003) was one of the clear gainers from devolution. Since then, a certain disillusion has set in, as the political parties and the civil service have shown their resilience. Local government remains a rival for the sector in the control of services and resources, and strongly insists on its representative and democratic credentials. Voluntary groups, on the other hand, complain that initiatives from the centre are not always carried through locally as local authorities use their discretion to set their own priorities. Trades unions, while supportive of volunteering in principle, are wary that it might be used to substitute for full-time jobs and are strongly attached to traditional modes of service delivery. So there have been some conflicts over Community Planning, which the Executive has placed under the responsibility of local councils to the discomfort of the voluntary sector, and over the policy of transferring housing stock from local councils to housing associations, which the trades unions and many local councillors oppose.

The Churches

Scotland has traditionally been seen as a religious country, although like much of Europe it has secularised in recent years. Since religion is often worn lightly or is a matter of family tradition, it is difficult to get a precise idea of its importance in people's lives. In the 2001 census, two-thirds of the population described themselves as being of one of the Christian religions, slightly below the numbers in England and Wales.[3] Twenty-eight per cent declared that they had no religion, although only 17 per cent had been brought up without a religion. The Scottish Social Attitudes Survey showed rather lower religious identity, with 40 per cent declaring themselves without a formal religion.

The Church of Scotland is established as the state religion but, unlike the Church of England, is not subject to state direction or intervention. Its democratic traditions have been a strong influence on Scottish civic and political life, and at one time it was commonly said that its annual General Assembly was the nearest thing that Scotland had to its own parliament. Since the nineteenth century, however, its dominance has declined as a result of the Disruption of 1843, the immigration of Irish Catholics and, later, secularisation. In 2001, 42 per cent of the population identified with it, although active participation is much lower, at just over 5 per cent (*Whitaker's Scottish Almanack* 2003). It continues to speak out on public issues, including both international and domestic affairs, notably through its Church and Nation Committee, and plays an important role in social services with its care homes. In recent years it has abandoned its former conservative positions for more socially progressive ones, although on modern lifestyle questions it is often divided and unable to articulate a single view.

The Catholic Church has a substantial presence in Scotland and traditionally has spoken for a section of the working class, bringing it onto the same ground as the Labour Party. By 2001 it accounted for some 15 per cent of the Scottish population, notably higher than in England and Wales. Only a third of these attend church regularly, but this still gives it a slightly higher number of practitioners than the Church of Scotland (*Whitaker's Scottish Almanack* 2003). It tends to be conservative in social doctrine but left of centre on economic and welfare state issues, a combination personified in the late Cardinal Winning of Glasgow.

There is a range of smaller Presbyterian churches, tending to be more socially conservative than the Church of Scotland, and smaller Jewish and Muslim communities.

Religion has in the past been a divisive issue in Scotland, and there is a history of sectarian hostility. In the early days of the Scottish Parliament a speech by Catholic composer James MacMillan sparked a debate on whether sectarianism was still a factor in Scottish society and, while neither side in the argument ceded much ground, the bulk of academic commentators have concluded that sectarian divisions have greatly diminished. Most attribute this to social change, including the decline of the old skilled trades, which were sometimes reserved for Protestants, and urban redevelopment, which mixed formerly segregated neighbourhoods. Secularisation has accelerated in recent years, so that more people decline to accept a religious identity at all. Nonetheless, there have been accusations of sectarian favouritism in Labour Party politics in the west of Scotland, and there are professional societies and networks still bound by religious affiliation.

The Christian churches were active in the devolution debate and generally in favour of the Scottish Parliament, and were quick to organise themselves to deal with it. Action of Christians Together in Scotland (ACTS) groups all the main Christian denominations to promote common interests and maintains a Scottish Churches Parliamentary Office. Given the differences among the various denominations, this does not seek a common line, but assists its members in gaining access to ministers and MSPs. The Catholic Church also has a parliamentary officer of its own. Access to politicians is not difficult given the standing of the churches in society, and issues raised are very broad, including education, social inclusion and poverty, homelessness and international peace. A Scottish Churches Social Inclusion Network deals with issues of poverty, while the

Scottish Churches Commission deals with common interests in temporal matters like property taxes on their buildings or charity law.

Relations between the Parliament and the churches got off to a rather bad start with the debate on the repeal of Section 28/2A, the legislation passed under the Conservatives banning the 'promotion' of homosexuality by schools and local governments. The Catholic Church was outspokenly opposed to repeal, while Protestant businessman Brian Soutar organised a private referendum against it. The Parliament stood firm on repeal, supported by most of the Labour, SNP and Liberal Democrat MSPs, but the debate left a residue of suspicion of the role of the churches in public life, and a wariness about taking on such emotive issues in the future. It is notable that after the 2003 election, the Executive preferred to leave the question of civil partnerships to Westminster through a Sewel motion.

Devolution and Policy Communities

Devolution has, as expected, reinforced the Scottish level of interest-group activity and led to changes on the two dimensions mentioned earlier (see Chapter 1): the territorial dimension, between Scotland, the UK and now Europe; and the horizontal dimension, within Scotland. It has also forced British groups operating in Scotland to make a clearer distinction between UK and Scottish matters, along the lines of the allocation of powers to the Scottish Parliament, and to give their Scottish branches more autonomy in policy matters. There has been a corresponding, but weaker, tendency for Scottish groups to play less of a role at the UK level, leaving that to their parent or sister bodies. Perhaps surprisingly, Scottish groups have not been particularly active in European matters, apart from the obvious cases like the farmers and fishermen. Europe was often seen in the 1990s as a form of substitute for being excluded from influence in London, a way of bypassing the centre to get at least some symbolic recognition and even some resources. After 1999 this seemed less urgent and Scottish groups were absorbed in their own affairs, tending to leave Europe to their London counterparts. This in turn may be changing again, as groups are drawn into European networks of collaboration and partnership, along with the Scottish Executive and Parliament themselves.

Within Scotland, channels of access to the policy process have increased with devolution, although different groups take distinct paths. 'Insider groups', including the main economic interest groups and the professions, have close contacts within Executive departments and are consulted about policy on a regular basis. Voluntary groups and campaigning bodies pay more attention to the Parliament and its committees, where they can expect a more sympathetic reception. The Scottish Parliament with its 129 members and specialised committees has provided a focus for group lobbying that did not exist when Scotland was represented by seventy-two MPs who spent most of their time in London. Groups have also become active in and around the conferences of all the main parties, knowing that the parties are sensitive to the public mood and less confident of their loyal core vote. The media are another channel which has grown in importance with the increased coverage of Scottish affairs and the inability of the parties to supply a good story every day. There is also the Civic Forum, an effort to institutionalise group activity and broaden participation.

One sign of the new activity is the habit of groups to prepare manifestos for the Scottish elections, setting out their priorities and asking the parties to respond. At the 2003 elections, sixty-one manifestos were published to try to influence the electoral agenda. These included the main parties, minor parties and fringe parties. Sixteen party manifestos were issued in all. Seven parties stood without publishing a manifesto, and there were eleven independent candidates, issuing local election addresses. Campaigning groups on rural affairs, fisheries and hospital closures entered the electoral arena putting up candidates, one of whom won.[4] Forty-five interest groups also issued manifestos setting out their views on the issues without endorsing any party.

Table 3.3   Manifestos for the Scottish Elections, 2003

Parties with manifesto	Groups with manifesto
Labour	Advocates for Animals
SNP	Age Concern Scotland
Liberal Democrat	Amnesty International
Conservative	ASH Scotland
Scottish Socialist	Association of University Teachers
Green	Asthma
UK Independence	British Dental Association
Scottish People's Alliance	Cancer Research Scotland
Scottish Senior Citizens Unity	Carers Scotland
Scottish Unionist	CBI Scotland

Table 3.3 *continued opposite*

Table 3.3 *continued*

Communist Party Peace
  Democracy Socialism
Pro-Life
Protect Rural Scotland
Pensioners'
Countryside Party Fighting
  Rural Issues
British National Party
  Scotland

Other Parties
Adam Lyal's Witchery Tour
Christian Independent
  Alliance Upholding
  Community Values
Fighting Hospital Closures
  and Downgrading Fishing
Liberal Party in Scotland
Rural
Save Local Hospitals
Socialist Labour

Independent Candidates
Campbell, Helen
Canavan, Dennis
Gatensbury, Peter
Gray, Tom
MacDonald, Margo
Mathers, Steven
Quigg, Damien
Robbie the Pict
Robertson, Arthur
Scott, Alexander
Turner, Dr Jean

Chambers of Commerce Scotland
Chartered Institute of Housing
CHESS – Coalition of Higher Education
  Students in Scotland
Children First
Children in Scotland
Conservative Christian Fellowship
Council of Mortgage Lenders
Dementia Scotland
Disability Agenda Scotland (umbrella)
EIS – Educational Institute of Scotland
Energy Action Scotland (with Transco and
  UNISON)
Engender
Epilepsy Scotland
Equality Network
Federation of Small Businesses
Friends of the Earth
Highland Community Care Forum
Independent Green Voice
Pharmaceutical Industry Council
Royal College of Nursing
RSPB
SACRO
Scottish Building Federation
Scottish Civic Forum
Scottish Environment LINK (25 organisations)
Scottish Human Rights Centre
Scottish SPCA
Scottish Tourism Forum
Scottish Youth Parliament
SCVO
Sector Skills Alliance Scotland
SFHA – Scottish Federation of Housing
  Associations
UNISON
Victim Support
Volunteer Scotland

Groups which review party manifestos
Advertising Association
Charter 88

Others
Roger Crofts

Source: own compilation

There has been an increase in staffing and policy-making capacity but not always enough to meet the needs of the new system, so that groups are not always in a position to generate a distinctive Scottish response to policy issues.

The system is undoubtedly more pluralist, going well beyond the former 'insider' groups like the business community, the professions and (under Labour governments) the trades unions.[5] Determining the patterns of winners and losers is more difficult. Big business interests, having generally opposed devolution, initially felt rather detached, emphasising their links into the economic departments of Whitehall; they also point to the lack of business people among the ranks of Scottish politicians. Yet over time the private enterprise voice has grown, and business gained some significant concessions in matters such as transport policy and business rates. This is a pattern common to devolved and regional governments everywhere, who are increasingly obliged to emphasise the needs of economic growth and competitiveness and hence to listen to business demands. The trades unions have gained more access, although this may have as much to do with the change of UK government in 1997 as with devolution in 1999, and there has been no return to the 1970s when unions were regarded as an equal partner in tripartite bargaining over public policy. Access for the voluntary sector, which had few institutional channels of access before 1999, improved greatly, especially in the Parliament, where it is well represented among MSPs. Voluntary organisations were also able to appeal to 'new politics' themes, as an alternative to conventional political action or bureaucratic administration.

This increased pluralism, while positive from a democratic perspective, has raised problems of its own. Groups have complained of consultation fatigue, as they are constantly asked their opinions and government even comes back to them for clarification. Scottish policy communities, previously organised as a territorial lobby to get more for Scotland out of whatever policy was going, now have to adapt to making policy. There is also a problem with excessive expectations, as not everyone who is consulted is going to get their way. This is exacerbated by some unrealistic expectations of devolution from many groups in Scotland, especially those in the voluntary sector who had previously exercised little influence. New politics advocates made much of the potential for consensus, assuming a common interest across Scottish society. For some, indeed, the flourishing of 'civic Scotland', the range of groups that had developed in the 1980s and 1990s, made a Parliament almost redundant. It was in this spirit that a Civic Forum was created to be the voice of civil society alongside the politicians. Yet much of the unity of the 1990s concerned what Scotland was against rather than what it was for. Constitutional change mobilised a broad consensus, but this could not always be extended to substantive policies. Politics is intrinsically about setting priorities, distributing resources and testing competing ideas, with winners and losers. Devolution has also introduced a new class of politician to Scotland and a new institution, the Parliament, ending the political void that had allowed civic Scotland to thrive. The same phenomenon has been noted in Spain, where political devolution has crowded out the voluntary sector. The Civic Forum has continued but mainly to provide a voice for those who have not found a place in the new parliamentary politics, and remains a rather marginal force.

Yet, even conceding this, politics in Scotland has still been more consensual than in England. There is a willingness to negotiate with groups and stakeholders and less tendency to confrontation, whether with public-sector professionals, trades unions or the poor and deprived. The strength of vertical devolution, from Westminster to Holyrood, has had an effect on the horizontal dimension of power within Scotland. Given the extensive powers of the Parliament, it is not possible for even the most powerful or UK-oriented to opt out of the Scottish political arena altogether, or to bypass Scottish institutions. This has strengthened Scotland as a political arena, rather than as a series of sectoral arenas linked only at UK level. Business must therefore have something to say about social exclusion, unions must be aware of the need for firms to be competitive, and social welfare groups need to be aware of the economic dimension. This in turn has encouraged a social dialogue within Scotland, with agreement here, disagreement there and compromise elsewhere. It would be an exaggeration to say that Scotland has developed its own version of corporatism, binding government, business and unions, since the Scottish Parliament does not control all the relevant powers and business is strongly opposed. Yet in a weaker sense, there is developing a form of social concertation and a shared agenda on certain issues, notably around economic development (see Chapter 7). Some groups are better represented in this process than others, with the professional networks and business in a stronger position than the poor and powerless. Yet there has certainly been a change, and this does affect the policy process and its results, as we will see in later chapters.

Think Tanks

Since the 1970s much new policy development in Britain has come from foundations or institutes colloquially known as think tanks. They were largely responsible for propagating the monetarist and free-market ideas that formed the basis of Thatcherism in the 1980s, and a decade later a new generation of centre-left think tanks laid the basis for New Labour. Scotland does not have the same range of think tanks as London, and those that exist do not command the same resources, from business, trades unions, foundations or wealthy individuals as their UK counterparts. The Institute for Public Policy Research, cradle of New Labour thought, has done some work on devolution and public policy but has no formal presence in Scotland and has not sought to promote a distinct Scottish agenda, rather than exporting English New Labour ideas to Scotland. Since devolution, there has, however, been a modest increase in Scottish-based policy institutes. The Scottish Council Foundation (SCF), which for a while described itself as a social democratic think thank, is sponsored by the Scottish Council (Development and Industry) and has a number of corporate funders for its activities – often UK- or London-based companies. In its scope, it is closest to the London-based think tanks, producing policy papers and organising longer-term projects, as well as organising seminars and conferences. A smaller body, the Scottish Forum for Modern Government, is explicitly New Labour and aims to steer the Scottish Parliament and Executive away from the traditional public-service ethos which they have tended to follow (see Chapter 7) and closer to the line followed down south. The David Hume Institute is an older body, generally promoting free-market policies in the Scottish context, and has provided an outlet for serious academic work. Further to the right is the Policy Institute, founded by Andrew Neil and housed in the *Scotsman* offices, promoting a neo-liberal agenda. Centre for Scottish Public Policy was established in 1990 as the John Wheatley Centre, changing its name in 1997. It organises meetings and conferences for which it is able to attract ministers as speakers, but does not have a sustained research programme of its own. Big Thinking is a small unit emerging from the *Big Issue* magazine and concentrates on conferences and publications rather than research. It is broadly centre-left, with New Labour tendencies. Policy work is also done in university-based institutes. The Fraser of Allander Institute at the University of

Strathclyde is a long-established body working on the Scottish economy. Its economic research and forecasts have been very influential, it has good contacts with the Scottish Executive and since devolution it has sponsored a number of conferences and lectures on what the Scottish Parliament could and should do with its economic powers. At the University of Edinburgh, the Institute of Governance undertakes independent and commissioned research and sponsors meetings and conferences on Scottish issues.

Most of the think tank work, then, is from a centrist political perspective close to the ideas of New Labour or from the free-market point of view. In this it reflects the balance of think tank opinion in London, although the absence of a more left-wing strand in Scotland, given the state of public and political opinion, is striking. There is not always a great deal of attention given to how Scotland could do things its own way, rather than borrowing from London or, sometimes, the United States. Outside the university-associated bodies, the European dimension is rather weak, although the Scottish Council (Development and Industry) has devoted attention to this over the years. It is also notable that there is no think tank associated with the nationalist perspective, despite the SNP being the second party of the country. This perhaps explains why the debate on independence has remained trapped in the old categories of national sovereignty, when elsewhere in Europe nationalist parties are exploring the range of post-sovereignty options available in the new international order (Keating 2001).

The Media

Scotland stands out among the nations and regions of the United Kingdom in having its own media, consumed by the majority of the population. Since the 1970s these have had a stronger Scottish focus, serving to strengthen Scottish political identity and emphasise the Scottish dimension of policy issues. Since devolution they have helped set the Scottish political agenda and shape public perceptions of the new institutions and their performance.

Scottish newspapers have long constituted a distinct market (see Table 3.4). Among the popular daily papers, the Glasgow-based *Daily Record* accounted for a third of the total market in 2003, much as it had thirty years earlier (Kellas 1975). It is a stalwart supporter of the Labour Party, and although it is often mistakenly assumed to be a Scottish edition of the *Daily Mirror*, it is a distinct product, rooted in the Scottish environment. The *Scottish Daily Express*, which used to account for another third, collapsed in the 1970s and, although a Scottish edition of the *Daily Express* is now produced, it has ceased to be a distinctively Scottish voice. Since the 1980s these Scottish papers have faced competition from the English-based tabloids, although the *Sun*, owned by the Murdoch empire, is the only one commanding a similar share of both English and Scottish markets. It follows the general line of its English sister paper, guided by the economic and political priorities of its owner, but in the early 1990s surprised the world by coming out for Scottish independence.

The quality or broadsheet newspapers in Scotland have traditionally been regional, with the *Glasgow Herald* in the west, the *Scotsman* in Edinburgh, the *Dundee Courier* in that city and the *Press and Journal* in Aberdeen and the North-east. This makes the overall Scottish readership figures misleading, as the qualities are quite dominant in their local markets. Until the 1950s they tended to be Conservative and unionist in their politics, but during the 1960s the *Scotsman* adopted a liberal line and was the first Scottish paper in modern times to take up the devolution issue (Kellas 1973). The *Glasgow Herald*, previously the voice of the local business community, evolved under successive owners in the 1980s and 1990s to a centre-left and pro-devolution position, and sought to break out of its local market by dropping 'Glasgow' from its banner and subtitling itself 'Scotland's Newspaper'. The *Scotsman* also tried to broaden its geographical appeal, but under the direction of Andrew Neil from 1996 moved back to the right, adopted a more sceptical tone on home rule and went somewhat down-market. More competition is provided by London-based quality dailies with varying amounts of Scottish input, the *Guardian*, *Times*, *Independent* and *Financial Times*, although their penetration of the Scottish market is limited, reaching less than half the readership of the Scottish qualities, a situation that has not changed since 1970 (Kellas 1973; Schlesinger et al. 2001). Particularly noticeable is the weak penetration of the *Daily Telegraph*, widely regarded as the house paper of the English Conservative middle classes.

Sunday coverage is dominated by the popular *Sunday Mail*, sister paper of the *Daily Record*, and the *Sunday Post*. This last, once a Scottish institution with a readership estimated at 90 per cent of the adult population until the 1970s, reflects an older Scotland, socially

Table 3.4   Percentage of newspaper circulation in Scotland and rest of UK, 2003

Title	Scotland	Rest of UK
Popular Dailies		
Daily Record	31.3	0.2
Sun	24.6	25.6
Daily Mail	8.7	20.1
Daily Express	5.7	7.5
Daily Mirror	5.0	15.1
Star, Daily	0	2.0
Popular Sundays		
Sunday Mail	28.0	0.3
Sunday Post	27.0	na
News of the World	17.5	28.7
Mail on Sunday	6.2	18.4
Sunday Express	2.9	7.3
Sunday Mirror	1.2	3.5
Star, Sunday	1.3	5.8
People	0.7	1.7
Quality Dailies		
Press and Journal	6.3	na
Herald	5.9	na
Scotsman	4.6	na
Times	1.8	5.1
Daily Telegraph	1.5	7.7
Guardian	1.1	2.9
Financial Times	0.5	1.2
Independent	0.4	1.8
Quality Sundays		
Scotland on Sunday	4.0	na
Sunday Times	1.7	9.7
Sunday Herald	3.0	na
Sunday Telegraph	1.2	5.6
Observer	1.2	3.5
Independent on Sunday	0.3	1.4

Source: Audit Bureau of Circulation

and politically conservative, traditional and replete with everyday stories of ordinary folk. Among the qualities are *Scotland on Sunday*, under the same ownership as the *Scotsman*, and the *Sunday Herald*, although with two papers competing for such a small market, it is a constant struggle to survive. London-based qualities have much smaller circulations.

All this makes Scotland one of the most competitive newspaper markets in the world, and one quite different from England. This is not to say that all parties are equally represented. No quality paper supports the SNP, and a pro-Conservative bias in the 1970s gave away to an anti-Conservative one during the 1980s and 1990s. At the General Election of 1983, five of the eleven Scottish papers supported the Liberal–Social Democrat Alliance. Individual proprietors and managers exercise considerable influence (Kellas 1989). In the 1930s, Lord Beaverbrook saw advantage in swinging his *Scottish Daily Express* briefly behind Scottish nationalism, as did Rupert Murdoch with the *Sun* in the 1990s. Hugh Fraser's adoption of nationalism preceded the *Glasgow Herald*'s conversion to home rule (Brand 1978), while the installation of Andrew Neil as editor-in-chief of Scotsman Publications resulted in a shift the other way. Yet there has been nothing like the domination of English popular newspapers by Rupert Murdoch that forced successive Conservative and New Labour governments to pander to the Murdoch empire in return for editorial support. Nor has the Scottish press sustained the strident anti-Europeanism that has dominated coverage south of the border. Ownership and control of the press remains a sensitive political issue in Scotland, as Scottish papers have progressively come under external control (Smith 1994). The publishing empire of D. C. Thomson in Dundee remains locally owned. The *Scotsman*, formerly part of the other Thomson empire (of Lord Thomson of Fleet), ceased to be registered as a Scottish company in 1993 (Smith 1994) and was taken over in 1996 by the Barclay Brothers. The *Herald*'s owners, Outram, came successively under the control of Hugh Fraser (and later his son, also Hugh) in 1964 and then Lonrho in 1979, but the newspaper was bought out by its management in 1992 in an effort to retain independence (Linklater 1992). In 1996, Scottish Television purchased it by playing the Scottish card, arguing the need to keep decision making in Scotland (Schlesinger et al. 2001). When the *Herald* was sold again in 2002, a lot of political pressure was brought to bear from the Scottish Executive, the Parliament and Scottish MPs to prevent it falling to the same owners as the *Scotsman* and generally to maintain its independence and sympathetic stance towards devolution. In the event it was taken over by an American group, Gannett. In 2004, uncertainty over the future of the *Scotsman* again prompted concern about the need to sustain media pluralism.

There has been a steady growth in Scottish political coverage since the 1970s, as the devolution issue has rarely been off the agenda and the parties have emphasised the Scottish context of their appeals. This may have given the media something of a vested interest in home rule, since a Scottish Parliament would give them so much more to report on. During the election campaign of 1992, coverage in Scotland diverged widely from that in England, with a strong emphasis on Labour's plans for devolution and the expected demise of the Conservatives, and there was widespread shock when the Conservatives not only returned to power but registered a small increase in support in Scotland. During the 1997 election campaign, the devolution issue was sidelined by Labour's promise of a referendum, giving the campaign more of a common British feel, but by this time the assumption of a Labour victory was so strong that devolution was almost taken for granted. Yet for all this preparation, the media seemed unprepared for devolution when it happened and relations between the press and the Scottish Parliament got off to an extremely bad start. This partly reflects tendencies in British journalism generally, where price competition and cost cutting have reduced resources available for in-depth reporting and investigation into policy issues and increased reliance on spin doctors and insider gossip on who is up and who is down (Reid 2003). It may also be the result of an excessive concentration on the issue of devolution itself, rather than on what a Scottish Parliament might do. As a result, coverage of the new institutions was dominated by a series of mostly trivial 'scandals', starting with the so-called Lobbygate affair, set up as a sting by the media themselves. There is also an almost universal tendency to describe devolution as a disappointment and a failure, and to extrapolate from criticisms of individual policies to condemnation of the institutions themselves.[6] In comparison with the 1970s and 1980s, there is much less detailed examination of policies and issues and little concern with the longer-term implications of Scottish devolution. This presents a marked contrast to other stateless nations such as Catalonia, Quebec or the Basque Country, which have sustained a much higher level of serious debate in the printed media.

The ability of the media to shape or reflect a distinctly Scottish policy agenda is also hampered by the confusion between devolved matters dealt with in the Scottish Parliament and equivalent English matters dealt with at Westminster and treated as 'national' news. As well as reporting on Scottish initiatives, the Scottish press gives some prominence to those of Whitehall departments, even when these only apply in England and Wales. UK papers circulating in Scotland often simply report these as coming from 'the government', although now more care is taken to specify which level is meant. Even so, there are examples such as the *Herald* of 31 July 2003, summing up the record of six years of Tony Blair's British government, which listed measures of the Scottish Executive under crime, education and health, while under environment and transport there was a mixed list of British and Scottish policy initiatives. Equally confusing was an article the previous month about a speech by John Reid, a Scottish MP appointed as minister for health in England, who happened to give his first major speech at a (UK) NHS confederation meeting in Glasgow: 'on the eve of the Scottish Executive unveiling its NHS Reform Bill, Dr Reid said he would increase capacity, choice and diversity within the NHS' (MacLeod 2003). Readers would hardly know that Reid's model had actually been rejected for Scotland (see Chapter 7). Given the asymmetrical nature of devolution, with the UK government doubling up as the government of England and the weight of England in the whole, this tendency may be built in, but it does not help clarify the terms of debate in Scotland and may reinforce the tendency for Scottish policy debates to follow on from those in England.

Broadcasting in Scotland has become more distinctive over the years, although this is a contentious issue. BBC Scotland is one of the UK's 'national regions', with a degree of local control of programming and content. Since the 1970s its Scottish political content has steadily increased and there is regular television reporting of the Scottish Parliament (Lynch 2001). Arguments about the right balance of Scottish, UK and international coverage have periodically focused on the idea of a 'Scottish Six', an evening news bulletin made in Scotland that would incorporate all three levels (Schlesinger et al. 2001). Supporters argue that this would provide Scottish viewers with information on domestic matters without swamping them with stories only applicable in England, while still keeping UK and international news. Opponents criticise the idea as parochialism and suspect that it is a nationalist plot; opposition has been particularly strong in Labour Party circles. In the meantime, Scotland, along with other parts of the UK, makes do with an opt-out slot from *Newsnight* devoted to local news, while the main news bulletins continue to be standard across the UK. Radio coverage is more clearly differentiated, with Radio Scotland providing a mix of Scottish and wider stories alongside Radio Four, which does the same for the UK.

Independent television, from its inception in the 1950s, has been regional and there are three Scottish franchises. Scottish Television covers the central belt, Grampian the north and Borders Television combines the Scottish and English border territories. For a time, both Scottish Television and Grampian were part of a Scottish media empire, SMG, covering the *Herald* and a large share of Scotland's local radio stations. Hopes, or fears, that this would emerge as a global media player from a dominant Scottish base, however, did not materialise. In an increasingly deregulated media world, control of broadcasting in Scotland is in constant danger of falling under outside control and this has become a recurrent political issue.

Broadcast media have helped sustain a distinct Scottish political arena in recent decades although, like the press, they are responsible for a certain confusion over what items are Scottish, English or UK-wide. At the same time, responsibility for broadcasting policy is firmly reserved to Westminster, and unionist politicians regard the prospect of devolution here with considerable alarm. They have been equally wary about strengthening the Scottish level or focus within the existing broadcasters, since this might weaken the UK or British political community. The BBC has long contained 'national governors' with advisory councils in the non-English parts of the UK, and a similar arrangement applied to the Independent Television Commission. The new regulatory framework established in 2003 under the Office for Telecommunications (Ofcom) is UK-wide, and it took serious lobbying by Scottish interests and the Scottish Executive to secure a territorial dimension in the form of a Scottish Advisory Committee (Schlesinger 2004).

The Scottish Policy Arena

Over the last thirty years, Scottish civil society has become more distinct within the United Kingdom. Interest groups and organisations have strengthened their Scottish profile, a development that both sustained the momentum for devolution and was further encouraged after devolution came about. The media are much more concerned with Scottish issues. Within the broad confines of British politics there is a distinct Scottish political agenda, and the Parliament has become a significant focus of interest-group activity. Yet policy networks, despite the stronger horizontal dimension, are still predominantly vertical, linking people and groups within the same policy field, rather than across fields. There is a great deal more consultation, although this does not always lead to concrete results, to the frustration of some. Scotland is often described as a village community, in which all the policy actors know each other, and there is some truth to this. Lines of communication are short and, at least in the central belt, people are likely to have a great deal of casual face-to-face contact. Scottish papers are given occasionally to publishing league tables of the 100 most powerful people in Scotland. These are quite meaningless, but reflect an expectation that there is a power elite in charge of the country, who can be named.[7] This myth of the village community is prevalent across small nations and regions in Europe, although every example is held up as though it were unique (Keating et al. 2003). At its best it can lead to common purpose and action for social advance. At its worst it stifles change and excludes outsiders. Devolution is gradually opening up the old networks and encouraging different ways of thinking about power, but the process is a slow one.

Notes

1. I do not propose to enter the theological debate about the differences between policy communities, policy networks, issue networks and the rest. Policy community here is a rather simple descriptive concept to capture those involved in the policy process. The degree to which they have a common set of attitudes or interests is an empirical one.

2. In private, business leaders concede that devolution has not been the disaster that some of them had predicted.

3. The 71 per cent figure in England and Wales may not be very different. Respondents there were given only the generic category Christian, which may have encouraged those with loose religious affiliations or a nominal attachment to the Church of England. Scottish respondents had to identify with the Church of Scotland, the Catholic Church, or 'other Christian'. In both countries the question was voluntary.

4. Dr Jean Turner, standing against hospital closures in Strathkelvin and Bearsden.

5. In over a hundred interviews with interest groups in connection with this research, there was unanimity that devolution had improved access to government, including ministers, officials and backbenchers.

6. I would lay good odds that sections of the press will treat this book as another 'devolution fails' story.

7. An example is *Scotland on Sunday*, 2 May 2004, which promises to expose 'Scotland's power elite', the 'people who exercise the most influ-

ence on daily life'. This is an eclectic list of business people, public servants, writers and entertainers with nothing in common except being known to the people on the selection panel. Politicians were excluded from the list.

CHAPTER FOUR

Executive and Parliament

The Executive

Scotland has a Cabinet system of government, with a First Minister
(FM) elected by the Parliament and ten or eleven ministers responsible for the main policy areas. Together with deputy ministers these
comprise the Scottish Executive, a somewhat confusing term on
which unionists insisted to distinguish it from the British Government (although the Welsh equivalent has simply called itself a
government). Ministers are chosen by the First Minister and,
although they must be approved by the Parliament (unlike at
Westminster), the FM in practice has almost complete freedom in
hiring and firing, as was shown when Jack McConnell took over
from Henry McLeish and removed most of the Labour members of
his predecessor's Cabinet. At least in the first two sessions of the
Parliament, no Labour notables had established an independent
political base strong enough to make them undismissable. The First
Minister also has a free rein to intervene in policy domains according to his/her own priorities. Much depends on the personality of the
individual FM. Donald Dewar, the first incumbent, was cautious, a
long-serving member of the Labour front bench at Westminster and
former Secretary of State, and was preoccupied in his year and a half
in office with setting up the new institutions. His successor, Henry
McLeish, who served only a few months, was keen to put a distinctive Scottish stamp on policy, the main result being the implementation in Scotland of the Sutherland recommendations on free personal
care for the elderly, and signing the Declaration of Flanders with the

'constitutional regions' of Europe demanding more say within the European Union. Jack McConnell, who took over in 2001, lessened the ambitions with his slogan about doing 'less, better' and tended to cleave more closely to New Labour at Westminster, keeping his ministers on a similarly tight leash. McConnell did, however, seek to make a personal mark by elevating the environmental issue, with the curious phrase 'environmental justice', which was to be a cross-cutting theme informing the work of the Executive as a whole.

Yet there are limits to this picture of First Ministerial government. Ministers must be MSPs, whereas British Prime Ministers can and do send their friends to the House of Lords and then appoint them to government. Coalition government, made almost inevitable by the proportional electoral system, allows the partner party to select its own ministers and gives it a veto over their dismissal. A post of Deputy First Minister has been created for the leader of the junior party, who has a wide-ranging brief over general Executive policy as well as being a departmental minister. Coalition also obliges the Executive to negotiate a policy programme at the beginning of each session. In 1999, this was subject to difficult bargaining, especially over the issue of university fees, which was passed on to a commission of inquiry. By 2003, the Liberal Democrats were in a stronger position, and the parties more used to the idea of coalition negotiations, producing in a few days a programme of fifty-one pages. Apart from specific pledges on proportional representation in local government, university top-up fees, GM crops and nuclear power, there was a general commitment to the environment, while a Labour proposal to gaol parents of delinquent children was diluted almost to the point of disappearance. Some of these may have come in any case – the First Minister had highlighted the environment as a priority area. In others, like university fees, Liberal Democrat pressure helped push Scottish Labour away from the line pursued by its counterparts in England. Cabinet government also seems to be more important than its counterpart in London, which has largely been reduced to a cipher. This is certainly a change from the Scottish Office, in which the departmental ministers were few in number and served the Secretary of State. Now they head departments of their own and will fight a departmental corner. Finally, the First Minister is limited by the absence of a substantial department or anything equivalent to the expanding policy units at 10 Downing Street, which have been at the forefront of policy innovation in London.

The balance of knowledge and policy capacity thus remains

within the departments. Unlike in Whitehall, the boundaries of departments and ministerial responsibilities do not coincide precisely. This is a hangover from the Scottish Office days, when there were not enough ministers to go round, but is defended as a way of achieving more coherence across government and combating departmentalism and closed thinking. The Scottish Executive has also bundled functions differently from its Whitehall counterparts. It created an Environment and Rural Affairs Department (SEERAD), an idea later taken up in England. Education is divided, with higher education put together with economic development in the Department of Enterprise, Transport and Lifelong Learning. Not all these innovations achieve a real policy coherence, as the functional divisions remain within the merged departments and there may even be conflicts of interest among them. Rural Affairs seems to have retained three distinct elements, for agriculture, rural policy and the environment. Enterprise and Lifelong Learning, on the other hand, seem to have achieved more synergy. Cross-departmental working is also achieved through Cabinet committees.

Devolution has meant an increase in Scottish ministers from four or five to twenty-two, and thus greater ministerial control and policy direction. On the other hand, the high turnover of ministers in the first term meant that few, the two Liberal Democrats apart, had a chance to master their briefs. In four years, a total of thirty-six MSPs occupied the twenty-two ministerial posts. Ministers are, moreover, overwhelmed with management issues and recurrent crises in service delivery, partly as a result of the greater visibility and coverage of government in Scotland, so that their time for policy work is limited. Indeed, when Wendy Alexander quit the Cabinet in 2002, one of her reasons, remarkably, was to spend more time on public policy issues. Many Scottish ministers have come to office without previous experience and, while this may be healthy in renewing the political class, they have taken time to master their briefs and learn the folkways of government and the relationship with civil servants.

The two Scottish law officers, the Lord Advocate and the Solicitor General, are in a rather different position from the other ministers, as was the case before devolution. They do not need to be MSPs and, in their legal capacity, have a degree of independence, for example in matters of prosecution, despite being members of the Scottish Executive. They act as legal advisors to the Executive and, even if they are not MSPs, may participate in parliamentary proceedings where necessary, although without a vote. This dual

Table 4.1   The Scottish Executive, 2004

First Minister
Head of the Scottish Executive, responsible for development, implementation and presentation of Executive policies. Also responsible for strategic relationship with the UK Government, the European Union and other external relations.

Deputy First Minister
With First Minister, responsible for development, implementation and presentation of Executive policies. In 2004 the DFM is also:

Minister for Enterprise and Lifelong Learning
Economy, business and industry, including Scottish Enterprise, Highlands and Islands Enterprise, European Structural Funds, trade and inward investment, energy (including renewable energy), further and higher education, lifelong learning and training, and science.

Minister for Justice
Criminal justice, youth justice, victim support, criminal justice, social work, police, prisons and sentencing policy, courts, law reform.

Minister for Health and Community Care
NHS, community care, health service reform, health improvement, health promotion, public health, allied healthcare services, acute, primary and mental health services, addiction services, pharmaceutical services, performance, quality and improvement framework, and food safety.

Minister for Education and Young People
School education, nurseries and childcare, Gaelic, children's services, social work.

Minister for Finance and Public Services
Scottish Budget, public service delivery, modernising government (including civil service reform), local government, cities and community planning, and external relations issues.

Minister for Environment and Rural Development
Environment and natural heritage, land reform, water, sustainable development, agriculture, fisheries, rural development (including aquaculture and forestry).

Minister for Communities
Antisocial behaviour, poverty, housing and area regeneration, the land-use planning system and building standards, equality issues, voluntary sector, religious and faith organisations, and charity law.

Minister for Parliamentary Business
Parliamentary affairs and the management of Executive business in the Parliament.

Minister for Tourism, Culture and Sport
Tourism, culture and the arts, sport, major events strategy, built heritage, architecture, Historic Scotland and lottery funding.

Minister for Transport
Transport policy and delivery, public transport, road, rail services, air and ferry services.

Lord Advocate

Solicitor General

Source: Scottish Executive

Table 4.2   Scottish Executive departments, 2004

Office of Permanent Secretary
Support for First Minister, Deputy First Minister and Cabinet; relations with rest of UK; analytical services including research; Changing to Deliver; Performance and Innovation.
Corporate Services
Personnel policy, propriety, recruitment, staff appraisal and interchange; pay, employee relations, training and development; equal opportunities and welfare; accommodation and estate management issues; communications and information facilities; security.
Finance and Central Services Department (FCSD)
External relations including Europe; local government; Scottish Budget and accounts; advice on financial matters for other departments and agencies.
Scottish Executive Development Department (SEDD)
Housing; land use planning and building control; social justice agenda; economic and statistical advice.
Scottish Executive Education Department (SEED)
Pre-school and school education; children and young people; tourism, culture and sport.
Enterprise, Transport and Lifelong Learning Department (ETLLD)
Support for business, encouraging enterprise, skills and employability; energy; transport and communications; higher education, skills and lifelong learning.
Scottish Executive Health Department (SEHD)
NHS Scotland; development and implementation of health and community care policy.
Justice Department
Police and fire services; criminal justice; aspects of criminal and civil justice and civil law; courts administration; legal aid; liaison with the legal profession.
Scottish Executive Environment and Rural Affairs Department (SEERAD)
Agriculture; rural development; food; environment; fisheries.

Source: Scottish Executive

political/judicial role, a carry-over from the pre-devolution system, has come under some criticism from people who think that the two realms should be more clearly separated (McFadden and Lazarowicz 2000).

In addition to the ministerial departments, there are executive agencies, staffed by civil servants, but self-managing and entrusted with the management of those services provided directly by the Executive, as opposed to local governments or health boards. In 2004, the agencies shown in Table 4.3 existed. Some of these are long-standing. Communities Scotland, on the other hand, was formed in 2000 out of Scottish Homes, itself descended from a variety of Scottish and UK bodies. The aim was to integrate housing

Table 4.3   Executive agencies in Scotland

Accountant in Bankruptcy
Communities Scotland
Fisheries Research Service
Historic Scotland
HM Inspectorate of Education
National Archives of Scotland
Registers of Scotland
Scottish Court Services
Scottish Fisheries Protection Agency
Scottish Prison Service
Scottish Public Pensions Agency
Scottish Agricultural Science Agency
Student Awards Agency for Scotland

Source: Scottish Executive

into a broader community regeneration framework, although it got off to a shaky start and did not really establish itself as a powerful policy generator.

Beyond these agencies is a range of non-departmental public bodies (NDPBs), colloquially known as quangos, which are not staffed by civil servants. Some of these are advisory, while others exist to insulate tasks from direct political control. These include business development bodies like Scottish Enterprise, commercial concerns like Highlands and Islands Enterprise, the funding council for universities and colleges, and professional regulatory agencies. In 2001, responding to popular concerns about the 'quango state' as well as issues of administrative reform and modernisation, the Executive undertook a review of agencies, which recommended the abolition of fifty-two of the 180 then existing. Some were to be abolished, some merged and others, like Scottish Homes, incorporated as executive agencies. By 2004 the number of NDPBs was down to 144. Under the public Appointments and Public Bodies etc. (Scotland) Act 2003, a Scottish Commissioner for Public Appointments was established to ensure transparency in procedures; this followed a similar initiative from the UK Government in response to the Nolan Report on standards in public life.

The Civil Service

A strong element of continuity in Scottish government was provided by the civil service, which was taken over from the Scottish Office.

It was decided from the beginning that there should not be a separate Scottish civil service, so that the staff of the Executive are part of a Britain-wide system, with the possibility of moving to and from Whitehall departments. In practice, the Scottish Office was dominated by Scots, who tended to remain in that department, apart from short spells working in London, often for the Treasury or Cabinet Office, where they learned the ways of Whitehall (Kellas 1975), a practice also common in other departments. Such movements as occurred tended to be at the senior level, as individuals were promoted across departments. Scottish Office civil servants were often educated at Scottish universities, although in 1968 some 20 per cent of the administrative class had degrees from Oxford or Cambridge, a lower percentage than for Whitehall but still well above the Oxbridge contribution to the total graduate pool.

These patterns have largely persisted after devolution. In 2004, 60 per cent of the Scottish Executive senior civil servants were born in Scotland. Twenty per cent of the senior civil servants in the Scottish Executive were educated at Oxford or Cambridge, rising to a third in the case of heads of department.[1] Sixty-three per cent of all senior civil servants, but only 44 per cent of heads of department, were graduates of Scottish universities. Mobility is still limited, as 70 per cent of the senior civil service and three-quarters of heads of department have never worked in Whitehall, while a further 15 per cent have spent less than three years there as part of the standard learning process. Some concern has been expressed that, after devolution, Scottish civil servants may become detached from their counterparts elsewhere, and the need to maintain mobility was one reason for keeping a unified civil service. While the evidence is that mobility was never high, there have been some efforts to encourage it after devolution to keep the networks intact (see Chapter 5).

In recent years, many senior civil service positions have been filled by open competition in an effort to bring in outsiders, while career civil servants have been encouraged to spend time working in the private sector. Fifteen per cent of the Scottish Executive senior civil service in 2004 had been appointed from outside since 1999, although many of these had come from other parts of the public sector. Top civil servants still tend to come from upper middle-class families and to be male. A quarter of the senior civil servants and a third of heads of department in 2004 were educated at private schools and 80 per cent of the senior civil servants were men. While socially exclusive, this is perhaps a little more representative than Whitehall, where over 80 per cent of the officials at grade 1/1a between 1990 and 1995 were privately educated (Kavanagh and Richards 2003).

Civil service appointments are made by a non-political recruitment process, and the Scottish Executive enjoys considerable scope over recruitment, grades and pay settlements, although not just because of devolution, as individual Whitehall departments have also gained more freedom. The most senior appointments are made through the Senior Appointments Selection Committee, a British body that makes recommendations to the Prime Minister, even for the devolved administrations (Parry 2001). In practice, the First Minister has a strong say over the appointment of the Permanent Secretary and civil service heads of departments, although there is no suggestion that this has been politicised.

Relationships between British ministers and civil servants have been the subject of much analysis, from the most serious to the popular television show *Yes Minister*, which plays on the inherent tension between their need for each other and their competition for influence. Matters are no different in Scotland, but devolution has introduced some new elements. Ministers are now more present in Edinburgh, rather than spending their weekdays in London, so that civil servants have gone from being the least ministerially controlled in the UK to being perhaps the most. Civil servants, used to the Scottish Office world of lobbying for Scotland or adapting policy to local needs, are now faced with the challenge of helping to make policy, a task for which they have not always been equipped. While it is common to put this down to the culture of the old Scottish Office, Kavanagh and Richards (2003) detect a more general tendency among the senior civil service during the Thatcher and Major years away from policy making and advice and towards efficiency and service delivery. There was also something of a culture gap, at least in the early days (Parry 2001). Ministers in London come to office after a parliamentary apprenticeship in which they learn the folkways of Whitehall and the conventions of the constitution. Scottish Executive ministers who came from Westminster had usually absorbed these values; but the majority of ministers were from local government or had not been in elective office at all, and the experience was often jarring. Even an experienced Westminster hand like Henry McLeish caused an upset when he became First Minister, with a suggestion that civil servants could brief back-bench MSPs as well as ministers, in defiance of all the conventions – the idea was quickly abandoned.

Relationships between civil servants and MSPs have also taken time to evolve. Civil servants were not used to the everyday scrutiny of a body of local politicians in Edinburgh, and MSPs in turn were not always familiar with the conventions by which civil servants answer to ministers rather than parliamentarians, and avoid taking partisan stances. Over the course of the first session of the Parliament, there was a process of mutual learning and, while relations differ from one area to another, most civil service departments have established a fairly stable relationship with 'their' parliamentary committee, providing policy briefings and information where requested. Similar difficult relations have also occurred with interest groups, who now have several channels of access, including the Parliament and ministers, where previously most contact was with the civil service. Civil servants may resent some ministers escaping from their care and talking directly to groups or outside advisors, while feeling that their skills and experience are being undervalued.

Civil servants have similarly had to learn a whole new game of dealing with interest groups, now better organised, more vocal and with an outlet in the Parliament. New institutional identities need to be formed in a civil service which still remains part of the Whitehall network (Jones 2001). It would be fair to say that some have coped better than others, with a younger generation finding the experience quite exhilarating, but some of the more established figures are more resentful of the change. Hierarchical ways of working inherited from the past persist and politicians continue to complain, as before, that civil servants are good at thinking of reasons not to change.

Policy Capacity

One of the greatest constraints on policy making under devolution has been the limited policy capacity of Scottish departments, more used to adapting Whitehall initiatives than to making their own. For historic reasons there was a large research capacity in agriculture, through in-house research, sponsored research institutes and funded research in universities. There was also some capacity in housing and education, but less in other fields like health policy or the environment. The Scottish Executive is the direct descendant of the old Scottish Office and many traces of the former structures and practices have remained, while it has evolved into a government in its own right. Over the years there were repeated efforts to bring the

Scottish Office departments together and to encourage a more corporate approach, but it remained a federal department with a relatively weak centre. After 1999 the departments took on a new life of their own, but the centre remained underdeveloped. The Department of Finance and Central Services plays an important role in the budgetary process (see Chapter 6) but does not have the policy role that the Treasury has come to play for domestic policy in Whitehall. A Policy Unit existed after devolution but did not have the broad role and influence of its London counterpart. Gradually, there have been moves to provide more central leadership and address cross-departmental issues. A new Permanent Secretary in 2003 came in committed to creating a 'policy powerhouse' at the centre. An Office of the Permanent Secretary was set up, with divisions for Analytical Services including research, a Ministerial Support Group and the Office of the First Minister. The Policy Unit was divided into two (the Strategy and Delivery units) and placed within the Ministerial Support Group. New units were set up for Changing to Deliver, a temporary body to improve the synergy between statisticians and analysts, and for Performance and Innovation, headed by an outsider on a part-time contract. The Research Unit itself had been reorganised earlier in order to bring research to bear more directly on policy issues. Within departments there has been an effort to bring together analysts, responsible for data, with researchers looking at policy issues. Also at the centre is the Management Group of senior officials, with some outside membership, to deal with common issues across the Executive, and subgroups have been created within this in order to allow the Group as a whole to focus on strategic issues. The resulting structure looks complex but in practice involves rather few people, with short lines of communication. The result has been a more cohesive centre within the Executive, but the balance of influence and policy capacity remains with the departments. There is nothing equivalent to the Treasury's role in UK government and most insiders feel that too powerful a centre in such a small administration could unbalance the system. So policy tends to be developed across departments and through policy networks rather than being laid down from above.

There is provision for the appointment of Special Advisors from outside government, limited to a total of twelve for the whole Executive. This is a small number compared with Whitehall, and they are not assigned to individual ministers, although the Liberal Democrats are allowed to nominate their own. Their role is to bring in outside expertise and link ministers to the political world. Compared with Whitehall, however, the role of policy advisors is rather limited and they work with ministers on political and presentational matters, rather than within the policy machinery of the civil service.

There has been some increase in policy-related staff across the departments. Other policy input is gained from interest groups and professional associations, from consultation, which has grown since devolution, and from the think tanks and universities. Local government has also been a source of policy advice, with its considerable staff working on matters like housing, planning and urban deprivation, although the abolition of the regional councils in 1996 had done some damage there. This dependence on outside bodies for knowledge and policy ideas is one factor encouraging a more consensual policy style in Scotland and militating against the accumulation of power in the hands of the Scottish Executive and, within the Executive, in a central department.

Policy making at the centre is also affected by a move, within British government more generally, towards a less overtly ideological style of government and a focus on service delivery and performance. New Labour politicians claim to be in favour of 'what works' irrespective of its political origins, although this often hides a preference for market-style mechanisms and a disdain for traditional modes of public service delivery. Jack McConnell, on becoming First Minister, promised to 'do less, better', and the very names of the new policy units indicate the emphasis on a rather technical style of government.

The Scottish Parliament

The Scottish Parliament was intended to improve the political representation of Scotland and, in providing for an enlarged number of members, directly answerable to the Scottish voters, it has done so. Representativeness, however, also has another meaning, that the elected members should resemble their constituents in their backgrounds and experience. During the Constitutional Convention, the main emphasis was on better representation by gender, which has largely been achieved. Some 40 per cent of MSPs in 2004 are women, compared with only 15 per cent of Scottish MPs at Westminster and 18 per cent of non-Scottish MPs. This is to a large extent down to the Labour Party, which has operated a policy of gender parity (in practice there have been slightly more women than men). There is less gender balance in Cabinet, where 27 per cent of Scottish ministers serving in 2003 and 2004 were women, slightly above the Westminster figure of 20 per cent. Another concern that has been expressed has been for ethnic representation, but the Scottish Parliament has not (up to 2004) had a single member drawn from an ethnic minority.

Much less attention has been given to the class and occupational background of Scottish politicians. For many years, Scottish MPs, more so than their English counterparts, were drawn from the class backgrounds traditionally associated with the two main parties (Keating 1975a). Scottish Labour MPs were more likely to be working class and Conservatives to be landowners or military officers. Devolution appears to have broken this hold, drawing in more people from professional backgrounds, and MSPs now resemble politicians in England and, indeed, Europe more generally, while Scottish MPs still have more traditional backgrounds. Taking first occupations, we find that 52 per cent of MSPs in 2004 are drawn from the professions, against just 40 per cent of Scottish MPs, but only slightly above the figure for non-Scottish MPs, which is 48 per cent. Between 1945 and 1970, by contrast, only 39 per cent of Scottish MPs had a professional background, and a quarter of these were military officers in the Conservative Party, a category that has almost disappeared. People from teaching and academic-related occupations alone account for a fifth of all MSPs. Manual workers are just 6 per cent, compared with 16 per cent of Scottish MPs and 9 per cent of non-Scottish MPs. Between 1945 and 1970, 17 per cent of Scottish MPs and 20 per cent of non-Scottish MPs had been manual workers; and among Labour MPs, two-fifths had a working-class occupational background.

If we use the occupation that took most time in a politician's career, the 2004 figures are even more biased to the professional classes, as some of the politicians have been upwardly mobile, especially in the Labour Party. Teachers and academic-related jobs now account for 26 per cent of Labour MSPs, and social and community workers for another 16 per cent. Civil servants and local government officers account for another 12 per cent. This picture is not, in broad terms, dissimilar to that at Westminster, although there Labour MPs are more likely to be university academics and less likely to be school-teachers, social and community workers or local government officials. The increased representation of women in the Scottish Parliament may explain much of this difference (Shephard et al. 2001).

More than half of Scottish ministers and no less than 80 per cent of Scottish Cabinet ministers are originally from professional backgrounds, with more than half being teachers, academic-related or community and social workers. No Cabinet minister has a manual background. Devolution has also reduced the proportions of Scottish politicians with substantial experience in the trade union movement. Only 15 per cent of MSPs have held office in a trade union, compared with over 30 per cent of Scottish MPs and a fifth of non-Scottish MPs.[2] Nearly all of these are Labour politicians, with the SNP failing almost completely to recruit among this constituency despite its efforts to challenge Labour on this flank.

Business groups have consistently complained about the lack of business experience in the Scottish Parliament. There is truth in this, since only 19 per cent of MSPs have worked in private business, and only 11 per cent had this as their main occupation. Not surprisingly, this is higher than the figures for Scottish MPs (10 per cent), as the latter are predominantly Labour. It is also, however, slightly higher than among non-Scottish MPs, so that Holyrood is at least no worse than Westminster on this score.

There is a substantial 'miscellaneous' category, whose composition has changed considerably over the postwar decades. Farmers, previously a substantial presence on the Conservative benches, have declined steeply in numbers. A surprising number of Scottish Labour MPs in the past had worked as insurance salesmen, presumably as an occupation compatible with politics, giving flexible hours and an opportunity to knock on doors. In recent years, there has been a rise in professional political workers, some of whom have had no other occupation than working for their party or for a Westminster or European politician. Nearly 10 per cent of MSPs had come into politics this way, a similar figure to that at Westminster. The voluntary sector was another source of recruitment, accounting for nearly 5 per cent of MSPs. Journalism has always supplied politicians and 6 per cent of MSPs have had this as their main profession.

A marked trend in recent years has been the rise of the professional politician, with a career trajectory going from service on a local council, to entry into Parliament at a relatively early age, followed by long service terminated only by defeat or retirement due to age. MSPs are on average younger than Scottish MPs, but this reflects the recent establishment of the Parliament. If we look at their age on first election, MSPs are somewhat older, with a third of them being over fifty when first elected, compared with about one in ten

Table 4.4   Occupational background of MPs and MSPs, 2004: percentage first occupation

	MSPs	Scottish MPs	Scottish ministers	Non-Scottish MPs	UK ministers	Scottish MPs, 1945–70
Professional	53.2	40.3	61.1	48.1	40.0	39.1
Business	12.1	9.7	5.5	15.1	22.2	14.0
Blue-collar and junior white-collar	7.3	16.7	5.5	10.1	7.7	24.0
Other	27.4	33.3	27.9	26.7	30.1	22.2

Source: own compilation

of Scottish and non-Scottish MPs. This suggests that the Parliament has recruited a cohort of people experienced in other fields, and may also reflect the increased opportunities under PR for non-Labour politicians who have been waiting a long time for an opportunity for election – Labour MSPs tend to be a bit younger. Members of the Scottish Executive also tend to be young. Over 80 per cent of those serving in the Cabinet in 2003 and 2004 were under fifty, compared with 56 per cent of their UK counterparts.

It is sometimes suggested that the Scottish Parliament is dominated by the municipal element. It is true that 40 per cent of MSPs elected in 2003 were former councillors, but this is lower than the figure for Scottish MPs, at 47 per cent, while for non-Scottish MPs it is higher still, at 54 per cent. This is a reversal of historic trends. Between 1945 and 1970, 53 per cent of Scottish MPs were former councillors, compared with 43 per cent of non-Scottish MPs. In that period, a seat in Parliament was the customary award for long-serving councillors, especially in west-central Scotland; few of them went on to ministerial careers. The Scottish Parliament has given an opportunity for people without a council background to get into higher-level politics, while in Scotland as elsewhere, those councillors who do proceed to national office are often the younger and more successful ones. This is true even for Labour politicians. Forty-four per cent of Labour MSPs are former councillors, compared with 53 per cent of Scottish Labour MPs and a remarkable 65 per cent of non-Scottish Labour MPs. The figure for Conservative MSPs is identical, with 44 per cent being former councillors, accounting for many of the rather older entrants to the Scottish Parliament identified above. Less than a third of nationalist MSPs, however, are former councillors, although many may have stood unsuccessfully for local office (Shephard et al. 2001). Council service is no longer a handicap for ministerial office in Scotland, again suggesting that it is the more ambitious councillors who are coming through. Just over half of Scottish ministers in 2004 were former councillors, almost the same as the figure for the UK government.

Table 4.5   Former local councillors, percentage, 2004

MSPs	39.5
Scottish ministers	55.5
Scottish MPs	47.2
Non-Scottish MPs	54.2
UK minister	56.6
Scottish MPs, 1945–70	53.0

Source: own compilation

MSPs and Scottish MPs have overwhelmingly (84–87 per cent) been educated in the state sector, compared with around two-thirds of non-Scottish MPs at Westminster. Among Labour MSPs the figure reaches 96 per cent, against 80 per cent for non-Scottish Labour MPs. About four-fifths of all ministers at both levels have been state-educated, although the UK Cabinet does contain a significantly higher proportion of privately-educated politicians, including the Prime Minister. Even the Scottish Conservative Party shows a pre-ponderance of state-educated politicians. Two-thirds of Conservative MSPs attended state schools, compared with two-fifths of non-Scottish Conservative MPs. This profile shows a marked change, as between 1945 and 1970 the proportion of state-educated Scottish Conservative MPs actually fell from 54 per cent to 18 per cent as the party lost its popular urban base. The figures for MSPs[3] suggest that the Scottish Parliament has not only allowed the party to re-enter elective politics, but has also broadened its representative standing. Not surprisingly, the Scottish Parliament does not show the bias to Oxford and Cambridge found at Westminster, where 27 per cent of all backbenchers and 37 per cent of Cabinet ministers attended those two universities. At Holyrood the figures are 3 per cent and 9 per cent (just one individual) respectively. Again, the most dramatic shift is among Conservatives. In 1970, 65 per cent of Scottish Tory MPs were Oxbridge graduates, against just one Conservative MSP in 2003.

Table 4.6. Percentage educated at state schools

MSPs	84.5
Scottish ministers	78.0
Scottish MPs	87.3
Non-Scottish MPs	67.9
UK ministers	79.0
Scottish MPs, 1945–70	70.0

Source: own compilation

Devolution has thus accelerated changes in the Scottish political elite, which has gone from being more based in the traditional catchments of the main parties than Westminster, to being less so. There is a preponderance of the professional classes. Party differences in the background of politicians are generally less pronounced, as the professional middle classes predominate. The Conservatives incline slightly towards business and Labour towards public sector occupations, especially in teaching and social work. The SNP are somewhere in between, having slightly more business people than Labour but even less working-class representation. More balanced representation has been achieved with reference to gender, although at the cost of class representativeness, as women MSPs are even more concentrated in the professional and business categories than are men; 64 per cent of female MSPs and 46 per cent of male MSPs have a background in the professions. We cannot read simply from an individual's occupational background or experience to their views on issues, but the presence of large numbers of politicians who have come up through the public sector, teaching and social work in the public or voluntary sector is likely to be significant. It is likely that Scottish politicians will be inclined to the public sector and be well-connected with professional networks. They are also likely to be in tune with the prevailing ethos of public provision and of consultation.

The Legislative Process

The legislative procedure in the Scottish Parliament is based on Westminster precedent, with its three elements of general consideration of the principles of a bill; detailed scrutiny and amendment; and final consideration of the revised bill (McFadden and Lazarowicz 2000; Winetrobe 2002). Scottish procedure, however, aims to address repeated criticisms that the Westminster system spends too long on formal debates between the parties, repeated at all stages of a bill, at the expense of detailed scrutiny. The main remedy is the system of subject committees. Whereas at Westminster select committees, with their investigative role, are separate from legislative committees, set up for individual bills, in the Scottish Parliament the roles are combined. Bills introduced into the Parliament are first referred to the relevant subject committee, which produces a report on the general principles; a second committee may also contribute if the bill covers its area of interest. The whole Parliament then debates the bill, takes a vote on the principles and refers it back to the committee. This is Stage 1. The committee then considers the bill clause-by-clause and discusses and votes on amendments. This Stage 2 is equivalent to the Committee stage at Westminster, except that any MSP may introduce an amendment and speak, although only members of the committee may vote. Finally, the bill is referred back to the Parliament for consideration of the amended version (Stage 3). At this stage (equivalent to Report and Third Reading at Westminster) further amendments may be introduced or those passed earlier can be reversed; the member in charge of the bill may also move that sections be referred back to the committee for reconsideration.

Most bills are introduced by the Scottish Executive and known as Executive Bills. In the spirit of legislative reform, these must be accompanied by an explanatory memorandum setting out the aims of the bill, how they are to be achieved, and the extent of consultation conducted in advance. It must also certify that the bill is within the powers of the Scottish Parliament and does not contravene European Union or European Convention for the Protection of Human Rights provisions. Committee Bills, introduced by subject committees, go through essentially the same procedure, except that the committee does not have to consider the bill at Stage 1, since it has already done so by introducing it. Backbench MSPs may also introduce bills, known as Members Bills, although they are restricted to two in any one session. As at Westminster, legislation providing for public expenditure can only be introduced with the sanction of ministers, in the form of a Financial Resolution. These regularly accompany Executive Bills and are needed in the case of other bills if they have financial implications. In the first parliamentary session, 1999–2003, just over 80 per cent of all bills were sponsored by the Executive.

A peculiarity of the Scottish devolution settlement is that, while certain powers are reserved for Westminster and thus beyond the competence of the Scottish Parliament, there are no limits on Westminster itself, which retains the right to legislate even in devolved matters. At the outset, a convention was established, named after its sponsor, Scottish Office minister Lord Sewel, according to which Westminster would only legislate in devolved matters with the agreement of the Scottish Parliament. This was intended to be an occasional occurrence, but in the first session (1999–2003) forty-one Sewel motions were passed, leading to criticisms that the Scottish Parliament was abdicating its legislative role (Hassan 2002). Closer examination shows that this headline figure is misleading (Cairney and Keating 2004). Most of the motions were passed to deal with matters where devolved and reserved matters were entangled, notably in the area of criminal law, and there was a need to avoid loopholes or ambiguity. In other cases, they were used to regulate cross-border or UK bodies whose responsibilities fall within both fields. Sometimes the device has been used where the responsibility for the function is not clear and, rather than concede the issue or leave it to the courts, the Scottish Executive has passed a Sewel motion to allow Westminster to act while at the same time safeguarding Scotland's own powers. This reflects a general practice in intergovernmental relations in the UK, of not testing the division of powers legally, but going instead for a political compromise or accommodation, a habit that might be criticised for leaving so many issues in constitutional limbo. Finally, the Executive has sometimes used Sewel motions for reasons of political expediency, to let Westminster take the criticism for controversial measures. Early in its life the Scottish Parliament repealed the legislation banning the 'promotion' of homosexuality by schools and local authorities, against a ferocious campaign by the Catholic Church and a privately funded referendum by millionaire Brian Soutar. Chastened by the experience, the Scottish Executive passed on to Westminster the responsibility for the Sexual Offences Act of 2001 and, in the second session, legislation on same-sex partnerships.

Sewel motions have been criticised for not allowing proper parliamentary scrutiny of the legislation involved (Page 2002; Page and Batey 2002). It may happen that Westminster abandons the legislation for lack of time or because there is an election, or the bill may be changed in its passage to look rather different from that anticipated at the time the motion was passed. So while the effect of Sewel motions in weakening the Scottish Parliament has certainly been exaggerated in much reporting, they do raise some questions about the role of the Parliament in the policy process.

An important difference with Westminster is the provision for constitutional review, since Scottish legislation must conform with the Scotland Act, EU law and the European Convention for the Protection of Human Rights (ECPHR). Ministers and the Presiding Officer must attest that bills are compliant with these legal provisions. After passage of a bill, the Lord Advocate, the Attorney General or the Advocate General may refer it to the Judicial Committee of the Privy Council for a ruling on compliance. The Judicial Committee, in turn, may refer the matter to the European Court of Justice. In addition, a party in a legal dispute can at any time claim that a Scottish law is ultra vires, and should be disallowed; such cases are known as devolution issues. The court in question can make a ruling, subject to appeals, ultimately back to the Judicial Committee of the Privy Council, which thus remains the ultimate arbiter of constitutionality. All this might appear to open the Scottish policy process to a large degree of judicial intervention, as has happened in the United States and Canada and, to an increasing extent, in other European countries. In practice, the Scottish Executive has taken great care to remain within the law, minimising court challenges. Ministers and law officers who might challenge Scottish laws at passage have themselves been members of the Scottish Executive or UK ministers of the same political party as Scottish ministers or its coalition partners. The same applies to a further provision, allowing UK ministers to veto bills on the grounds that they adversely affect the international obligations of the United Kingdom, or impinge negatively on reserved matters.

A centrepiece of the Consultative Steering Group proposals was a powerful system of parliamentary committees, which would break with the Westminster model of docile backbenchers and foster consensus and interparty cooperation (Arter 2002; Procedures Committee 2003). They were to combine two roles. First, in the legislative process, they were to bring a more informed and constructive perspective than the Westminster Standing Committees, which tend to reproduce the partisan posturing found on the floor of the House (see above). Second, they were to have an investigatory role, undertaking inquiries into key issues and scrutinising the work of the Executive, a task undertaken at Westminster by Select Committees. Eight of the Scottish Parliament Committees are mandatory. Others are established according to the main areas of responsibility of the Parliament and generally correspond to the structure of Executive Departments. Committees in 2004 are listed in Table 4.7.

Table 4.7   Committees of the Scottish Parliament, 2004

Mandatory Committees
Procedures
Equal Opportunities
Public Petitions
Standards
Finance
Subordinate Legislation
Audit
European and External Relations

Subject Committees
Health
Communities
Justice 1
Justice 2
Education
Enterprise and Culture
Local Government and Transport
Environment and Rural Development
Health

Source: Scottish Parliament

Membership is chosen to reflect the party balance in the Parliament as a whole, giving the coalition parties a majority on all committees but, especially since 2003, this has been a very small one. In 2001, the size of most committees was reduced from eleven to seven members, in order to reduce the strain of multiple committee memberships. Convenorships are shared among the parties, and the party leaderships are able to determine who will occupy the role. This has also been the practice at Westminster, but there in recent years the leaderships have sometimes had to back down from efforts to install their own nominees as backbenchers have become more independent-minded.

Committees took some time to work out their role, determine their priorities and use their time effectively. Many members were new to politics and had little idea about parliamentary procedure, or the distinction between the executive and legislative roles. Relations with civil servants were often difficult, as parliamentarians sometimes thought that the civil service answered to them, and civil servants could be patronising about the learning difficulties of MSPs. There was a high turnover of committee membership, preventing committees building up expertise. On the other hand, as committee service, unlike at Westminster, is an essential part of the job, committees have drawn on ex-ministers as well as those ambitious for future ministerial status. This has avoided the Westminster syndrome where committee work is often for those who cannot make it into government or who are out of the political mainstream. Gradually, committees have found their feet; by the end of the first session they were more confident in their role, and have significantly increased public involvement in policy making (Hazell 2003).

In their legislative role, committees do not represent a radical break from Westminster, since party whips are applied and the governing parties usually get their way. Indeed, as the Parliament has developed, they seem to have become rather more partisan (Arter 2004b). Nonetheless, the whole process is taken more seriously than at Westminster because of the broader role of the committees, their ability to take evidence and the small majority for the governing coalition, which can lose an amendment if just one of its members fails to toe the line. Departments of the Executive certainly pay them great attention and spend much more time keeping them on side than they needed to do with the old Scottish committees at Westminster.

In their investigatory role, committees are less beholden to the Executive or the Opposition line, and have some scope for developing their own ideas. They need to balance long-term inquiries with addressing pressing issues. Sandford and Maer (2003) cite three types of review. Strategic policy reviews are large-scale and forward-looking investigations into broad areas. Forward policy proposals focus on particular issues or policies. Event inquiries are backward-looking reviews of particular happenings, such as the crisis in the Scottish Qualifications Authority in 2000. Some tasks are predictable, such as scrutinising the budget proposals (see Chapter 6), while others are more difficult to plan, as when a committee is awaiting a bill whose publication has been delayed. Knowing that their report will carry more weight if it is unanimous, committee convenors seek consensus and to keep their distance from the Executive (Arter 2004a). The Executive is obliged to respond to committee reports within a set time period, which enhances their influence in setting the policy agenda. On matters not raising issues of party policy, committee reports have sometimes made a real impact. Arter (2004a) cites the Local Government Committee's inquiry into non-domestic rates; the Enterprise and Lifelong Learning Committee's report on the prison estates review; and the Health and Community Care Committee's inquiry into free personal care for the elderly. One might also add the Enterprise and Lifelong Learning Committee's report on the enterprise support network. The effect of committee reports is not always direct. Sometimes they may shift the political agenda and force the coalition parties into adjusting their positions, or in some cases may reinforce the position of one coalition party against another.

The experience of committees points to some of the ambiguities in the concept of the new politics and its application. Much attention in the run-up to devolution was given to the Parliament as an institution and how it could be the engine of change. Powerful committees could provide more information and authority, while a new culture could promote consensus and policy based on evidence and needs rather than pre-set ideology. In such a dispensation, the lines between government and opposition, and between ministers and backbenchers, would fade in importance. This idea was in fact incorporated into the original design of the National Assembly for Wales, in which there was to be no difference between executive and the assembly itself. In contrast is the parliamentary model, in which backbenchers are separate from the executive and can scrutinise it, and in which opposition members are there to oppose (albeit perhaps constructively). It is revealing that the Welsh Assembly has moved in this direction, during the passage of the devolution legislation and since. The Scottish Parliament was designed on parliamentary lines from the outset and so it has remained. A suggestion made by the Procedures Committee (2003) that MSPs from opposition parties could participate in Executive Task Forces was not taken up, since the parties thought that this would blur the lines between government and opposition and between the Parliament and the Executive (Arter, 2004a). Within the limits of a parliamentary system, however, the Scottish Parliament committees do mark an advance in scrutiny, control and accountability, providing mechanisms that did not exist before and forcing policy makers to anticipate criticism.

The main difficulty in enhancing the role of the Parliament in policy making is really not institutional but party-political. All the parties maintain tight control over candidate selection, resulting in some surprising omissions from the Labour lists in 1999 and those of the SNP in 2003. There has been little effort to bring in experienced people from other walks of life who might come and go in politics. Instead, Holyrood has followed Westminster in the development of a class of professional politicians. There are few of the independent-minded backbenchers who often survive at Westminster with the support of their constituency parties, even when they are a thorn in the flesh of the party leadership. On the other hand, party control can backfire. Dennis Canavan and Margo MacDonald, both excluded or demoted on their party lists, stood and were elected as independents, while minor parties gained substantially in 2003 in a backlash against the big parties. This has brought into the Parliament a group of MSPs not beholden to the old political class and who might well hold the balance in future parliaments. In that case, policy would increasingly have to be negotiated across party lines in shifting coalitions, and the place of the Parliament in the political system would grow further.

Notes

1. Strict comparability between the two periods is hampered by changes in the categories involved. The old administrative class encompassed the senior staff as well as young high-flyers recruited directly into it.
2. This may be partly connected with the decline of manual workers, but nowadays trade union density is highest among the white-collar public-sector workers.
3. There is, in 2004, only one Scottish Conservative MP, who was educated at a state school.

CHAPTER FIVE

Intergovernmental Policy Making

Interdependence and Cooperation

On paper, the division of powers between Westminster and Holyrood looks fairly clear, with each tier free to act within its own competences. In practice, there is considerable overlap and mutual dependence, so that a great deal of policy must be made by cooperation between the two levels. European integration creates a third level, with many European Union (EU) policies impinging on both reserved and devolved matters. Economic development, for example, is a devolved responsibility but general economic policy, including taxation and monetary policy, is reserved. The Scottish Executive makes policy on industrial assistance, but the boundaries of assisted areas are reserved and subject to European rules. Transport policy is also divided in a complicated way. Initially, railways and air transport were reserved, since it was thought that these affected the UK as a whole, while road transport was devolved. Later the scheme was revised to give the Scottish Executive responsibility for franchises and subsidies for rail services entirely within Scotland, enabling it to plan rail and road policy together but raising problems about the relationship between rail services (devolved) and rail regulation and the network (reserved). Inevitably, the Scottish Executive has taken an interest in air transport and airports, although only the airports in the Highlands and Islands (regarded as an essential social service) are devolved. Airports and airlines operating in Scotland can also claim regional assistance from the Scottish Executive and have not hesitated to threaten to withdraw services if they do not receive it. Agricultural policy is largely devolved to Scotland, but in practice regulated at European level. This requires the Scottish Office to work not only with the Commission in Brussels, but also with the Whitehall department that takes the lead in agriculture and fisheries matters. Welfare state matters are divided between the Scottish and UK levels, with Scotland largely responsible for social service and London for cash payments, but the interface between the two creates areas of shared responsibility. Responsibilities are particularly entangled in the area of criminal and civil law, where bills frequently cut across devolved and reserved matters and both levels are anxious to avoid loopholes that could be exploited by wrongdoers.

Further interdependencies are created by new, transversal policy initiatives, responses to new problems or new ways of framing social questions. So, as labour-market policy has been linked to welfare policy and to social services in the effort to get people into work, both levels of government have had to work together. The broader social-inclusion agenda, the focus on rural affairs or the theme of 'environmental justice' are other transversal issues, which require a coordinated approach not only across Scottish Executive departments but among all levels of government – European, UK, Scottish and local – as well as the voluntary and private sectors. The UK Government's policy to introduce identity cards affects both reserved matters, like immigration, and devolved matters of access to public services. As the Liberal Democrats in Scotland opposed identity cards, a compromise was reached that in Scotland they would be valid only in reserved matters. There is also a general concern, reflected in the devolution White Papers and legislation, that devolved governments should not upset UK policies in reserved areas and should adhere to European regulations.

Interdependence is a common feature of systems of federal and devolved governments, and there is a large literature on the theme of intergovernmental policy making. What is unusual about the UK case is the highly asymmetrical nature of the system. Other countries, like Germany, Spain, Belgium or Canada, have a central level with its own competences, facing a set of federated or devolved governments, with an area of reserved powers, an area of devolved powers and a third area where powers are shared. In the United Kingdom, the central government doubles up as the government of the largest part, England. Whitehall departments are sometimes predominantly English, where their responsibilities correspond to devolved powers in Scotland, Wales and Northern Ireland, for example the Department for Education and Skills or the Department of Health; although in legislative matters, these are English and Welsh. In other cases, they are predominantly UK departments, like the Foreign Office, Department of Work and Pensions or Department of Defence. A third category is mixed, with some functions applying only in England, others in England and Wales, others to Great Britain and yet others to the United Kingdom; a prime example is the Home Office. Further confusion is added when Scottish MPs are appointed to UK departments dealing predominantly with England, as in the case of John Reid, made Secretary of State for Health in 2003, on the grounds that any MP can serve in any 'UK department'. The result can be seen from two perspectives. We could say that, in policy fields like education or agriculture, there is no 'central government', merely a group of territorial departments for England, Scotland, Wales and Northern Ireland, coordinating where necessary on common issues. Alternatively, we could argue that there is a centre and that it is England, whose government and departments dominate and lead the policy process, to which the other administrations must adapt. There is in fact some truth in both perspectives, but the world of intergovernmental policy making is rather secretive as most of it is conducted through informal channels rather than the official machinery. This is not because the machinery does not exist – there is in fact an elaborate set of legal and administrative mechanisms to resolve intergovernmental conflicts, clarify roles and facilitate joint working.

Legal Mechanisms

Under the Scotland Act, the courts have the right to strike down Scottish legislation or administrative action as ultra vires, where it breaches the Scotland Act, European Union legislation or the European Convention for the Protection of Human Rights. The ultimate court of appeal on these matters is the Judicial Committee of the Privy Council (JCPC).[1] Either level of government can also refer legislation to the JCPC for a ruling on vires. While in countries like Spain or Canada, a substantial jurisprudence has developed over the years to shape the pattern of intergovernmental relations, nothing like this has appeared in the United Kingdom, since the UK Government has not referred any cases to the courts, preferring to rely on political or administrative mechanisms. Often, there is not even an attempt to clarify responsibilities between the law officers at the two levels. Instead, Sewel resolutions are used to take the matter at Westminster, or there is a practical compromise on who will do what, without the Scottish Parliament surrendering its claims to its own jurisdiction. For example, on the question of offshore wind farms, the Scottish Executive position was that the matter fell within its jurisdiction up to the twelve-mile limit and that it could be devolved administratively up to 200 miles. Whitehall took a different view. The compromise, which sidestepped the question of territorial jurisdiction, was that the entire zone should be treated as one, with regulations made by UK ministers and consents given by Scottish ministers. Another case in which the limits were unclear was over genetically modified crops. Instead of testing in the courts whether it could ban these, the Scottish Executive chose a political compromise, going along with a UK-wide permission on planting but calling for a voluntary moratorium on planting (see Chapter 7).

Administrative Mechanisms

There is little provision in the Scotland Act for intergovernmental machinery, but devolution was accompanied by a Memorandum of Understanding between the UK Government and the devolved administrations. This was supplemented with a series of concordats in various policy areas, providing for exchange of information, collaboration and resolution of conflicts. Concordats are codes of practice, not legally binding on either level, but intended as constitutional conventions. Although quite elaborate and detailed in some cases, they give the last word to the central government. In practice, the concordat mechanism has been little used, as the two governments have preferred informal ways of working.

A related mechanism is the Joint Ministerial Conferences (JMCs), consisting of ministers from Whitehall and devolved administrations, which can both debate broad policy issues and act as conflict-resolution mechanisms. There is an annual plenary JMC, attended by the Prime Minister and First Ministers of the devolved administrations, as a rather formal occasion. A JMC for European Affairs meets twice a year to discuss the agenda for the forthcoming EU presidency, and it was used to provide a joint input of the Foreign Office and devolved administrations to the Convention on the

Future of Europe in 2003. A series of JMCs was held in 1999–2000 under the impetus of the Chancellor of the Exchequer to discuss poverty, and for a time there were regular meetings on health (House of Lords 2002), which seem to have been among the most useful. Other JMCs seem to have reflected the whims and immediate concerns of the Prime Minister and Chancellor, but none established themselves (Trench 2004). JMCs might help shape the policy environment, and emphasise the presence of UK ministers in the devolved territories, but they are not decision-making bodies. Indeed, sometimes such general meetings have been convened as the British–Irish Council (sometimes known as the Council of the Isles), set up under the Northern Ireland peace agreement and which also includes the Republic of Ireland, the Isle of Man and the Channel Islands. More common are informal interministerial meetings, summoned and chaired by UK ministers on issues of the day. The most regular are those in advance of the meetings of the European Council of Agricultural Ministers, to agree a common UK line. Whether a meeting is summoned under the JMC framework or not does not seem to be particularly important and there are no set rules. JMCs have never been summoned to resolve policy conflicts, as was originally envisaged, and these are instead resolved by informal contacts between ministers and civil servants. Such an ad hoc and informal approach has been possible while the two governments have been politically close, but it has been criticised by the House of Lords Select Committee on the Constitution (2002) for failing to develop institutional procedures which might be needed in the future.

Following devolution, the Secretary of State for Scotland was retained as a Cabinet minister with a much-reduced department renamed the Scotland Office. It was thought that Scotland still needed its own voice in Cabinet – indeed the possible loss of this voice was one of the principal arguments of opponents of devolution over the years. The Secretary of State was also responsible for following the work of Parliament and Executive and referring acts as needed to the courts, and for handling the block grant to fund the devolved administration. In practice, the Scottish Executive has taken the main role in fighting Scotland's corner in the United Kingdom and in dealing with UK departments. There have been no referrals to the courts, and the Barnett formula (see Chapter 6) has removed most of the negotiation over funding. As a result, the Secretary of State was distinctly under-employed and the post only avoided abolition in 2003 when it was realised that it was legally required. Instead, the Scotland Office was wound up and the Secretaryship of State transferred to another Scottish MP and minister. This rather added to the confusion since the MP in question, Alastair Darling, was also Secretary of State for Transport, a largely English brief but with some responsibilities for railways and air transport in Scotland. In the event of the Secretary of State for Scotland needing to make representations about these reserved matters, Darling would then have to lobby himself! Even more confusingly, the junior Scotland Office minister and civil servants were accommodated within the Department of Constitutional Affairs (DCA). This would logically be the place to accommodate a new department or division of intergovernmental relations, but this does not seem to have been thought through at the time.

Civil Service and Departmental Networks

A crucial link between Whitehall and the devolved administrations is the unified civil service. Prior to devolution, Scottish Office civil servants were involved in joint committees and working parties on a wide range of matters and were in frequent contact with their Whitehall counterparts to apply common UK policy to Scotland. Despite the distance, they were to some degree part of the Whitehall 'village', sharing assumptions and attitudes and exchanging experiences on a regular basis. Cabinet and departmental papers were regularly copied to the Scottish Office and civil servants, answering to the same government, could share information and ideas. Much of this spirit survived devolution, as the same civil servants were doing much the same work, and there was a good relationship between the political leaderships at both levels. Yet much also changed. Civil servants are conscious that they have different political masters, and coalition arrangements in Scotland mean that they may even serve different parties. Papers are not circulated unless there is a specific reason to do so, especially across party lines. There are many fewer joint committees on policy work, except where cooperative policy making has been adopted or there is a need for a common position in Europe. On the other hand, most departments in Scotland have made a conscious effort to maintain contact with their Whitehall counterparts, to exchange ideas about policy and practice. For example, there are regular meetings in the field of health, which are particularly useful to the devolved administrations, although the English department is not always involved. More generally, enthusiasm for networking tends to be stronger on the side of the territories.

There is a recurrent tendency in Whitehall to forget about Scotland, to issue statements or policies purporting to apply to the UK or Britain as a whole, or to neglect to consult the devolved administrations. The Curry Report on farming following the foot-and-mouth outbreak caused some distress by proposing changes for the UK, when its remit had been limited to England. There have also been complaints about the Department of Trade and Industry. Informal networks can pick up English policy initiatives by chance, but some items slip through and are not noticed until too late. The establishment of a Department of Constitutional Affairs, with a Supreme Court for the United Kingdom, was announced in 2003 as part of a hasty Cabinet reshuffle, without proper consideration for the huge effects this would have on Scots law and the devolution settlement. Only afterwards did London open discussions with the Scottish Executive. Proposals for universities, including the imposition of top-up fees in England, were also launched unilaterally, although this has ramifications in Scotland and Scottish MPs were expected to toe the government line. Issues of taxation can also impinge on devolved matters, such as urban regeneration or land, but the Treasury does not always bring the devolved administrations in on the consultation since they are no longer part of the Whitehall network. This linkage of devolved or federal units into state-wide policy making has been identified as a weakness in many systems of government, but is exacerbated in the UK case by the asymmetrical nature of the settlement, which means that functional departments dealing with England have the advantage of insider status. To address this problem and to ensure that the networks were sustained, a new UK relations unit was established in 2003 within the Office of the Permanent Secretary. This does not handle working contacts, which are still conducted among departments and sections, but seeks to facilitate working and to build links at both political and official levels.

Some joint policy making has been encouraged through the strengthened central policy structures that have grown up around 10 Downing Street and the Treasury. The Performance and Innovation Unit, the Social Exclusion Unit and the Centre for Management and Policy Studies, coming under the Prime Minister, have emerged as important centres for policy innovation and transversal initiatives, and have drawn in the devolved administrations in their deliberations (Parry 2001). Since 1997, the Treasury has become a powerful force in domestic policy making across the board, drawing in UK departments and imposing strict requirements on them in the form of Public Service Agreements. Scotland and the other devolved administrations are not subject to this, and continue to manage their block funding autonomously; but they are involved in many of the Treasury research and policy development initiatives, and can bid for funding under them. Yet Treasury dominance over devolved administrations should not be exaggerated.[2] It is less a matter of issuing them orders than of giving advice and providing for the circulation of ideas.

Party Links

In the absence of regularly used formal networks of collaboration, a great deal of intergovernmental relations is conducted through party networks. Labour remains a single political party, albeit with devolution to its Scottish level, and there is an ideological consistency to its stances on Scottish and English matters. Labour politicians are in regular contact and will often clear matters through bilateral contacts, phone calls or meetings in various party contexts. London ministers have not hesitated to let their Scottish counterparts know when a policy threatens to cause them trouble at home, although their complaints are not always effective.[3] The same happens in the Liberal Democrats, although their Scottish party has always had a larger degree of autonomy. Coalition politics can complicate matters in other ways, since Whitehall ministers might be reluctant to share information with the Scottish Executive, where it might be available to the Liberal Democrats, an opposition party at Westminster. This in turn may reinforce the tendency to rely on Labour Party networks. The presence of Scottish ministers in key UK departments often facilitates such contacts, with, at various times, Gordon Brown at the Treasury, Robin Cook at the Foreign Office and Alastair Darling at Work and Pensions. At other times, ministers less sympathetic to, or knowledgeable of, Scottish conditions have hampered understanding. In the early days of the Parliament, many ministers were former Westminster MPs with close contacts with colleagues in London and sharing their ways of working, but by 2003 the only survivors were the Liberal Democrats Jim Wallace, Deputy First Minister, and Nichol Steven, who had briefly been an MP. A new generation of leaders had come up through the Scottish system, owing nothing to preferment by the London leadership and often lacking the networks of contacts in London. Yet Jack McConnell chose to cleave closely to the New Labour government, carefully avoiding criticism or comment where things were done differently in England, and maintaining a strict ban on ministers making their views known on reserved matters. Even where Scottish policy diverged, as in the system of public service provision, the issue was not played up, in contrast to Wales, where First Minister Rhodri Morgan made great political capital out of traditional or 'Old Labour' values and ways, putting 'clear red water' between himself and London. The Welsh example and other evidence indicate that Scottish Labour's low profile is not the result of dictat from the centre, but from the decision of the local leadership to maintain a united front. In return, Scottish Labour is regarded as a loyal ally and team player, and included in the Whitehall policy networks to a greater degree than might have been otherwise; a tactic reminiscent of the old Scottish Office system. A more independent-minded leadership might choose to build up political capital in Scotland by running against London, but this might play into the hands of the SNP, and damage the Scottish Executive's standing in Whitehall.

With different political parties in charge at the two levels, this would all change and formal mechanisms for negotiation would become more important. It is fair to say that we do not know how this would develop, since the legal and formal machinery has not been tested and broken in. Overseas experience is some guide, suggesting that intergovernmental committees and conferences would become more important, but not an elected second chamber for the regions and nations. However, the asymmetrical nature of UK devolution means that Whitehall, speaking for both the UK and its largest part, would still play the larger role.

Scotland in Europe

Scotland's policy-making system is not only embedded within a wider UK system, but is also part of an emerging European polity. The Scotland Act incorporates the Council of Europe's European Convention for the Protection of Human Rights (ECPHR), which the courts may use to strike down laws of the Scottish Parliament.

So Scottish law becomes part of a developing system of European human rights law, which in turn is adapted to Scottish traditions, without passing through Westminster. ECPHR issues, like devolution issues, can be appealed to the Judicial Committee of the Privy Council, which should bring Scottish interpretations into line with those elsewhere in the United Kingdom (O'Neill 2001), but the ultimate appeal is to the European Court of Human Rights in Strasbourg. In this way, Scottish, UK and European law are increasingly intertwined, influencing each other mutually.

A more pervasive influence on Scottish policy making, however, is the European Union (EU), also recognised in the Scotland Act. The European Economic Community (later EU) was committed from the beginning to the free circulation of goods, services, capital and workers, and from the late 1980s this was deepened to a 'single market', removing all barriers, explicit or implicit. This means that governments, central or devolved, must refrain from measures that would hinder competition. Industrial assistance is allowed only within designated areas and up to fixed levels, designation of areas is reserved to Westminster, which negotiates these with the EU, and aid ceilings are set by Brussels. Subsidies must be justified and subject to competition, so that the Scottish Executive has found itself negotiating at length about the conditions of support for the socially necessary ferry services in the Highland and Islands. Public procurement is similarly subject to strict rules for competitive tendering.

More broadly, the single market intensifies competition among countries and regions of Europe, all seeking to attract capital and technology, gain markets and improve their competitive advantage. This is one factor enhancing the importance of economic development as a task of the devolved institutions, but requiring new approaches to achieve it, given the limits on traditional industrial policy posed by European regulations. It has also stimulated, right across Europe, new forms of 'paradiplomacy', in which sub-state governments link up to exploit complementary advantages and forge strategic alliances on matters of common interest.

Many EU sectoral policies also impinge directly on Scotland's devolved competences. Agriculture is a prominent example, a matter almost entirely devolved but in which most policy is made in Brussels. Reform of the Common Agricultural Policy, with a move away from support to farmers towards more general measures of rural development, has caused several differences between England and Scotland, which is more dependent on subsidies to support small and hill farmers (see Chapter 7). Fisheries has been another point of contention, as Scotland has around half of the UK fishing industry, and its interests are not always consistent with those of England and Wales. Environmental policy has become highly Europeanised over recent years, and Scotland must adapt to European environmental regulations. There is a European transport policy, focused on trans-European networks, and a research policy of interest to Scottish universities and research institutes. Like the ECPHR, EU laws take precedence over Scottish laws, and the courts can strike the latter down if they conflict. Over a broad range of matters, Scotland must implement EU directives, and there are European funding programmes, notably the Structural Funds, which may have a direct impact on Scotland. As the EU expands its sphere of activity, both through Commission initiatives and through the 'open method of coordination' whereby governments agree on parallel policies, it impinges more on Scottish devolved matters. In recent years, there has been a development of common policy in police and justice matters (Pillar 111 of the Union), which are devolved in Scotland, but are centralised in many other countries. Under the 'Bologna process', educational qualifications are being coordinated with a view to mutual recognition and transfer. Again, Scotland is unusual in having its own system, which is entirely devolved, with no direction from the centre. The Scottish legal system, too, is largely separate from that of England and Wales, requiring a distinct approach in coordinating and applying EU laws. Other Scottish interests are touched in unpredictable ways, as when in 2003 the statistical agency Eurostat classified the kilt as 'womenswear', only to beat a hasty retreat in the face of protests across Scotland.

Yet in spite of the penetration of devolved nations, regions and localities by European policies, the EU remains fundamentally an organisation of member states. Its most powerful body is the Council of Ministers, an intergovernmental body, and the Commission is chosen by member states, although acting independently of them. This has raised a steady stream of demands for more sub-state participation in EU matters, both 'upstream', in the making of European policy, and 'downstream', in its implementation. Three principal channels of representation have emerged: via national governments; intermediary associations and consultative mechanisms; and directly to Brussels.

Under the provisions of the 1992 Maastricht Treaty on European Union, it is possible in federal or regionalised states for a representative of the regional level to represent the state, where devolved matters are at stake. This happens regularly in Germany, where the sixteen Länder will agree on a common position, with one of their number then participating in the Council of Ministers, and in Belgium, where there are three regions and three language communities. The main difference is that in Germany the Länder will decide their common position, where necessary, by a vote in the Bundesrat (the federal chamber), while in Belgium there needs to be unanimity among the governments affected. In both cases, participation in the Council of Ministers depends on the mix of federal and regional matters on the agenda, so the delegation might be purely federal, purely regional, or joint. A similar but weaker arrangement exists in Austria. The devolution legislation in the United Kingdom makes provision for Scotland, Northern Ireland and Wales to use this possibility, but with two critical differences. First, the presence of devolved administrations in the Council of Ministers is not a right, but at the invitation of the UK Government. Second, the absence of a federal government or English devolution means that the Whitehall departments speak both for the United Kingdom and for England. So the need to strike a common position in Europe draws Scotland and the other devolved administrations back into the Whitehall networks. In practice, the arrangements put into effect in 1999 were designed as far as possible to continue the pre-devolution system in which the Scottish, Welsh and Northern Ireland Offices (as part of the single UK government) participated in European affairs. Some modifications, however, had to be made in recognition that the new administrations do not share the political responsibility of the UK government.

Relations with European institutions are covered by a concordat, supplemented by more detailed Departmental Guidance Notes (DGNs). These provide for a sharing of information on European matters and for an input into the UK position from the devolved administrations, although none of them is binding or in legal form. On information sharing, it is provided that devolved administrations should be told of relevant issues coming up and be copied the relevant correspondence. On the other hand, as they are no longer part of the same government, they do not get Cabinet or other papers of political sensitivity. There is a Joint Ministerial Committee on Europe, which in December 2003 took over the Ministerial European Coordination Committee, which deals with presentational aspects. This allows discussion of broad European issues or matters like the Convention on the Future of Europe, but is not an authoritative decision-making body.

In the determination of the line to be pursued by the UK delegation in the Council of Ministers, the concordats provide for collaboration and input. Normally, a functional department in Whitehall will take the lead, bringing in the territorial administrations, as happened with the old territorial departments in the past (Bulmer et al. 2002). Experience here is mixed. In the case of agriculture, where there is need of a constant input, there are meetings monthly before the Council of European Agricultural Ministers. It appears that at one time at least, the lead UK Cabinet minister (from 2001, the Secretary of State for Environment, Agriculture and Rural Affairs) would represent the United Kingdom, with one of his/her junior ministers speaking for England alongside the Scottish and Welsh ministers. In other cases, there have been complaints that Whitehall departments have forgotten to take Scottish opinion on board. If there is a conflict, the matter can be referred to the Joint Ministerial Committee on Europe. Here the UK Government has the final say, and, like the other JMCs, it has proved less important than informal contacts between the relevant departments and politicians.

Ministers from the devolved administrations can attend the Council of Ministers by invitation of the UK Government. In fisheries negotiations, there is always a Scottish minister and others have participated from time to time.[4] In contrast to the situation in Belgium, the lead is almost always taken by the UK department, although occasionally the Scottish Executive is allowed to take the lead as part of a single UK delegation. This gives influence but at the cost of being drawn into a London-dominated policy team. Scottish ministers are not allowed to discuss with the Parliament the details of negotiations or where they have had to give way, and may not share information about the UK negotiating position which has been given in confidence. There are sometimes considerable tensions here, as when the Scottish fisheries minister was negotiating as part of the UK team on the closing of fishing grounds, and had to support the UK line, while signalling to fishermen back home that he was fighting their corner.

Even where Scotland is represented in the functional formations of the Council of Ministers dealing with individual matters like agriculture or transport, it, like other sub-state governments, may lose out when trade-offs and bargains are made across functional fields, in the Council of Foreign Ministers or European Council, where there is no Scottish presence. There is a devolution unit in the Foreign and Commonwealth Office and the devolved administrations have their own European units, responsible for overall policy and some coordination work. General European work is done in the Central Services department in the Scottish Executive. These can be useful channels for information and warning, but defence of Scottish interests within the general-purpose European councils depends mainly on political contacts and the sensitivity of the UK Government to opinion in Scotland.

Since 1999 the Scottish Executive has taken a cooperative line in European matters, seeking to exercise influence behind the scenes by being an active player in the Whitehall networks but a loyal member of the UK negotiating team. This care to remain an 'insider' in the policy networks is consistent with its general position on intergovernmental relations and is made possible by the shared party affiliation of the leadership at both levels. It rules out Scotland publicly taking a different line on EU policies, or doing anything that might embarrass the London departments. The Scottish Executive, for example, did not press for differential treatment in the export of meat to Europe following the BSE crisis, although Northern Ireland politicians did seek to differentiate themselves from the rest of the United Kingdom. The Scottish Executive insisted that they could not ban trials of genetically-modified crops in Scotland alone and, at one time, that modulation of agricultural payments could not be applied differently from England (see Chapter 7). In the event of a difference in political control in Edinburgh and London, these conditions would no longer apply and the present informal system of bargaining inherited from the Scottish Office days would have to give way to something more formal and regulated, as in Germany or Belgium.

Within the Scottish Executive, general European matters are the responsibility of a minister, who combines this with another portfolio. There is a division of External Relations, reorganised in 2003 and separated from the division dealing with intergovernmental relations within the UK. In the Foreign and Commonwealth Office, the Parliamentary Relations and Devolution Department is responsible for overall relations with the devolved administrations. Generally speaking, the attitude of the Foreign and Commonwealth Office to Scottish initiatives has been tolerant, since these do not challenge the UK position and help to demonstrate British ability to accommodate national diversity, but on the understanding that Scotland does not stray from the UK line. This has been a very sensitive issue (McLeish 2004), although there have been successes like the joint paper prepared for the Convention on the Future of Europe (see above). For the Convention on the Future of Europe, the Scottish Executive, the UK Government and the devolved administration in Wales produced a joint paper under the aegis of the Joint Ministerial Committee on Europe. Another sensitive area, in Scotland as elsewhere, has been cultural promotion. Scotland has access to the network of the British Council, which has even sponsored seminars on devolution around Europe, but the Foreign Office is sensitive to anything that looks like promoting nationalism. This issue has caused endless conflicts between Canada and Quebec, and could prove a flashpoint between London and a future Scottish administration. Relations with functional departments have sometimes been more difficult, given the differences of interest in Scotland and England, the pressure from interest groups and the political sensitivity of matters such as fisheries. There is also cooperation with local government, and the Scottish Executive produced a joint input with the Convention of Scottish Local Authorities for the White Paper on European Governance.

Scottish interests in Europe are also represented by a variety of intermediary and consultative bodies. The Committee of the Regions (CoR) was set up by the Maastricht Treaty as a consultative body for sub-member state governments, including federated units, devolved regions and nations, and municipal governments. There are 317 full members and the same number of alternates, who may attend if a full member is absent. Scotland has four of the twenty-four UK seats, and in the early years its representatives were chosen from local government. Representation is now shared by the Scottish Parliament and local authorities. CoR has two main roles. It must be consulted by the European Commission, the Council of Ministers and the Parliament in certain policy fields impinging on regional responsibilities, and it can issue reports on its own initiative. Under the proposals of the Convention on the Future of Europe, it would also have the right, in the name of the subsidiarity principle, to bring European institutions before the Court of Justice should they impinge too much on regional competences. There were those in the early days of CoR who dreamed of a powerful 'third level' in Europe, representing the regions and stateless nations, and indeed it counts among its members some of the leading regional politicians of Europe, presidents of German, Spanish, Italian and Belgian regions. In practice it has been a disappointment. The top-ranking politicians rarely attend, preferring instead to send their alternates; Scottish First Minister Jack McConnell achieved the same aim another way, opting to become an alternate rather than a full member. The CoR's powers are weak as, while it has to be consulted, it does not have to be heeded. The membership is highly diverse, from small municipal governments to powerful legislative regions and federated states and nations. Common interests are often hard to find, since regions differ so much and often have quite different visions of the future of Europe.

As a result of this, a group of stronger regions has sought to carve out a distinct role, calling themselves the Regions with Legislative Power (RegLeg). An earlier, similar, initiative was that of the Constitutional Regions. Parallel to this is a conference of the parliaments of legislative regions (CALRE). Their main contention is that there is a fundamental distinction between unitary states, where local government has an essentially administrative role, and federal or regionalised states, in which regions share the basic tasks of the state itself and must play the main role in adapting European legislation to the local environment. Scotland has been active in this movement, under both the Constitutional Regions and RegLeg banners, and was a signatory of the Flanders Declaration of 2001 calling for recognition of its position.[5] In 2004, First Minister Jack McConnell served as president of RegLeg. Yet the Scottish Executive has been wary of the more radical demands and of the nationalistic tone of some of its partners, fearing for its strategy of playing close to the UK line. It has consequently trodden a narrow line, supporting a stronger regional role, but in close partnership with member state governments.

This is only the most recent of a series of inter-regional networks that have arisen over the years and in which Scottish local governments were involved before 1999. The Assembly of European Regions is a general-purpose body whose heyday was the early 1990s. The Conference of Peripheral Maritime Regions is an established body whose influence has waxed and waned over time. Scotland is also involved in networks of industrial regions (RETI), for environmental policy (ENCORE) and for other policy fields, their importance at any time depending on the quality of their leadership and the effort their members are prepared to invest.

Since the 1980s many European regions have sought a more direct input into European policy making by opening offices in Brussels, of which there were 160 in 2002 (Marks et al. 2002). Of course, since it is member states who are the building blocks of the EU, these cannot negotiate for their own interests, but they can seek to penetrate the complex policy networks in Brussels, to get advance notice of upcoming initiatives, and to cooperate with other regions. The question of the representation of Scotland in Brussels first arose in the 1990s, following skirmishes between the Scottish Office and the Whitehall departments. Eventually it was agreed to set up offices to provide a base for interests within Scotland, Wales and Northern Ireland. This was all carefully arranged to make clear that the offices were not a form of political representation and that the UK political line in Europe remained a single one. Following devolution it was agreed that the three devolved administrations should have their own presence in Brussels. Scotland chose to keep the existing representation, Scotland Europa, as a platform for Scottish interests generally and to add its own Brussels Office, representing the Scottish Executive.[6] Both are housed in the same building and work closely together. The Scottish, Welsh and Northern Ireland Offices in Brussels are treated as part of the 'UKREP family', named after the UK Permanent Representation in Brussels, and work closely with it. They participate in its weekly meetings, are on the circulation list for papers, and try not to pursue conflicting lines on European policy. They liaise with offices of other European regions, follow issues of concern to their respective administrations and brief ministers on matters coming up in the EU generally. This network has proved particularly important in matters of environmental policy, where most of the initiative now comes from Brussels and most of the application is done by the devolved administrations.

Downstream, the Scottish Parliament and Executive have an important role in implementing European laws and directives. In the case of EU initiatives requiring domestic legislation, the Scottish Executive must decide whether to present its own legislation or to opt into a UK bill via a Sewel resolution. Similarly, it can decide whether or not to adopt its own administrative instruments, if the matter lies within the devolved field, and must inform the relevant UK department within a time limit. There is a grey area concerning the issue of whether, where the United Kingdom has some discretion in how to implement an EU directive, this discretion also applies within the UK, so that Scotland could adopt a different approach. This matter was not cleared up in the European Constitution produced by the Convention in 2003 and the position seems to differ from one area to another. In any case, any failure to meet EU requirements is laid to the member state, so that the UK Government could be taken to court over any lapse by the Scottish Executive. The

UK Government has made it clear that, if this should happen, any fine would be deducted from the block grant paid to the Scottish Parliament. Correspondence about directives and implementation therefore tends to go via London, although the Scottish Executive may consult the Commission on details of what a regulation or directive means and how it is to be interpreted.

In its 2001 White Paper on Governance, the European Commission opened the door to more contacts with sub-state authorities in the form of tripartite contracts, by which regions could become partners of the Union, taking on broader responsibilities for policy delivery in particular fields. This addresses a problem felt in many regions, that EU directives come down via the national government. If there is a failure in implementation, the national government is responsible, tempting states to exercise more detailed control than might be necessary and desirable. The Scottish Executive is one government that has expressed interest in the idea of partnerships – including Europe, the UK and Scotland in matters of environmental policy – but the Commission has not followed through with any enthusiasm or determination.

Within the Scottish Parliament, the European and External Affairs Committee has a dual role: a *reactive* role, responding to items on the EU agenda; and a *pro-active* one, taking initiatives to debate issues of general importance. The quantity of European legislation that needs to be translated into Scottish law is so large that it threatens to overwhelm the system, and a balance has to be struck between this routine scrutiny and the more future-oriented work – trying to influence the development of European policy. Gradually the balance has shifted, and the committee has been able to give some time to general policy issues, such as the consequences of enlargement for Scotland and the European constitution. It has also entered the European arena itself and in 2002, along with the Parliament of Catalonia, was responsible for setting up a joint forum of European committees of regional parliaments.

A link to Europe is also provided by the European Parliament, where Scotland is represented by seven members (MEPs) elected by proportional representation from party lists. This has meant that all four main parties are represented, providing interlocutors who are able to raise Scottish issues both in the Parliament generally and within the party groups.

Scotland's external policy has developed and expanded over the years into a form of paradiplomacy comparable to that of other stateless nations and regions. This is less than a foreign policy, which only independent states can have, but more than a simple extension of domestic policy. Rather it is focused on promoting Scotland in the world and forging links and partnerships wherever they may be useful. In line with this expanded brief, the relevant minister's title was extended in 2001 to Europe and External Affairs, with a civil service division concentrated on this task. By 2003 the Scottish Executive had signed cooperation agreements with Catalonia, Tuscany, North-Rhine Westphalia and Bavaria, and there were proposals for links with a French region and one in a new EU member state, as well as regular cooperation with Flanders. There have been initiatives with the Nordic countries on common issues, including the EU Northern Periphery programmes, and with EU accession countries, including the Czech Republic and Estonia, on structural fund matters. Links have also developed beyond Europe. A Scottish Executive civil servant was attached to the British Embassy in Washington, DC and there has been official involvement in the celebration of 'Tartan Day' in the USA. In 2002, the First Minister attended the World Summit on Sustainable Development in Johannesburg, following the emphasis on environmental policy as an Executive priority. One spin-off from this was a link with the Eastern Cape region of South Africa.

Europe was not a major theme in the early years of devolution, despite the link that had been made between the two issues in the 1990s. Gradually, however, it grew in importance, as politicians and civil servants recognised the external dimension of their domestic policy responsibilities. Such had the salience of European issues become that in 2004 the Executive published a European Strategy (Scottish Executive 2004). This set out a list of issues in substantial policy fields like fisheries, the environment and economic development, and a series of avenues for approaching Europe, including working with the UK Government, contacts with the Commission, MEPs, the Committee of the Regions and the Regions with Legislative Powers. All of this has drawn Scotland into new policy networks and introduced new ideas into the policy debate. Formal relations with the EU are a reserved matter and negotiations are conducted via the UK Government, which has the last say on British input into EU policies. Yet Scotland's exposure to European influences has grown, enhanced by Scotland's reputation for being rather more pro-European than the UK as a whole. This has moved policy debate beyond the usual Scotland–England comparison and encouraged learning and exchange with other European countries. In the longer run, this is likely to lessen dependence on London for policy leadership and to increase Scotland's own policy capacity.

Patterns of Intergovernmental Policy Making

Intergovernmental policy making is crucial in many fields of government, where boundaries are unclear or responsibilities are entangled across the four levels of local government, the Scottish Executive, Whitehall and Europe. Yet the system for intergovernmental policy making since devolution has been characterised by informality, and constant changes in responsibilities. Broad forums for negotiation such as the JMCs have been downgraded in favour of informal arrangements at the departmental level and personal links among the politicians. Much of this stems from the asymmetrical nature of the devolution settlement and the weight of Whitehall departments, which have not always seen the devolved administrations as equals and have had some difficulty in adapting to new ways. Another factor is the coincidence of Labour-dominated administrations at both levels, which has encouraged the use of political and party mechanisms to resolve disputes, rather than formal or legal ones. This all helped devolution to evolve smoothly in the early years, in contrast to examples in other countries, and provided a flexibility to policy making that enabled issues to be addressed in what seemed the appropriate way. Yet it has also meant that the intergovernmental institutions are still to be tested, presenting a challenge for the system in the future, should different parties come to office at the two levels of government.

Notes
1. It is not clear at the time of writing just how this will be affected by the new UK Supreme Court, which was announced with little thought for devolution questions and which has been heavily criticised by Scottish lawyers.
2. Adams and Robinson (2002) exaggerate its role in portraying the Treasury as a new domestic policy centre for the UK. In fact, its main instrument for centralisation of domestic policy, the Public Service Agreements, do not extend to the devolved administrations.
3. See McLeish (2004) for Alan Milburn's attempts to get the First Minister to back down on free personal care for the elderly.
4. Critics have suggested that these numbers may be manipulated by a

system of rotation, in which devolved ministers get twenty minutes each in a meeting, so that they can tell their constituents that they were present (Walker 2002).

5. While participating in these regional networks, the Executive is aware of the sensitivity of the word 'region' in relation to Scotland, referring instead to sub-member state governments.

6. Scottish Executive EU Office, or SEEUO.

CHAPTER SIX

Getting and Spending

Determining Scottish Expenditure

One of the most difficult aspects of the devolution settlement was the financial provision for the Scottish Parliament, and this remains an item of keen contention. There are two aspects to the debate: whether Scotland gets a fair share of resources; and the discrepancy between Scotland's large discretion over how money is spent, and its very limited say over how it is raised. In fact, while devolution has led to huge changes in the political relationship between Scotland and Westminster, the fiscal relationship has remained largely unaltered. It remains an extreme case of path dependency, to be understood in relation to its evolution over time, rather than to any coherent set of principles. Yet, while many people find the arrangement unsatisfactory, it has proved impossible to get agreement on an alternative, since any change would create obvious and visible winners and losers.

The issue has a long history. In the nineteenth century, various government grants were attributed to Scotland on a basis derived from its percentage contribution to probate duties in 1886 (Heald and McLeod 2002b). Known as the Goschen formula after the Chancellor of the Exchequer who first formulated it, this gave Scotland 11/80 of any general increase, a proportion that happened to be roughly in line with its share of population. It was sporadically extended to other services during the early twentieth century but never formed a comprehensive basis for allocating spending (Mitchell 2003). As Scotland's share of the UK population fell throughout the twentieth century, the Goschen ratios gradually produced higher spending per capita. After the Second World War, the formula gradually fell into disuse, although it was used in educational funding as late as 1959. Thereafter, changes in Scottish Office spending were negotiated with the Treasury like that of other departments. Yet shades of the old formula remained, as the Scottish Office negotiating position was to take the Goschen share of expenditure increases as a minimum and then make a case for additional spending on individual items where it could advance a plausible claim (McLean and McMillan 2003). Having established its total, it then had a certain margin of discretion in reallocating the money according to its own priorities (Haddow 1969). There are, of course, endless arguments about exactly how much Scotland does get and whether or not this is 'fair' in relation to its needs or its contribution to the UK Exchequer, but the system does seem to have worked to its advantage during the 1960s and 1970s (Heald 1983; 1992). It also came to be generally accepted that Scotland's relatively generous treatment for expenditure and its distinct voice in Cabinet were a form of compensation for the absence of home rule (Keating 1975a).

It was this consideration that underlay the opposition of many Scottish MPs to the devolution proposals of the 1974–9 Labour government, as they feared that the implicit bargain would be undermined. English MPs, especially from northern constituencies, opposed Scottish devolution for the opposite reason, that it would give Scotland a further advantage. For the first time the territorial distribution of expenditure became a major political issue and the government's response was to commission a Needs Assessment Study to try to work out what the proper distribution of funds should be; and, separately from this, it introduced a new (supposedly provisional) distribution formula. The Needs Assessment Study found that, while Scotland should indeed get more than England on account of its greater social needs and the costs of providing services in remote areas, the differential should be reduced, while Wales should get more. Yet the methodology was rather crude and the data inadequate, and the main finding was that a proper needs-based formula would need much better information and more sophisticated treatment. Cutting Scottish expenditure down to English levels at a time of general restraint and nationalist sensitivity was clearly a political impossibility and, after the devolution proposals were repealed in 1979, the Needs Assessment Study was shelved.

The new formula to govern allocations to the Scottish Office later became known as the Barnett formula after its author, Treasury minister Joel Barnett (Heald 1983). It did not govern total Scottish expenditure, merely the changes from year to year. Unlike Goschen, it was based explicitly on population relativities, providing that any increase or cut in government expenditure on relevant services would be allocated in the ratio of 10:5:85 among Scotland, Wales and England (later Northern Ireland was brought into the formula). Relevant services included most of the responsibilities of the territorial offices and, as these increased, the scope of the formula was broadened. The Secretaries of State would then have discretion to reallocate the money within their own territories. The formula was not statutory, merely a working practice of the Treasury, and was not even made public until 1980. Even then, details of the formula, the relevant expenditure items and the calculations were shrouded in mystery, emerging only slowly in the subsequent twenty years (Heald and McLeod 2002a). Now the Treasury publishes the list of comparable English services and the percentage of comparability under a series of headings. As we have seen, Whitehall departments and programmes are a complicated mix of English, British and UK elements, so for comparability purposes it is necessary to separate out the purely English spending. For example, university expenditures are seen as 100 per cent comparable, so giving Scotland, Wales and Northern Ireland their full percentage share. Trade and Industry, on the other hand, is only 20 per cent comparable, since it is not entirely devolved and the relevant Whitehall department does spend money directly in Scotland, so the Scottish Parliament gets 20 per cent of the population-based share. Social Security, on the other hand, is a UK-wide function, so that the Scottish Parliament gets a zero per cent allocation in that field. Intended as a temporary arrangement for the Scottish Office, Barnett has lasted over a quarter of a century and, for lack of any alternative, was carried forward in 1999 to determine the financial allocation to the Scottish Parliament and the Welsh and Northern Ireland assemblies.

Neither Goschen nor Barnett ever applied to anything like the whole of government expenditure in Scotland, or even to that of the Scottish Office. The coverage of Barnett has gradually been extended, and at present it applies to most of the expenditure of the Scottish Executive, making up what is known as the assigned budget or block grant, which the Scottish Executive and Parliament are free to spend at their discretion. This in turn makes up the bulk of the Departmental Expenditure Limit (DEL). Within the DEL but outside the assigned budget are Welfare to Work schemes (which fall between devolved and reserved responsibilities), which are set at UK level; and odd items like the European Hill Livestock Compensatory Allowances. Other items come within the category of Annual Managed Expenditure, and represent UK moneys passing through the Scottish Executive, without discretion on how they are spent. These include Common Agricultural Policy payments, determined by EU rules and local demand; Housing Support Grant, which is calculated by the Treasury on the basis of anticipated need; and National Health Service and teachers' pensions (Treasury 2000). Finally, there is the expenditure of UK departments in Scotland, set in London and subject to no territorial distribution formula. The structure is summarised in Figure 6.1.

Figure 6.1   Government expenditure in Scotland

Assigned Budget (Barnett)	Non-assigned Budget	Annual Managed Expenditure (AME)	UK Departments' Expenditure in Scotland
Departmental Expenditure Limit (DEL)			
Scottish Executive Expenditure			
Total Government Expenditure in Scotland			

The Assigned Budget (determined by the Barnett formula) now covers most of the expenditure of the Scottish Parliament and Executive, and nearly 60 per cent of all government expenditure in Scotland. UK departments administering non-devolved matters like Social Security or defence account for most of the rest. The DEL for the Scottish devolved institutions, along with those for Whitehall departments, is set for three years ahead, adjusted every two years in the Treasury's Comprehensive Spending Review, while the Annual Managed Expenditure is set yearly (Heald and McLeod 2002b).

In a gesture to those calling for taxation powers, the Scottish Parliament was also given a very small degree of discretion over the standard rate of income tax, which it can raise or lower by up to three pence in the pound. In practice, the cost of levying this tax would be rather high and the benefit small, about 5 per cent at most on top of the block grant (McFadden and Lazarowicz 2000). It would cause some political difficulties in Scotland, where taxpayers would ask why they should pay more than England, and in England where politicians would ask why they should pay for Scottish services through the block when the Scots could obviously afford to pay more themselves. So the coalition parties in the first two sessions of the Parliament agreed not to use the tax-varying power at all. The Scottish Parliament also has control over local taxation, including the national Unified Business Rate (UBR), which it sets and collects itself but distributes to local governments, and the council tax on residential properties, which is set by local governments subject to Scottish-level regulations. Although these are local taxes, it would be possible for the Scottish Parliament to benefit from them itself by reducing its block transfers to local government, and then increasing the national business rate or forcing councils to increase council tax in compensation. This, however, would be fraught with political difficulty as these are unpopular and non-buoyant taxes; the UBR accounts for about 7.5 per cent of the Scottish Executive's income, so even doubling it would not provide much additional cash to the system. Nor would this go down well with the UK Government, which has indicated that if this happened it reserves the right to reduce the block transfer accordingly. It would certainly violate the spirit of the settlement, which is that local government should be left alone. A final source of revenue is officially European funding, but this does not actually affect the total amount available, since it is part of the block (see below). Unlike other devolved or federated governments in the world, the Scottish Parliament and Executive do not have borrowing powers.

Barnett has been much misunderstood in England, where it is widely seen as a mechanism that gives Scotland a larger share of public expenditure. In fact, it is a mechanism to bring Scottish expenditure levels in line with those of England over time, and this is the aspect that has attracted attention in Scotland. Each territory gets a cash increase in line with its population but, as existing Scottish expenditures are higher, this represents a smaller percentage increase. The larger the annual increases in public expenditure, the more the overall difference between Scotland and England will diminish. Yet, curiously, over eighteen years of Conservative government, this 'Barnett squeeze' never materialised. There are several reasons for this. Population relativities set in 1978, already slightly above Scotland's population share, were not revised again until 1992, although Scotland had been losing relative population, so that it still in practice got larger per capita increases. Secondly, expenditure bases were recalculated regularly to take account of inflation. Third, allowances were made for public sector pay increases negotiated on a UK basis, since otherwise Scotland would have had to lay off staff to accommodate the increased wage bill. Fourth, in the late 1990s public expenditure was squeezed, reducing the scope for convergence. Finally, various increases were made outside the formula, a move known as 'formula bypass', where the Secretary of State was able to make side deals (Lang 2002). The underlying political reasoning remained as it had throughout the twentieth century, to allow the Scottish Office victories on public expenditure matters in order to assuage discontent and dampen demands for home rule. Since devolution in 1999, this reasoning no longer operates and the UK Government has taken the view that Scotland cannot have both devolution and a permanent spending advantage. So the formula has begun to bite, as opportunities for bypass have been removed and a larger proportion of total expenditure taken into the formula. From 2000, there were substantial increases in public expenditure and, as these are allocated by population, Scotland's overall advantage has decreased. The result is that the Assigned Budget or Barnett element of Scottish expenditure has increased less rapidly in percentage terms than expenditure in England (Heald and McLeod 2003). In 2003–4, Scotland's public expenditure total was calculated to be about a billion pounds less (out of a budget of eighteen and a half billion) than it would have been without the Barnett squeeze (Bell and Christie 2001). SNP politicians and others have tried to make political capital out of this, demonstrating that the Scottish percentage increases are lower than those in England, but since public expenditure was rising quite rapidly from 1999, there were still large absolute increases in Scotland, dulling the impact.

Governments before and after devolution have declared that expenditure is allocated to the various parts of the United Kingdom after a judgement about relevant needs and services. For example, the Scottish Executive (2003a: 15) has claimed that 'Within the United Kingdom the levels of public expenditure vary from one constituent part to another, reflecting the needs rather than the tax capacity of an area.' This was expressed even more strongly by the Scottish Council Foundation in a report before devolution: 'A process of "equalisation on the basis of need" underpins the UK public expenditure system.

That results in net transfers, broadly, from the prosperous South East to other parts of the country' (Scottish Council Foundation 1997: 27). In fact, there is no equalisation system, but rather an accretion of historic changes and compromises.

This all makes it both difficult and politically sensitive to try to calculate how well Scotland does out of public expenditure as part of the United Kingdom. Such a calculation needs to go beyond Barnett or even the Scottish Parliament and look at all government spending in Scotland. One measure takes into account all 'regionally relevant' or 'identifiable' expenditure, that is expenditure that can be attributed to the various parts of the UK, irrespective of which department or government is responsible. This covers most government expenditures, excluding items like foreign affairs, overseas aid and defence, which cannot be said to benefit any particular part of the country; defence accounts for about 60 per cent of this non-identifiable expenditure. Definitions of these terms, and the availability of data, vary over time, but it appears that up to 1920–1 Scotland's contribution to revenue and its share of expenditure were roughly in line with its population share (McCrone 1999). The recessions of the early 1920s and the 1930s hit Scotland hard and increased its dependence on revenue transfers from England. After the Second World War, it regained an advantage in spending, largely due to its falling population and then the regional policy initiatives of the 1960s. Scottish identifiable expenditure per head in 1973–4 was some 120 per cent of the British average across the board, with variations from law and order where it had 98 per cent, to agriculture, fisheries and forestry, where it reached 203 per cent (Short 1982). For items coming under the Scottish Office, the ratio was nearer 130. We do not have a consistent data set since then, because of differences in the method of calculation, but the Treasury has issued figures since the late 1980s. Figure 6.2 shows no long-term trends, but a fluctuation, with Scotland mainly getting between 1.2 and 1.3 times the amount spent in England. Much of this is explained by the varying impact of UK expenditure on Social Security. Scotland was not as badly affected as England by the recession of the early 1990s, hence Scots did not increase their demands on Social Security to the same extent. By contrast, by the end of the decade, Scottish employment conditions were worse than in England. The consequent increase in payments to Scotland cannot therefore be seen as a clear benefit, since it only came because of bad economic times.

Figure 6.2 Identifiable expenditure in Scotland compared with England, 1988–2003

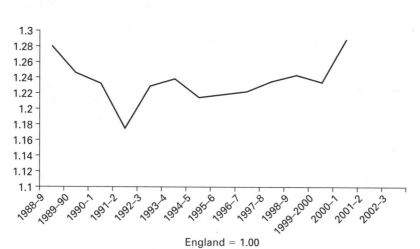

England = 1.00

Regionally relevant expenditure can also be broken down into functional categories, as shown in Table 6.1. So health and personal social services expenditure in 2001–2 was 17 per cent higher per head than in England, and on education was 20 per cent higher. In housing it was nearly three times as much, while in agriculture and fisheries (largely financed by the European Union) it was over twice as high, reflecting Scotland's predominance of small farms and the presence of most of the UK's fishing industry.

These figures fluctuate from year to year, especially on smaller programmes like culture and housing (and in the latter case the figure is adjusted for council-house sales). There are three large items. Social protection expenditure (a reserved matter) varies according to the state of the economy and the level of unemployment. The other two big programmes, both subject to the Barnett formula, are education, and health and social services. Here the Scottish advantage over the UK average has diminished between 1997 and 2002 from 24 per cent to 17 per cent (education) and from 21 per cent to 15 per cent (health and social services). These figures need to be taken with due caution, and are subject to revision, as happened in 2003 when the Treasury realised that it had been using the wrong population relativities and over-estimating Scotland's advantage (the revised figures are shown in Table 6.1) (Treasury 2003). Yet there does seem to be a Barnett squeeze, not

Table 6.1   Identifiable expenditure per capita, 2001–2 (UK=100)

	England	Scotland	Wales	N. Ireland
Education	97	117	106	125
Health and personal social services	98	115	108	110
Roads and transport	100	117	91	74
Housing	79	290	109	131
Other environmental services	90	172	154	90
Law, order and protective services	99	90	96	182
Trade, industry, energy and employment	88	169	135	200
Agriculture, fisheries, food and forestry	73	234	170	358
Culture, media and sport	98	135	100	44
Social protection	98	108	114	119
Total	96	120	113	127

Source: HM Treasury

in the form of cuts to Scottish spending, but through a lower percentage rate of increase.

Critics complain that the figure for regionally relevant expenditure is misleading, since it does not take into account general UK expenditures intended to benefit the UK as a whole, but which are undertaken disproportionately in the south of England. These 'non-identifiable' expenditures amount to about 20 per cent of all government spending, of which nearly two-thirds is attributable to defence and overseas services. They are included in the Government Expenditure and Revenue in Scotland (GERS), produced since 1992 by the Chief Economic Advisor (to the Secretary of State and now the Scottish Executive). It is assumed that Scotland gets a share of these proportional to its population, on the grounds that it is intended to identify the beneficiaries rather than the location of spending, but this is often a matter of judgement. It might equally be argued that the multiplier effect of these expenditures on jobs and supplies, as well as the spill-overs of research spending, benefit the region in which they are undertaken. There are also some items of expenditure in England that do not generate Barnett consequentials for Scotland. These exceptions do not, contrary to widespread opinion, include London transport, motorways, trunk roads or the old Urban Development Corporations, but do include the Channel Tunnel rail link. Scotland may also do poorly out of expenditure by UK corporations such as Network Rail, which has concentrated its investments in South-east England, leaving the Scottish Executive to pick up the bill for improvements in Waverley station in Edinburgh or the Borders rail link. Any calculation of how well Scotland does within the United Kingdom needs to take into account all these elements. There is also the question of 'tax expenditures', or tax breaks given to various activities. Until it was phased out, tax relief on mortgage interest favoured England, which had a higher level of owner occupation. Charitable status for private schools also benefits England disproportionately, and a move to tax relief for private medicine, as canvassed by the Conservative Party, would certainly do so.

A proper assessment must also take account of Scotland's needs, and whether these are greater than those of England, justifying higher levels of expenditure on devolved services. On the other hand, expenditure levels in the north of England, which also has high social needs, are lower than in Scotland, a matter which has become a political issue in the region. For example, in 2001–2 North-east England had an identifiable expenditure per head of £5,793, against £6,246 in Scotland. London in fact did better than North-east England, at £5,874 (Treasury 2003).

There is another argument about how much Scotland contributes to the UK Exchequer and whether it therefore has a 'fiscal deficit' that needs to be covered by transfers from England. It does seem that, after the First World War, Scotland's serious industrial recession hit tax revenues hard, reducing its contribution to government expenditure, although with some recovery during the Second World War and from the 1970s (Lee 1995). GERS calculations include both spending and revenues and have consistently shown Scotland to be dependent on transfers from the rest of the UK. For example, in 2001–2 GERS shows that the deficit between taxation and spending in Scotland was 10.3 per cent of GDP, while for the UK as a whole it was 0.6 per cent (Scottish Executive 2003a). Yet this, too, is fraught with methodological and measurement problems. Attributing corporation tax to the nations and the regions of the UK is very difficult, and in practice estimates are made from the Regional Accounts. Critics say that this may exaggerate the contribution made by London, where many firms have their headquarters. Excise on Scotch whisky is allocated according to consumption, which is mainly in England. Were it allocated according to place of production, Scotland would be credited with higher revenues (Lee 1995).

Oil revenues are the most controversial item of all. By convention they are allocated to a statistical region known as the Extra Regio, rather than to England or to Scotland, but nationalists claim that most of the wells lie in Scottish waters. Since Scotland is not an independent state, there is no such legal concept as Scottish waters, but it is reasonable to take those areas in which Scots law applies. GERS includes estimates as to how much difference oil would make to the balance, depending on what share of the revenue is assigned to Scotland. For 2001–2, if all the oil revenues were assigned to Scotland, there would have been a deficit, but of just 2.8 per cent of GDP. On a more reasonable estimate of 66 per cent of the revenues, Scotland would have had a fiscal deficit of 5 per cent of GDP. Of course, oil revenues fluctuate greatly from year to year, so that the balance depends on exactly which years are taken. In 1997, a Scottish National Party MP extracted from the Treasury the admission that, on the assumption that 90 per cent of the oil revenues were attributed to Scotland, then in the period 1978–95 Scotland had contributed a net £27 billion to the Exchequer (Taylor 2002). Closer examination revealed that the Scottish contribution all came from a single exceptional year, with Scotland remaining in deficit for the rest of the period.

It should also be noted that all these calculations are based on rather static assumptions. Nationalists would argue that the Scottish economy has been held back by UK policies that advantage the interests of London and South-east England, for example the high exchange rate of the pound in the late 1990s and early 2000s, which hit manufacturing in Scotland (as well as Wales and northern England). In the longer term, it has been argued that 'stop go' macroeconomic management geared to preventing economic overheating in the south has persistently damaged other parts of the United Kingdom.

Business taxation has been another bone of contention. Since 1987, business rates, previously raised by local government, have been centralised as the Unified Business Rate (UBR) and distributed back to local governments on a population basis. This has the effect of spreading the business tax take between rich and poor communities, an equalising measure. The UBR, however, is set and distributed separately in Scotland, so that there is no redistribution between England and Scotland. A major source of grievance for the Scottish business community has been the higher rates for the UBR in Scotland. Yet merely looking at this is misleading, since the amount paid by business depends on a combination of the rate (or poundage, the amount paid per pound of value) and the rateable value. Until 2000, the English and Scottish rates were the same and rateable values were comparable, but then a revaluation raised rateable values almost twice as much in England and Wales. Consequently, Scotland has a higher rate and a lower valuation, while England and Wales are the other way around (Heald and McLeod 2002b; Young 2003b). These effects will roughly balance each other, and the overall burden was not affected by revaluation. Business rates in Scotland in 2000 were 2.07 per cent of GDP against 1.82 per cent in England and had been slightly higher for a number of years, although this might reflect lower recorded Scottish growth figures in that period (Young 2003a) (see Chapter 7). The trend from 1990 to 2003 is very similar in Scotland and England. In 2003, a rates relief scheme reduced the burden further for small businesses (overwhelmingly Scottish-owned, see Chapter 3), financed by a 0.6p supplement for larger companies. Taking the measure of comparability preferred by the business community, which includes all business taxation, including rates, corporation tax and transport taxes, the figure for England and Scotland has been identical, at 10.4 per cent of GDP in 2000 (Scottish Executive 2003b). Whether Scotland as a whole gains from setting and keeping its own business rates, as opposed to having them set and pooled across the UK, will depend on how well its economy is doing relatively. In booming times, with new businesses setting up, it does not need to share its increased revenues, but in bad times it cannot share the burden with other nations and regions. Developments since devolution seem to confirm the findings from other parts of Europe, that devolved governments will tend to keep their business taxes in line with those in other parts of the same country since if they lower them sharply they will lose revenue, and if they increase them too much they will lose businesses.

European Structural Funds

A great deal of political attention in Scotland is given to the Structural Funds distributed by the European Union to secure economic, social and territorial cohesion across the Union. The idea is to bring lagging regions up to a state in which they can compete within the single market, by investing in infrastructure, human capital and business services. Scotland has an obvious interest in this policy, especially since 1975 when the European Regional Development Fund (ERDF) was introduced precisely to offset the losses the United Kingdom was expected to sustain from other European spending instruments, notably the Common Agricultural Policy. In 1988, the ERDF was brought together with earlier development instruments (hence the term Structural Funds) and spending was more than doubled to make this the second-biggest item in the budget of the European Commission.

There are now four Structural Funds:

ERDF – European Regional Development Fund for regional and economic conversion
ESF – European Social Fund for training and employment
EAGGF – European Agriculture Guidance and Guarantee Fund for rural development
FIFG – Financial Instrument for Fisheries Guidance for adapting fisheries structures

In the early years of the ERDF, funds were allocated to states on a fixed basis, giving them a free hand to spend the money as long as they had some programmes vaguely corresponding to European priorities. Since the 1988 reforms, the Commission has sought to forge them into a consistent policy instrument, meeting European policy objectives and with similar criteria applied in all states. Eligible areas are decided according to economic criteria, although there is some negotiation at the margin between national governments and the European Commission. Areas can qualify under one of three Objectives, laid down by European regulations:

Objective 1 is for regions seriously lagging behind the EU average
Objective 2 assists regions or areas affected by industrial decline and the redevelopment of rural areas
Objective 3 is non-territorial and helps improve the prospects of the long-term unemployed, young people and the socially excluded

The Commission has, over the years, sought to increase its control over the funds at the expense of national governments, and has found allies in the regions, who like the idea of a source of funding independent of their respective capital cities. Its principles have been: additionality, that is ensuring that the money goes to the regions; transparency, so that it knows where the money is going;

and subsidiarity, taking decisions at the lowest level possible. Since 1988, plans must be drawn up before the money is allocated and partnership agreements made involving the regions themselves as well as the social partners. Yet national governments have always found their way back in, creating a three-way tussle for control. In Scotland, the Scottish Executive is the main agent for managing the funds and putting in place partnership arrangements with local government, business and the voluntary sector, but it is the UK Government that negotiates the funds from Brussels.

Table 6.2   Scottish percentage share of Structural Funds, 1975–2006

1975–88	1988–94	1994–9	2000–6
24.9	12.0	13.7	10.8

Source: Scottish Parliament European Committee (2000)

Much heat has been generated over the question of how much Scotland gains from these funds and whether governments have been doing enough to attract them. The raw figures (Table 6.2) would seem to show that Scotland did well in the early years but lost out significantly in the 2000–6 round. Yet contrary to most popular and political opinion, it makes almost no difference how much Scotland is allocated, due to the workings of a highly technical provision known as 'additionality'. The Commission has taken the view that Structural Fund moneys should be distributed among regions on the basis of eligibility and well-designed projects, and be additional to national funding. National governments, however, have preferred to have an informal understanding about how much goes to which state under the various objectives. The UK Treasury, moreover, has insisted that additionality applies only at the national level, and that to allow regions to benefit from European funding in addition to national spending would upset their public spending control system. So in practice, the UK is allocated a rather predictable share of overall Structural Fund spending and a share of this is notionally allocated to Scotland. Since changes in Scottish expenditure levels are determined by the Barnett formula, however, it does not make any difference whether Scotland's 'share' of the Structural Funds goes up or down. Instead, the amount that goes to Scotland depends, like other items in the Scottish block, on how much England receives. The only additional money involves the 5 per cent of

Structural Fund spending under Community Initiatives (see below). Scotland, however, has to provide spending cover for the European money out of its assigned budget. In addition, European projects are rarely financed 100 per cent, and there needs to be 'matching funding' from local sources, which could be the Scottish Executive, public agencies, local government or the private sector.

Many people have argued that Scotland should receive its allocation directly from Brussels, or at least that it should get the amount dedicated to it in the European plans. Yet this might not always be in Scotland's interests. This was dramatically illustrated at the beginning of the 2000–6 programming period, when Scotland 'lost' eligibility, generating widespread concerns. The government response was not to worry since, effectively, they had not enjoyed additional spending before, so had nothing to lose. On the contrary, since they no longer had to provide the matching funds as required by the Commission, they were in some ways better off! Wales, on the other hand, which had 'gained' eligibility, was told it would get no more, precipitating the fall of the First Minister and forcing the Treasury into making special provision, although the precise terms of this remain obscure (Bache and Bristow 2003). Given that Scotland and Wales get their Structural Fund money through the Barnett formula, indeed, their best strategy for maximising their receipts would be to argue for the designation of more areas in England and fewer in Scotland and Wales (bizarre though this seems), since it is the English total that determines the Barnett consequentials.

The Treasury has never liked the idea of spending that it does not entirely control and as the UK is a net contributor to EU funds, it always favours budgetary retrenchment. So it is not surprising that in 2003 the UK Government announced that it favoured the repatriation of regional policy in the more developed EU member states, meaning that it would no longer receive any money under the Structural Funds. This caused some disquiet in Scotland, as it would seem that it would lose out. Yet as long as regional policy spending in England was replaced by national spending, then Scotland would still get its Barnett consequentials.

The fact that many Scottish politicians appear to believe that Structural Fund moneys are additional and come directly from Brussels is partly down to ignorance, but perhaps more to considerations of political advantage. Governments like to show how successful they have been in getting European money, while the opposition parties berate them for not getting more. In the Scottish

Parliament debate on the Structural Funds in January 2002, Labour tried to show how well they were doing for Scotland, while an SNP member insisted that the money coming to the Highlands and Islands under the old Objective 1 designation had been to the credit of 'Madame Ecosse', Winnie Ewing, former MEP for the Highland and Islands division, and lambasted Labour for losing the designation. One effect of all this has been that the EU is widely seen in Scotland mainly as a source of funding, seriously distorting the debate on its broader impacts and potential.

Structural Funds do not determine the amount of money that comes to Scotland, but they do influence how it is spent. In order to draw down its funding, the UK Government needs to demonstrate that it has programmes satisfying EU criteria, and the Scottish Executive, as the managing authority for the funds in Scotland, has to cooperate here, since part of the block is earmarked as European money and, in accordance with European rules, the Scottish Executive has to match it with an equivalent amount, also out of the block. This has produced a complex tripartite relationship among the Commission, the UK Government and the Scottish Executive, and a lot of direct contact between Scotland and Brussels over details of programmes and delivery. For the 2000–6 programming period, management of the funds is entrusted to four regional partnerships within Scotland, and one thematic partnership to look after Objective 3 funding. Each has representation from the Scottish Executive, the European Commission, local government and the social partners, as required by European regulations. In addition, local governments have formed European consortia in the east and west of Scotland to promote awareness of European opportunities. European programmes have introduced into Scotland new ideas about partnership and local development, and come with requirements on environmental matters and equal opportunities. They have also helped to forge networks with other European regions sharing similar circumstances and opportunities (see Chapter 5). This has exposed Scotland to European influences, imported new ways of thinking, and created a European consciousness. These factors are more important than the rather unreal debate about whether Scotland gets additional money from Europe.

In addition to the main programmes, there are four Community Initiative programmes in Scotland. INTERREG sustains interregional collaboration, including the Northern Periphery initiative. URBAN addresses problems of decline in urban areas. LEADER is a programme for sustainable development, and EQUAL combats discrimination. These funds are allocated competitively and, although they only amount to 5 per cent of the total, are received directly by the beneficiaries in addition to national funding.

The Structural Funds are by no means the only source of EU spending in Scotland. Substantial amounts come in through sectoral programmes in fields such as agriculture and fisheries. Scotland could potentially attract more European funding by pressing for more spending in these areas or for new programmes. Its ability to do so, however, is constrained by the Treasury, as custodian of the Fontainbleau agreement, negotiated by the Thatcher government, which provides for a rebate on the British contribution to the EU. Hailed as a triumph at the time, this has another side, which is that the United Kingdom does not benefit from new EU spending programmes, as these are deducted from the rebate. It was said that efforts in 2003 to get more money for Scottish fishermen were blocked in Whitehall because they might put the rebate at risk (*Herald* 21 February 2003).

Allocating Funds

The UK system of devolved public finance is unique in combining tight central control over expenditure totals, with total freedom of allocation within the assigned budget. The Treasury has never surrendered its belief that macroeconomic management requires control of the totals, and all public expenditure comes under its purview. Only local government expenditure financed through council tax and the Unified Business Rate and any spending met by the (so far unused) Scottish tax-varying power is not directly determined by it. In the first two cases, the Treasury has reserved the right to adjust the block grant if they are used to increase total spending beyond its limits, but this does not apply to the income tax-raising power. The Scottish Executive also allocates rights to borrow for capital investment to local authorities, but these count as part of the Scottish block so that if the Executive were to increase such borrowing, it would lose out on the block allocation; the effect is to keep borrowing within the limits set by the Treasury. There is some scope to levy charges on public services, for example road tolls, which do not count as taxation and could therefore bring extra revenue in. So far, the main example of this is the graduate endowment, by which university graduates pay a retrospective fee for their courses, but this merely helps compensate for revenue lost by the abolition of up-front university fees. The scope for increasing revenue is thus highly constrained. On the other hand, the Treasury has no influence over how the money is spent once it comes to Scotland. This is determined by the budgetary procedures developed by the Scottish Executive and Parliament.

Scotland's system of allocating resources needs to fit into the sometimes rather different requirements of the UK budgetary process (which determines how much money will come and when) and the procedures of the Scottish Parliament. UK Government expenditure is planned in the Comprehensive Spending Review (CSR) every two years. The CSR in fact projects expenditure forward for three years, the third year becoming the first year of the next CSR and thus subject to revision. As these decisions generate Scotland's Barnett consequentials, the result is that the Scottish expenditure total is known for two years ahead, with a general indication also of the third year. The Scottish Executive uses this as the basis of its own two-yearly Spending Review, and for the annual budget. Logically, the Westminster spending review, the Scottish spending review and the annual budget should link together in a single process. In practice, they follow slightly different rhythms and procedures, since the Barnett consequentials are known only after spending has been allocated among English programmes (Christie 2004).

The annual procedure was based on the report of the Financial Issues Advisory Group, part of the Consultative Steering Group process before devolution, and was intended to give the Parliament and its committees a larger role in the expenditure process than is the case at Westminster. There are three stages. Discussions first seek to identify key issues and prepare a proposal for Cabinet, leading to Stage 1, the Annual Expenditure Report, giving a breakdown of the Executive's spending plans for the succeeding year and the remaining years of the three-year forward projection. These plans go to the subject committees of the Parliament, whose responses are coordinated by the Finance Committee and debated before the summer recess. In September, the Executive produces firmer plans, the draft budget, taking into account the Parliament's suggestions. Again, the Finance Committee and subject committees can comment and propose amendments, provided that they stay within the overall expenditure limit. They then produce a report, which is debated by the Parliament before the Christmas recess. In January or February, the Executive introduces the Budget Bill to authorise expenditure for the financial year starting in April. Since there has been extensive parliamentary debate and consultation already, the actual bill is usually passed rather quickly.

If it is a CSR year (every other year), there is a more elaborate process within the Executive. A high-level Spending Review Strategy Group reviews priorities and follows the process. This consists of senior ministers and officials representing the coalition parties, with a non-spending minister such as the Minister for Parliamentary Business (in 2004 the composition was First Minister, Deputy First Minister, Minister for Finance and Deputy Minister for Finance and Parliamentary Business, with the Permanent Secretary). Planning starts early in the year, but the Barnett consequentials are not normally known until July, so that firm plans are made only in the September draft budget. Although the Executive announced at the time of the 2002 Expenditure Review that 'these are firm three-year plans that will not be reopened until the next Spending Review', there are many smaller adjustments made in the course of the cycle. There are three opportunities during the year to reallocate money among departments in the light of spending trends and needs, although sometimes only two are used. Ministers may also reallocate money within their departments. Additional money may also come through the Barnett consequentials of decisions made by the Chancellor of the Exchequer outside the CSR cycle, either in the annual budget or at other times.

Within the Executive, procedures for the Spending Review year have evolved over successive exercises, in 2000, 2002 and 2004, away from the system inherited from the Scottish Office. Under the old system, there was limited discretion for the Secretary of State to reallocate resources and hence no need to develop a strategic capacity to determine priorities. Nor was there a Cabinet of departmental ministers with their own power bases and departments bidding for their shares. So at best there were marginal changes in programme priorities set in London. Now the process is much more politicised, interest groups are more alert and organised, and Scottish priorities need to be set.

The first review, in 2000, coincided with an increase in UK Government expenditure and hence in Barnett consequentials, and there was not much pressure to ration resources. So departments were encouraged to bid for extra money, which was rather easily allocated. By 2002, there was a more serious effort by the Finance

Minister to steer the process and departments were obliged to make a case for additional resources, based on the Executive's strategic priorities and the Partnership agreement of the coalition parties. Stress was also put on cross-cutting themes (involving more than one department), to discourage purely departmental thinking; the themes were 'closing the opportunities gap' and sustainable development. In 2004, the process was tightened up again, as departments were obliged to justify their existing budgets and how they contributed to overall policy and priorities. The general thrust of all this was an attempt, familiar to students of budgetary politics, to get away from incrementalism, merely adding or subtracting a bit from the existing budget, to a more innovative approach that would allow resources to be moved to where they are needed.

At the same time, there has been an effort to strengthen the central capacity of the Executive to set priorities and allocate resources, but this is much less developed than in Whitehall, where the Treasury has emerged as the dominant department in domestic policy making, encroaching on line departments, undertaking a lot of policy innovation itself, and binding departments to strict performance requirements. The Scottish Executive Finance and Central Services Department, lacking the power and status of the Treasury, or its policy capacity, is obliged to work more closely with the line departments. This also reflects the relative weakness of the centre within the Scottish Executive (see Chapter 4) and the overall Scottish policy style of working with institutions and seeking consensus rather than leading from the top (see Chapter 7).

The Parliament and its committees took some time to adjust to the task of budget scrutiny and made several complaints about the quantity and quality of the information they were getting from the Executive. In the first year (1999) the process had to be truncated following the elections and the subject committees made no input. In 2000, three proposals were made and all were accepted by the Executive. In 2001, no recommendations were made but in 2002, which was a Spending Review year, twelve recommendations were made. By 2004, more accessible information was provided in a new Annual Evaluation Report intended to show how spending was linked to policies, and it was suggested that the process could be simplified by adopting a streamlined procedure in years when there was not a Spending Review (Scottish Parliament Finance Committee 2004).

Approval of the budget is not the end of the financial process, as there is a need to monitor and control expenditure and to allocate much of it to outside bodies like the health service and local government. Here again, Finance also tends to work with departments. There are no Public Service Agreements, such as the Treasury has imposed on Whitehall departments. Rather, the Minister for Finance has bilateral discussions usually twice a year, to consider departmental targets and their achievement, and efficiency reviews (known in Scotland as Departmental Improvement Plans). Transfers to local government, which account for about a third of the Scottish budget, are largely in the form of block grants, which councils can allocate at their discretion. In practice, most of the money is taken up discharging their statutory responsibilities, with little left over for innovation, and they are subject to strong guidance from the Executive departments through circulars and other pressures. They are also subject to criticism from interest groups if they are seen to be squeezing their preferred form of expenditure in order to fund other priorities. Health boards account for another quarter of the budget and also have discretion over its allocation, although again subject to central guidance and pressure.

It is not easy to assess precisely the scope the Scottish Executive and Parliament have over expenditure allocation. Budgeting is typically incremental, as the weight of existing commitments allows few radical changes from year to year (Midwinter and Stevens 2001). The Barnett formula is calculated on the basis of functional allocations in England, and it is likely that similar pressures and priorities will exist in Scotland. Interest groups tend to look out for differences in spending decisions to claim that they are being short-changed compared with their equivalents on the other side of the border. If increased spending on a service in England generates a Barnett consequential, the relevant groups in Scotland will stake a claim to it, despite the fact that Barnett is a block grant. On the other hand, for technical reasons (see below) it is now very difficult to compare patterns of spending in England or Scotland or to know just where the Barnett consequentials have gone to, a situation that prevents the Scottish Executive from taking the English allocations as an easy default option, and forces it to make its own priorities. Sometimes, when a high-profile announcement is made by the Chancellor of the Exchequer, allocating money for a sensitive or hard-pressed service, the pressure for the Scottish Executive to apply the Barnett consequentials to the same service is overwhelming. For example, in the UK budget of 2002 increased spending for health was headlined and promised for five years ahead, as part of a long-term programme of investment. The Scottish Executive promptly agreed to spend the consequentials on health. Even here, however, there is some scope for choice, as the Minister for Finance later added that this did not mean the money would necessarily go to the health department but could cover fresh fruit for schoolchildren or breakfast clubs for poor communities (Kerr 2002). Similar reactions have greeted mid-year increases in Whitehall budgets. Press coverage also tends to favour this type of comparison, as shown by an article in 2003 leading with the line 'measures taken by Westminster to reduce council taxes in England will not apply in Scotland, the Scottish Executive said yesterday' (Ritchie 2003); several paragraphs later it was conceded that the situation was quite different, since council tax rises in Scotland had been well below those in England. An article in 2004 reported that for every pound per kilometre spent on roads maintenance in Scotland, £1.59 was spent in England, with motoring organisations claiming that 'Scots have been short-changed' (Williams 2004). In fact the comparison is almost meaningless, since Scotland has a huge network of lightly used rural roads in the Highlands; roads spending in Scotland fluctuates hugely from year to year depending on whether there is a big project under way; and most road spending is financed by local government. The Scottish Executive noted, moreover, that it had chosen to emphasise public transport, precisely the type of policy autonomy that devolution was supposed to achieve. This is confirmed by the figures showing that between 2003 and 2006 spending on roads was planned to remain steady, while public transport overtook it, with an increase of 26 per cent.[1]

The budgetary process is now much more open and politicised than before, and interest groups are learning to know how and when to intervene in private and in public. This may stimulate innovation and a debate about priorities. On the other hand, there is a tendency for interest groups to claim that their historical level of funding constitutes some sort of entitlement. The arts community, with its media savvy, has become a vocal player. An 'exclusive' newspaper article in 2004 claimed that 'senior sources warned last night' that 'the National Galleries of Scotland is facing unprecedented cuts in services and staff' (*Herald* 26 January 2004). A statement by the National Union of Students, the Association of University Teachers and Universities Scotland claimed that the higher education budget has gone up in percentage terms less than the whole Scottish budget (*Holyrood* 95, 22 September 2003). The implication of this complaint, taken to its logical conclusion, is that all services should be entitled to a fixed share whether the budget is expanding or contracting. This might also lead a cautious Executive to play safe and not to disturb the existing allocation of resources.

It is extremely difficult to know how much difference all this political activity makes in practice, or how far Scotland is setting different expenditure priorities from Whitehall. Efforts to map the effects of the Barnett squeeze on individual services in Scotland (for example, Cuthbert and Cuthbert 2001) are unreliable, depending as they do on the assumption that the Scottish Executive has simply applied the Barnett consequentials to the services from which they were derived in England. Spending is allocated by department, and these do not have the same mix of responsibilities in the two countries, with the possible exception of health – and as just noted, even health spending can be done outside the department. It is possible to look within the departmental allocations at individual programme headings, but these are not always comparable either, and there is some scope for ministers to move money among headings in the course of the year. Even where the headings are comparable, reporting conventions differ. So in some cases we find Departmental Expenditure Limits reported, while others include the Annual Managed Expenditure, which cannot easily be disentangled to produce comparable figures. Capital expenditure figures vary considerably from year to year, as in Scotland one large project can make a difference to the total, but be absent the following year, so that programmes appear to be fluctuating widely.

Then a lot of expenditure is handed on to local government as a block. While this total is calculated by reference to the expected spending by local governments on the main functions, local authorities are free to reallocate it and often do. Most expenditure on schools, for example, is undertaken by local governments, which may decide to give preference to social work, police or other matters. Some estimates can be made by using the Executive's Grant Aided Expenditure data, which indicates the pattern of local government expenditure which it expects to finance through grants (Midwinter and Burnside 2004). Local governments are not bound by these priorities and supplement the grant with council tax revenues, so that this only gives us a general picture of what the Executive would like to see happening.

Another way of trying to measure what the Scottish priorities are is to look at the GERS figures on total spending in Scotland by function over time (Midwinter 2004). These are outcome figures, representing what actually happened rather than plans for the future, and so might be thought to be more reliable. They also suggest that the Treasury has at its disposal rather detailed figures that could be used for more refined judgements. The published GERS figures, however, are of limited use. GERS categories are very general, with health and personal social services in a single category and all of education together. This is not the basis on which decisions are taken in the Scottish budgetary process, so these figures can hardly be used to read off those priorities. GERS figures also include local government expenditure, whether financed by local taxes or government grant.

No doubt it would be technically possible to break down expenditure by agency and by function to show just what the expenditure priorities are in Scotland and how they differ from those in England, but this is not done. Ministers and officials claim that they do not need this information, since their job is to make decisions for Scotland. Providing the information would certainly cause political difficulties, as it would increase the pressure to match English expenditure on each service and thus deprive them of the ability to determine their own priorities.

We can, then, only make limited inferences about expenditure priorities and how they differ from those in England. It is clear that the Scottish Executive has felt obliged to match English increases in health spending, which have been very considerable; this is by far the largest item coming directly under the Scottish Executive. There was a significant increase in spending on housing, which had declined under the previous Conservative government. On the other hand, spending on economic development promotion has tended to be steady or to fall. These figures have been affected by sharp increases in overall funding during the early 2000s, reducing the need for hard choices. As expenditure limits are tightened in the years to come, there will be greater competition over priorities and the patterns will become rather clearer.

Fiscal Autonomy

A number of politicians and academics, including home rulers, nationalists and Conservatives, have suggested a move to 'fiscal autonomy', in which Scotland would raise its own taxes and pass on an agreed sum to London for common UK services (Harper and Stewart 2003). Such a system operated in Northern Ireland under the Stormont regime and exists in the Basque provinces of Spain. Fiscal autonomy is supported by a range of political actors in Scotland, albeit for different reasons, and has sparked a continuing debate. Nationalists favour it as an extension and deepening of devolution and the Liberal Democrats, with their federalist tradition, are in favour in principle but cautious in practice. Some Conservatives have also come round to the idea that, as devolution is here to stay, then it should be completed and Scots weaned from dependence on the centre. There is also some support among academics and commentators.

Several advantages are cited in fiscal autonomy.[2] It could enhance responsibility by ensuring that those deciding on policy have to find the resources to pay. It would also widen the scope of policy discretion by allowing the Scottish Parliament to choose between public and private provision of services, or between charging and general taxation. This has been highlighted by the difference between England and Scotland over paying for long-term care for the elderly and over university fees, since the decision in England to charge for these items means that there are no Barnett consequentials. So Scotland either needs to follow England in levying charges or, as in these two cases, find the resources from its existing budget. The decision to impose additional fees in English universities put further pressure on the Scottish budget, forcing the Scottish Executive to find matching money for Scottish universities without being able to raise taxes instead. Further extensions of fee charging to services in England could strain the system to its limit. So could the introduction of tax relief for private health care, as proposed by the Conservative Party in England, since this would effectively subsidise private medical practice but without generating any Barnett consequentials. Such tax reliefs do cost the taxpayer and are classified by economists as 'tax expenditure', but would be available equally across the UK and so apply in Scotland. The Scottish Executive could not opt out of the tax relief and apply the money to public expenditure on health. Indeed, Scotland could be further disadvantaged, as the incidence of private health care is much less than in England, so that it would attract less tax relief. Similar constraints operate in the reform of local government taxation, which the UK Government was considering in 2004. Were Whitehall to make English local governments raise more of their own taxes, Scotland would lose the Barnett consequentials of transfers to English local government and so would have to make its own local councils raise more.

A second set of arguments concerns the economic effects of fiscal autonomy. Some figures on the political right argue that fiscal autonomy would allow Scotland to cut personal and corporate taxation, and thus attract more inward investment. In fact, there is some dispute about whether low tax rates are an effective means of attracting investment, especially of high technology and high value-added enterprises that need an attractive environment and a skilled workforce. These are expensive items, requiring heavy investment in public services. In the early 2000s, the SNP adopted a low-tax policy, promising to emulate the Irish economic miracle, which it attributed to its fiscal regime. Yet, while adopting the Irish economic model, it retained its traditional stance on social policy, modelled on the high-tax Scandinavian welfare state. It was not at all clear how this would be financed. A more sophisticated economic argument is that fiscal autonomy would allow Scotland to reap the benefit of successful economic policies and thus provide an incentive to focus on growth. Scotland might then be able to develop its own social and economic strategy, linking social and economic policies together, as happens in Scandinavia. It might also permit a more flexible approach to policy design, allowing incentives for particular types of activity and the ability to assemble packages of measures to deal with specific situations.

Any scheme for fiscal autonomy for Scotland under devolution would require a mechanism to determine the scale of transfers between London and Edinburgh to pay for UK services and to ensure equity among the various parts of the United Kingdom – the political value of the Barnett formula is that it has enabled this issue to be shelved. One option would be for Scotland to support all its expenditures from its own taxation and pay the UK Treasury for the value of common services. Yet, while this is in many ways the simplest solution, it would require a difficult and politically contentious calculation of how much Scotland owes for these services. A more sophisticated approach would involve fiscal equalisation, that is a calculation of what Scotland should receive and contribute based on principles of equity. There are two ways of doing this, either alone or in combination: to equalise for resources and to equalise for needs. Resource equalisation involves each part of the UK paying or receiving according to its wealth. Carried to its limit, this would allow the poorest part of the UK to provide the same level of services as the richest, as effectively happens in Germany, although in most other systems equalisation is less than complete. Again, there are technical problems, since wealth might be measured by GDP per capita, which might give a misleading and changing picture of Scotland when the oil wealth is included; or it might be measured by income or a combination of indicators.

The most difficult of all is equalisation according to needs, which would provide each part of the UK the resources it needs, given its social and economic conditions. Needs equalisation involves difficult judgements about the nature and definition of need and the indicators to be used. Such indicators are used in the distribution of finance to local government and the health service, but there is always a subjective and essentially political judgement to be made about what to include. People in the Highlands might argue that sparsity of population makes it more expensive to provide service, so that their need is greater. Those in the cities counter that dense population and urban conditions create greater costs and needs. Expenditure on universities in Scotland is higher partly because of the four-year honours degree course, in contrast to the three-year course in England. This could be defined as an indicator of need for spending in Scotland, or merely as a policy choice of the Scots, for which their own Parliament should pay. The controversy surrounding the only effort so far to calculate need across the UK, the 1977 Needs Assessment Study, shows how difficult these issues can be. Some commentators have argued that the task of equalisation should be entrusted to an independent board of experts, outside the political process, such as is the case in Australia. Others have argued, by contrast, that the judgements to be made are essentially political and must be made by responsible politicians, who will engage in normal political bargaining and compromise.

A final difficulty in moving to a system of fiscal equalisation is the transition. If a needs or resources formula were to show large discrepancies between what exists and what could be justified, major programme cuts would be indicated. The practical and political difficulties in doing this has meant that, where this has been tried, dampening mechanisms or adjustments have had to be applied to cushion the shock, so undermining the formula. Scottish ministers, believing that Scotland does well out of the present system, have certainly not been keen on such a new needs assessment, but if the Barnett squeeze leads to continued convergence of Scottish and English expenditure levels, they may change their minds in the future. Already, Welsh and Northern Irish interests, believing that they would do better from a needs assessment than from Barnett, are pushing for it. Barnett has come under political criticism both from those who think it is too generous to Scotland and those who, pointing to the 'squeeze', think that it is not generous enough. It determines Scotland's base expenditure and the annual changes on different criteria, neither of which is related either to a determination of need or to the amount Scotland contributes to the Exchequer, making it difficult to mount an intellectual defence of it. Looking at the political problems, informed observers thought it unlikely to survive the Parliament of 1992–7 (Heald 1992). On the other hand, it is possible that these pressures will simply cancel each other out, and that Barnett will remain as the least bad formula, illustrating the old proverb that there is nothing as permanent as the provision. Midwinter (2000) notably has defended the continued use of the Barnett formula as a way of settling the main financial issues and providing a degree of stability, while permitting an element of political bargaining around the margins. In any case, the process for determining Scotland's spending levels and allocating the money within Scotland will remain an essentially political exercise, balancing a number of distinct principles and founded on compromise.

Notes

1. This refers only to Scottish Executive spending, not that of local government.
2. A good review of this complex debate is given in Harper and Stewart (2003).

CHAPTER SEVEN

Policy Making in Practice

Policy Style and Innovation

Devolution represented the transfer to Scotland of powers across an important range of policy fields. While these largely corresponded to areas previously administratively devolved to the Scottish Office, there is now a greater scope for independent policy making and for divergence from the line set in London. Of course, this occurs within a broad set of assumptions about the role of government in the modern welfare state and market economy. The historic divisions about the role of government are less stark now than at any time since the consensus years of the 1950s, while European and international trends are pushing governments towards more broadly similar policy compromises. Yet, within this consensus, there are important choices to be made about how the welfare state is to be structured and on the balance between competitiveness and social cohesion. It is here that a distinct Scottish model may be emerging, even during a time when Westminster and Holyrood are dominated by the same political party. These questions are considered below under the general heading of public service delivery and reform.

More radically, devolution presents an opportunity not merely to produce distinct policies in familiar fields, but to define social and economic problems differently, to use the powers and resources available to fashion Scottish solutions to Scottish problems. This implies a capacity to look beyond traditional programmes and departments, to broaden the policy communities, and to question orthodox thinking. Two broad areas of government responsibility illustrate this challenge. The first is the promotion of economic development, growth and employment. The second is the task of social integration, the lessening of inequalities and providing equal opportunities for all. These are transversal responsibilities, cutting across regular departments and programmes, and drawing in other levels of government, and have a direct impact on the well-being of citizens. Rural policy is another cross-cutting policy area, and a new one, in which there is much scope for framing the issues and innovating solutions; it impinges not only on the Scottish and UK levels but also on the European level.

Public Service Delivery and Reform

New Labour in London has continued on the path of public-sector reform set by the Conservatives, inspired by the 'new public management' (Osborne and Gabler 1992). The emphasis here is on differentiation and competition in public services, and the separation of the service 'provider' (government) from the service 'producer' (the professionals doing the work). Sometimes this involves privatisation, or government contracting with private organisations to run a service. In other cases, it involves the introduction of quasi-market mechanisms into government itself, by forcing public service bodies to compete with each other. So schools may compete to attract pupils, or hospitals to attract patients, with the money following. Where it is not possible for services to compete to attract clients (or 'customers' as they are often now called), they have to compete to meet centrally-set targets. In this way, it is hoped, efficiency will be pushed up and waste reduced.

Critics of this approach have argued that it is likely to lead to greater inequality, as middle-class citizens have the means and skills to shop around for public services and to defend their localities. Competition, say the critics, may work in the supply of consumer goods but is unsuited to the provision of public services, which is why the services are public in the first place. Treating citizens as consumers may undermine the concept of citizenship itself, which is based on the notion of a shared public space and social cooperation. Professionals and other public service workers may perform better if they are accorded respect and listened to, rather than being made to feel insecure and threatened. Centrally-set targets may have perverse effects, as workers seek to meet the targets at the expense of the overall needs of the service. For example, if they are told to reduce hospital waiting lists, they may achieve this merely by making everyone wait the same time, irrespective of need. Output in schools and hospitals can be increased by not accepting difficult cases. League tables showing the performance of schools are unlikely to give a true picture of performance, as this is strongly affected by the social background of pupils, so that schools doing a good job might be stigmatised and penalised. The same may apply to hospitals, social services or policing. Target-setting has led to centralisation as central government determines the targets, monitors performance and allocates resources accordingly, without a detailed knowledge of conditions on the ground.

New Labour came into office in 1997 with a rather naïve belief in new public-management nostrums and a dedication to target-setting that perhaps reflected its inexperience in the business of government. In its second term, from 2001, there was some questioning of this approach, even from bodies like the Institute for Public Policy Research that had played a leading part in introducing the approach. New Labour, like the Conservatives before it, has also been rather hostile to public-sector unions and the professions, seeing them as an obstacle to change and a bastion of vested interests working against the interests of the consumer. Some of these trends have been common to Westminster and Holyrood. The public-service reform programme in Whitehall is closely linked to its Scottish equivalent, based on business practice, managerial efficiency and satisfying 'customers'. The Private Finance Initiative, renamed Public–Private Partnerships, has been used extensively to build schools and hospitals in both countries, and private prisons have been extended. On the wider agenda of welfare state provision, however, Scotland since 1999 has followed a more traditional social democratic model of public service delivery, based on universalism, egalitarianism and cooperation with public service professionals. This can be seen by looking both at examples of policy substance and at policy style.

In England, the government has largely abandoned the idea of comprehensive education, which was a flagship of Labour policy during the 1960s and 1970s, in favour of differentiation, keeping opted-out schools, publishing league tables of school performance and looking favourably on faith schools. The Scottish Executive has made an explicit commitment to comprehensive education, has brought back the only two schools that had opted out under the Conservatives, and has been cool on faith schools, although the issue has been raised. In 2003, the way that school examination achievements were reported was changed so as to prevent newspapers compiling simplistic league tables without taking into account differences in social conditions. A high-profile gesture to universalism in Scotland was the decision to implement the recommendations of the Sutherland Commission to provide free personal care for the elderly; in England this remains means-tested. In 2003, the Home Office floated the idea of neighbourhoods being able to hire additional police officers, with the government paying half the cost, a clear subsidy to the middle classes; the Scottish Executive made clear that it would not follow suit.

In England, local councils judged to be 'failing' can have all or some of their services removed and transferred to private contractors or non-profit bodies, and these powers have been used. Some powers have been taken which would allow the Scottish Executive to intervene in local education and social services, but they fall well short of those south of the border and are seen as available only in extreme circumstances. Scotland has rejected the idea of elite universities and differential fees, and has distributed research funding more evenly (see below). Foundation hospitals, with a degree of autonomy from the National Health Service, and borrowing powers have been rejected in Scotland, and there is no system of 'star hospitals' picked out as specially deserving and given better conditions (see below). Following the same logic into local government, England has introduced 'beacon councils', whose success in meeting performance targets allows them additional privileges; there is no Scottish equivalent. English and UK departments are subject to Public Service Agreements (PSAs) imposed by the Treasury, which requires them to meet detailed targets, and these have now been extended to other agencies, including the Regional Development Agencies. For constitutional reasons, the Scottish Executive cannot be subject to a PSA imposed by the Treasury, and it has not sought to impose them on its own departments or agencies. Instead, it works with departments and agencies to identify targets and address deficiencies. Targetry has attracted some criticism (Scottish Parliament Finance Committee 2004) and, while the Scottish style is somewhat different, targets apply across the departments of the Scottish Executive. The Scottish Executive also tends to work more closely with local government than is the case down south.

Some of these differences can be traced to differences in political conditions in England and Scotland. As noted above (see Chapter 2), there is generally more support for collectivist policies in Scotland, although the difference should not be exaggerated. Members of the professions may have a stronger public-sector ethos or civic commitment and show a greater willingness to engage with government (see Chapter 3). Strategically, the differences may stem from the need to adapt social democracy to changing conditions. A recurrent dilemma facing social democratic parties is the choice between selectivity (targeting resources on those most in need) and universalism (providing the same services to everyone). Supporters of selectivity argue that it is more socially progressive and redistributive, not wasting money on services for people who can provide for themselves. Universalists counter that benefits and services used only by the poor will not survive since the influential middle classes will not vote for them. More generally, if public services decline, the middle classes start to opt out, the sector will be residualised, used only by the poor, and will decline in quality, as happened with council housing.

New Labour in England is aware that the welfare state can only survive if the middle classes can be kept within it. It also knows that to maintain its majority it must appeal to a new middle class brought up on consumer values and with the ability to opt out. Hence, New Labour seeks to recast public services in such way as to provide a niche for the better off, while preserving the essential features of services that are, largely, free at the point of use. This is a 'third way' between the traditional uniform model of service provision, and a move to privatisation as favoured by the Conservative Party.

In Scotland, however, there is less of a problem of middle-class opt out. Only 10 per cent of Scots have private medical insurance, compared with nearly a quarter in London and over 20 per cent in the rest of South-east England (Wallis 2004). Even Wales and the northern English regions have significantly higher proportions than Scotland. Private schools enrol 3.4 per cent of Scottish pupils, against 6 per cent for the UK as a whole, and 10.8 per cent in London and the South-east. Hence there is less need in Scotland to provide differentiated services within the public sector as an alternative to opting out.

There is also a closer relationship with public service professionals in Scotland, with much less tendency for politicians to attack them or blame them for failings in the system. This, too, can be presented in two ways. Defenders of the approach will describe it as inclusive, consensual and see public service workers as 'stakeholders' deserving attention. Critics from a New Labour perspective describe the same process as pandering to 'producer interests' and blame the excessive power of trades unions and professional associations (Hassan and Warhurst 2002). Professionals themselves may be more strongly committed in Scotland to the public model of provision and, although concrete evidence of this is scarce, there are some indications. A survey in 2003 found that just under 60 per cent of medical general practitioners across the UK would like to charge for home visits, while in Scotland the same proportion was opposed (NU Health Care 2003).

The small size of the Scottish system may also explain the tendency of the Executive to work with professionals, local government and groups. In a country as large as England, it is impossible to manage the university system or the health service from a single point without creating a central bureaucracy so large as to be unmanageable. Hence the government has resorted to centrally set targets to try to ensure conformity, with incentives and penalties according to performance; or has set up competition among service providers in a quasi-market, in the hope that the best will prevail. In Scotland, policy and delivery systems are small enough to allow short lines of communication and a dialogue among policy makers, administrators and service providers.

This extends beyond the public sector into policy communities more generally. Policy making in Scotland is more consultative than in England and the Parliament and its committees have a role that is not performed in Westminster. Coalition government means that the Executive cannot behave like its counterpart in London and simply push through the First Minister's ideas. All of this is consistent with the recommendations of the Consultative Steering Group and the ideas of 'new politics'. The weakness of policy capacity within the Executive and the relative lack of think tanks in Scotland also forces more dependence on outside groups, professionals and stakeholders. Yet while this may make policy making more open and participative, by the same token it may be slower, less decisive and less capable of radical reform. This style of policy making is illustrated by reforms in health and higher education, which have taken strikingly divergent paths in England and Scotland.

Health Policy

Health is one of the most important responsibilities of the Scottish Parliament and Executive, accounting for about a third of expenditure just for the direct costs of the National Health Service (NHS). It is entirely devolved, including both public and private sectors, and excluding only medical education (which is shared) and the regulation of sensitive matters like xenotransplantation. The policy community, including the medical professions, research institutions and policy experts, has always been UK-wide, but for historic reasons these bodies have had a particularly strong presence in Scotland, which has four substantial medical faculties, teaching hospitals and the royal colleges (see Chapter 2). The 'national' in the NHS always referred to the British nation, with an expectation of equal treatment across the country (although in practice there were many inequalities) and very little scope for policy innovation or deviation on the part of the Scottish Office. The United Kingdom has also stood out since 1948 in the way the service is organised, with a single payer and provider for public health services, which are free at the point of use, in contrast to many continental systems, in which government regulates, but services are provided by multiple agencies and paid by a mixture of taxation, insurance contributions and direct fees. Health is a highly salient policy field, in which public expectations are high, and faces critical challenges. Demographic changes, with an ageing population, put more strain on the service and point to a change in priorities. Technical innovations impose constantly rising costs, while resources are never adequate and some means must be found to ration them. There are decisions to be made about the balance between preventive strategies or public health on the one hand, and clinical treatment on the other. Finally, there is a huge management challenge, since the British NHS (and now the English one) has long been the biggest single employer in Europe.

Devolution has not broken the old UK policy communities. The Scottish and English departments are constantly in touch about issues and developments, the Joint Ministerial Committee on health is one of the few that has met regularly, and there are meetings of the civil service heads of departments, although these seem to be more valued by the devolved administrations than by Whitehall. The medical professions still operate across the United Kingdom, exchanging ideas and innovations. Pay and conditions are negotiated at UK level in joint machinery, although this broke down in 2003 when the Scottish consultants accepted a deal that consultants in England, more concerned with their private practice, rejected. There had earlier been some tensions over the use of incentives to new and retiring doctors, on which a compromise was reached. Many of the issues, such as demographic change or new technology, are common to all four jurisdictions. Yet, on issues of organisation and delivery, England and Scotland have begun to diverge quite sharply.

Policy under the Conservative government between 1979 and 1997 was consistent across the United Kingdom, although its impact differed according to local circumstances. There was a stress on professional management in place of the self-regulation by which the system had operated since 1948, and increasingly on the introduction of market-like mechanisms within the NHS (Woods 2003). General practitioners were encouraged to become fund-holders, contracting for treatment with hospitals, which would compete for their custom, an option taken up much more widely by English than by Scottish doctors (Woods 2002). At the same time, while there was commitment to maintaining the NHS – and it did receive large increases in resources – government looked favourably on the growth of private medicine, which had been discouraged under Labour in the 1960s and 1970s. These policies were all extended to Scotland but, because of the distinct conditions, worked out a little differently here. Private medicine did not take off, and even a major private hospital built with government subsidies in the enterprise zone at Clydebank failed to generate the expected trade.

On its return to power in 1997, Labour announced the end of the 'internal market' across the UK. Its replacement in England, however, contained many of the old features, overlaid with an array of managerial systems and targets. Unable to manage such a huge system from a central point, and unwilling to go for territorial devolution, the Department of Health introduced a system of incentives and sanctions intended to drive up standards by competition (Greer 2004). GP fund-holding was abolished but replaced by Primary Care Trusts, which are responsible for general practitioner services and can buy in services from hospitals and other bodies, themselves organised into trusts. Hospitals are graded by inspectors and given star ratings, to encourage the best and shame the rest. Under controversial legislation pushed through in 2003 with the support of Scottish Labour MPs, the highest starred hospitals can apply to become Foundation Hospitals, freed from detailed government control and given greater financial freedom. Patients, treated now as 'consumers', have certain rights to decide where they will have their treatment and by which specialist. Care might be provided in an NHS hospital or, increasingly, in the private sector, depending on which can offer the best deal. Patients can also be referred abroad, and numbers have in fact been going to the (public) French health service to relieve overload in English hospitals. Alongside these quasi-market mechanisms is an elaborate regulatory and inspection regime comprising some thirty separate bodies (Greer 2004).

Policy in Scotland has taken a different direction, with an emphasis on professional leadership, consensus, uniformity and integration, rejecting the consumerist and market mechanisms of the English system (Davidson 2003). NHS Scotland is organised through fifteen regional health boards. Primary Care Trusts were introduced before devolution but, unlike their English counterparts, did not purchase care, and hospitals were reorganised into Acute Hospital Trusts (Woods 2002). In 2003, the Scottish Executive moved still further away from the internal-market model, and abolished the trusts. Responsibility now rests with the regional health boards. Common services and planning are managed by three regions (North, West and South-east) based on the major teaching hospitals, and the emphasis is on integration rather than competition. Priorities are worked out through Managed Clinical Networks, grouping professionals working on similar problems. Close links are maintained among the health boards, the professional bodies and the trades unions through the Scottish Partnership Forum, which has no counterpart in England, where such an institution would be seen as recalling the old corporatism. The royal colleges, while they insist on their UK and global role (see Chapter 2), provide a local source of advice, policy development and personnel to serve on various advisory and policy committees. In contrast to the English model, driven by consumer choice, patient interests in Scotland are represented by the NHS Forum, bringing together patients and carers. Local government is brought in through a health input to community planning and joint working groups with the Convention of Scottish Local Authorities (CoSLA) and the Society of Local Authority Chief Executives (SOLACE). Policy is developed by negotiation and consensus rather than central direction. There is no encouragement to private providers and, indeed, the HCI hospital at Clydebank was taken into public ownership as part of the NHS with the aim of bringing down waiting lists.

Performance management is also undertaken differently. There is no star system for hospitals, but a Performance Assessment Framework based on seven fields of activity with a set of indicators for each. Performance in each field is assessed, and where there are shortcomings these are discussed between the department and the boards to produce an action plan for improvement. A single-agency Quality Improvement Scotland, based on a merger of three existing bodies, has the responsibility for bringing up performance levels.

The most politically prominent divergence in health policy was the belated decision by the Scottish Executive to implement the report of the Sutherland Commission on free personal care for the elderly, rejected by Westminster on the grounds that the money could be better spent on other priorities. Although this is consistent with the Scottish emphasis on universal rather than selective benefits, it came about through a series of highly political events. A new First Minister, Henry McLeish, was eager to make his mark while, including the Liberal Democrats, there was a majority within the Scottish Parliament in favour of Sutherland. The Department of Health in England was opposed, fearing the pressure that would be brought to follow suit, and sought to dissuade the Scottish Executive. There was also internal opposition, notably from the Scottish Minister for Health. Following a confused day of manoeuvring in January 2001, it was announced that Scotland would provide free personal care, finding the money from within its existing budget. This was important as a symbolic divergence on a highly salient political issue, but in practice the difference between Scottish and English practice may not be as large as supposed, since it all comes down to a complex calculation of exactly who is entitled to what level of service in individual cases.

Health policy is a prominent issue at UK level, and the Westminster government has made a great deal of its recurrent (and often repetitive) announcements of funding increases. Scotland is under enormous pressure to match these, especially when they take the form of one-off announcements outside the normal budgetary cycle, or of long-term commitments, and it has always done so. Yet, given the different arrangements within Scotland, the priorities may not always be the same and could progressively diverge. The UK pledge to bring spending up to the EU average as a percentage of GDP did not have obvious and immediate repercussions, since Scotland was already there, allowing some choice in using the Barnett consequentials. In Scotland, more emphasis has been placed on preventive medicine, and ministers have made clear that, even where they match an English increase in funding for health, this does not entail increasing the NHS budget, since the money might more effectively be used elsewhere.

Higher Education

Higher education shows a similar pattern and set of contrasts. Scottish universities had distinct origins before the Union of 1707 and for centuries there were four of them (or five if we count the two in Aberdeen), while England had only two. There was a distinct intellectual tradition based on logic, philosophy and disputation, in contrast to the English focus on classics (Davie 1981). During the late nineteenth and early twentieth centuries, however, Scottish universities were drawn into the UK orbit, driven by the common needs of industrial society and the desire to equip their graduates to compete for British and imperial civil service posts. After a long battle, the Scottish Education Department lost its sponsoring role and the University Grants Committee, established in 1918 and responsible to the Department of Education in London, operated across Great Britain. This allowed government to fund universities without bringing them directly under the state as in other European countries, and respected academic autonomy. A distinct Scottish tradition persisted in the form of higher numbers of students and the four-year honours degree course, but the main policy developments were the same. In the 1960s, universities across the United Kingdom were expanded following the Robbins report and new ones founded. In the following decade, a second tier of higher-education institutions grew up, intended to provide more technical and vocational training. In England they were called polytechnics and were initially under local government control, while in Scotland their status varied, some coming under local government and others under the Scottish Office, but their role was much the same.

The early 1980s saw severe cutbacks for universities, followed by a further expansion of student numbers in the 1990s. At the same time government sought greater control over universities, achieved by a mixture of central regulation and inter-institutional competition comparable to that applied in health and other public services. The University Grants Committee, which had been dominated by the universities themselves, was replaced by the Universities Funding

Council, with a greater role for government and business interests. From 1988, the research element of government funding was distributed on a competitive basis via the Research Assessment Exercise (RAE), an effort to measure the quantity and quality of research in each department. Teaching-quality mechanisms were introduced, eventually leading to a highly intrusive regime of regulation and inspection. Universities were encouraged to compete for students, although government regularly imposed limits and quotas. Universities were encouraged to look for external funding, and to serve the needs of business and government more directly. In 1992, the binary line was abolished so that the polytechnics and degree-awarding colleges could call themselves universities. Since the latter were administratively devolved to the Scottish Office, the opportunity was taken to transfer the older universities as well and to set up a separate Scottish Higher Education Funding Council (SHEFC). Interestingly, Ian Lang (2002), then Secretary of State, claims in his memoirs to have made this decision himself, when it was transparently a consequence of a UK Cabinet decision with GB-wide implications. The higher-education system inherited by SHEFC was very similar to that in England, but still with higher student numbers, the Scottish four-year honours degree, and a closer link between universities and the further-education colleges, which provide Higher National Certificates and Diplomas equivalent to the first and second year of a degree course respectively.

Devolution in 1999 brought the whole sector under the Scottish Parliament, but the universities have remained part of a UK-wide policy community. Staff move freely between English and Scottish universities, pay bargaining is UK-wide (which in the past was true only of the old university sector), and the Scottish universities are very insistent on the need for UK standards of comparability. It was at their insistence that the Research Assessment Exercise remained a UK-wide one, and that the Quality Assurance Agency (QAA) was established in 1997 to replace the different assessment systems that had grown up. There is also a European dimension, as the Bologna process, intended to give university degree programmes and levels the same format across the European Union, unfolds.

Scottish and English universities face many of the same challenges. They have had to absorb a huge increase in student numbers without a concomitant increase in resources. Governments expect them to play a bigger role in economic development and to serve the needs of business, including those at the sub-state or regional level (Paterson

2001b). While providing mass education, they have to sustain world-class research excellence in the face of global competition. Under pressure from both government and commercial sponsors, they need to retain their academic autonomy. Scarce resources have to be allocated and new sources of funding found. A survey of academics in England and Scotland found similar attitudes towards the main issue, but with a persistent tendency for those in Scotland to favour a stronger 'civic engagement', with a role for universities in economic development, and a strong commitment to providing leadership within the nation (Paterson 2003). There was less suspicion of a government role in education, and academics were more likely to take on public roles. These attitudes were found throughout the system in Scotland, but in England were prevalent only in the newer universities, and even there they were less strong than in Scotland.

Faced with common challenges, but somewhat different attitudes among academics, English and Scottish policy makers have responded in different ways, leading to distinct models of university management and regulation. The English approach continues to emphasise management, regulation, differentiation and competition, while the Scottish approach stresses professional autonomy, consensus, egalitarianism and policy learning. In England change has been politically driven, while in Scotland it has emerged from professional networks, in collaboration with government.

England needs to manage a huge system of some 138 institutions funded by the Higher Education Funding Council for England (HEFCE). In this context, neither detailed planning nor close links with individual institutions is possible, so reliance is placed on targets and incentives. There has been an emphasis on differentiation and on broadening sources of funding, in line with previous Conservative policies. One sign was the decision by the Labour government in 1997 to abolish student grants and to introduce a fee (initially set at £1,000 a year) payable by all students in the United Kingdom, with exemptions for those from poorer families. In 2003, by which time it was responsible only for universities in England, the government proposed a system of 'top-up' fees chargeable at the discretion of individual universities and intended to give additional resources to the elite institutions so as to enable them to compete with the best internationally. It was another irony that this, like the Foundation Hospitals provisions, was voted into law only with the support of Scottish Labour MPs. Research funding was also to be allocated more selectively through the RAE, with HEFCE even inventing a new grade 6 after the 2001 exercise had been completed in order to achieve this.[1] At the lower end, the government proposed, also in the 2003 White Paper, to expand student numbers so that 50 per cent of the relevant age cohort were in higher education, by allowing further-education colleges to introduce two-year 'foundation degrees' and to call themselves universities. To address the problem of access for students from less-privileged backgrounds, the government toyed with the idea of quotas and targets, but retreated in the face of middle-class criticism. Instead, it proposed an access regulator, who would be able to penalise universities, and prevent them from charging top-up fees, if they failed to achieve social diversity in their student intake. The Teaching Quality Assurance exercise was initially stepped up but, in the face of the bureaucratic nightmares and mountains of paperwork that arose, the government pulled back in 2000 and agreed to reduce the burden of inspection and move to a less detailed Institutional Audit.

Scotland has a smaller and more manageable system of twenty institutions, and SHEFC was able to take on more of a planning role and establish closer relations with the institutions, although the latter have generally sought to keep SHEFC at arm's length and do not like the terminology of planning. At the same time, reform was less politically driven but emerged from discussion and negotiation among the Scottish Executive, SHEFC, the universities and other interested parties. One of the first decisions of the Scottish Parliament, and a condition of the Liberal Democrats for joining a coalition with Labour, was the abolition of university fees. In practice the solution was not simple and involved an independent commission (the Cubie Commission), and more negotiation after that, to arrive at a compromise in which no fees are charged while students are at university, but a 'graduate endowment' is charged afterwards, the proceeds of which are used to fund bursaries for poorer students. Part of the second coalition agreement in 2003 pledged the Executive not to introduce 'top-up fees' on the English model, and indeed all the parties in the Scottish Parliament are opposed to these. There is a general opposition to the idea of elite universities and a preference to achieve high standards through inter-institutional collaboration rather than concentrating resources in one place. Scotland remains part of the UK-wide Research Assessment Exercise, which universities regard as important in demonstrating their credentials, but SHEFC uses the results differently, and did not follow England in creating the new grade 6. Nor did it propose to concentrate future funding on a few elite institutions. Rather, it has provided mechanisms to allow emerging research fields in traditionally less research-intensive institutions to gain funding, and promoted networks among research teams across Scotland.

The teaching quality assessment process has also drifted apart, after the efforts to get UK-wide uniformity in the late 1990s. While the QAA remains a UK body, with offices in Gloucester and Glasgow, the Scottish body has formal responsibility in a range of Scottish matters and reports directly to SHEFC. There is a concern in Scotland to avoid creating league tables, punishing or shaming institutions, or being overly prescriptive. Instead, there is a focus on the institutional level and working with universities to improve performance. There is no list of requirements following review, but a narrative report intended to give a rounded picture. A student auditor is also part of the process in Scotland, but not in England.

By 2003, Scotland already had half of the age cohort in higher education, the target set for England, and the Executive announced that it did not intend to raise the participation rate beyond this. It had achieved this level partly by the presence of a higher-education sector within the further-education colleges, in the form of Higher National Certificates and Diplomas, with an articulation between the colleges and the universities and an ability to move from HNDs to degree studies. So Scotland did not follow the English 2003 White Paper in allowing colleges to become universities or for foundation degrees, opting instead to retain the HNC and HND as respectable qualifications. In 2004, the sectors were brought closer together again with proposals to merge the higher- and further-education funding councils. This is a sharp departure from the organisation in England, where the further-education colleges come under the Learning and Skills Council which, with its forty-seven local councils, is responsible for the volume job training which in Scotland comes under Scottish Enterprise. Improving access for students from less-privileged backgrounds is a priority in Scotland as in England, but Scotland has not gone for targets or a regulator. Instead, SHEFC works with four Wider Access Regional Forums and a series of local projects seeking to understand and address the problem on the ground.

Universities everywhere are increasingly expected to contribute to economic development, in particular by knowledge transfer and application of inventions. In Scotland, the economic link is marked by placing higher education along with economic development in the Enterprise and Lifelong Learning Department, which does allow for some cross-fertilisation. Specific initiatives (see below) include the Proof of Concept Fund and the Intermediate Technology Institutes that have no counterpart in England.

Policy since devolution has been developed through a three-part review by a team including representatives of the civil service, the funding council, business and universities (including people from English universities); a Lifelong Learning Strategy published in 2003; and a series of reports from the Scottish Parliament committee. The procedure is consensual and consultative, bringing in the various stakeholders, rather than politically driven as in England, and the result has been gradual policy evolution rather than radical change. The first review, published in 2002, focused on SHEFC and identified a number of issues, including the idea of merging with the further education funding council. The second review, in 2003, contained forty-four commitments by the Scottish Executive, twenty-nine rec- ommendations to SHEFC and twenty-one expectations for the uni- versities. Scottish developments were now overtaken by the English White Paper, itself delayed because of wrangling in Cabinet. A key recommendation of the English document, on top-up fees, was seen to have such strong implications for Scotland that the third phase of the review had to wait until this issue was decided before looking at the implications. This review was organised in four working groups, chaired by the Scottish Executive, the National Union of Students (Scotland), the Association of University Teachers (Scotland), and Universities Scotland respectively.

The issue of top-up fees was the most threatening to the consen- sus on university education in Scotland, as the universities insisted on additional funding being made available to compete with the elite English institutions. In practice, this issue may have been exagger- ated. The £3,000 fee for English universities represented only some £1,800 per head on the existing fee, and up to a third of this was to be devoted to bursaries for poorer students. The balance has to cover enhanced salaries, more staff, better equipment and new buildings, and most observers have considered that it will make a paltry difference. Additional government money was promised to increase the participation rate in England and Wales up to 50 per cent of the age cohort. As this level had already been reached in Scotland and the Scottish Executive had no intention of going beyond it, the Barnett consequentials of this funding will be avail- able for Scottish universities if they choose so to allocate them. In the short run, additional Barnett consequentials will be available from the start-up funding given to English universities to tide them over until fee repayments started. The Executive was therefore able to argue that there was no immediate crisis. Over the longer term, however, it is likely that universities in England will rely increasingly on fee income, and pressure on Scotland will develop. In any case, irrespective of what happens south of the border, Scotland needs to find its own way of financing world-class institutions competing in global markets.

Scottish universities have a long-standing fear of being parochialised and losing their UK and international links. On the other hand, the opposition to devolution which they expressed strongly in the 1970s had largely disappeared by the 1990s, and they have learned to operate the new system rather quickly. There are still close connections among higher-educational policy makers in England and Scotland, and the policy community is rather open and peopled by individuals able to work across different levels. The policy agenda has often been set by England, given its strongly politicised approach and the implications for Scotland of initiatives such as top-up fees. Yet the Scottish policy community has been strong enough and well enough articulated to come up with a series of distinct solutions to similar problems, as well as taking account of different circumstances.

Economic Development Policy

Economic policy in Britain was long the exclusive preserve of central government and Whitehall departments, managing the national economy as a whole. Monetary and fiscal policy have always been centralised and macroeconomic management, both in the Keynesian era and under the monetarist experiments of the 1980s, was run from London. There were regular complaints that policy was geared to the interests of South-east England and/or the financial interests of the City of London rather than those of Scotland, Wales or the north of England. In particular, restrictive financial policies intended to control inflation or manage the value of the pound were said to have a damaging effect on the economies of the more peripheral and industrial areas. Sporadically from the 1930s and more consistently from the 1960s, however, governments put in place a series of industrial and regional policies to encourage modernisation and growth, which had a direct impact on Scotland. Initially this took the form of 'assisted areas' benefiting from special measures to encourage investment. In the 1960s, the policy was expanded to a broad regional approach, with incentives to invest in designated regions; at its peak in the mid-1970s, these included the whole of Scotland as well as large parts of Wales and northern England. A strong emphasis was placed on diversionary policy, by which firms were induced to relocate major investments from booming areas to more needy ones through a combination of tax incentives, grants and the provision of sites and services. In principle, this was a national policy to benefit all. The development regions would get jobs, the booming regions would get a relief of inflationary pressures and congestion, and the national economy would gain from bringing into use otherwise idle resources. Policy was centralised and managed from London, but with the Scottish Office lobbying for special treatment. During the 1960s a series of flagship investments was brought north, including vehicle factories at Linwood and Bathgate, the aluminium smelter at Fort William and the steelworks at Ravenscraig. This last was a clear example of political pressure from the government which, unable to decide whether it should go to Scotland or Wales, resorted to the judgement of Solomon and sent half to each country. These investments were intended to act as growth poles, attracting ancillary industries and services and fostering an economic take-off for their localities and regions. To facilitate this, regional planning was introduced, with Scotland often leading the way in initiatives like the Clyde Valley Plan of 1948, its successor the West Central Scotland Plan (1974), and the Toothill Report of 1961.

In order to make and carry out these plans, the Scottish Office gradually built up its capacity, starting with the Scottish Development Department of 1962 and continuing with the establishment of the Scottish Economic Planning Department in 1972. Over the following years the Scottish Office gained the task of administering regional development grants, although the broad policy and criteria for eligibility were set in London. In 1974, the incoming Labour government responded to a long-standing demand and set up the Scottish Development Agency (SDA), with broad powers of industrial intervention and encouragement, and responsibilities in land reclamation and urban regeneration. A similar agency had existed in the Highlands since 1965, the Highlands and Islands Development Board. The regional councils, which came into being in 1975, also had broad planning and infrastructure responsibilities, aimed at fostering and facilitating growth. At local level, a dense network of agencies developed, sponsored by the SDA, local councils or private partnerships, to offer business advice and small-scale incentives. All this meant that by the 1980s Scotland had a long experience of regional policy and perhaps the most highly developed regional development machinery in Europe, although policy was still made within a centralised UK framework.

In the 1980s, Scotland underwent a serious recession, with the closure of all the big industrial plants brought in by the regional policy measures of the previous years. At the same time, the Conservative government turned away from both industrial and regional policy in favour of a market-based approach. Support for development shifted to smaller-scale initiatives in cities and areas affected by closures, and planning was de-emphasised. The Scottish Development Agency, having narrowly escaped abolition, lost its role in industrial investment and was focused more on urban initiatives and sustaining private-sector projects. It also lost its mandate to consider the social as well as purely economic implications of its programmes, and in 1991 it was recast and renamed as Scottish Enterprise, with a strong orientation towards the business community. Much of its work was both localised and privatised through the Local Development Companies, a Scottish equivalent of the English Training and Enterprise Councils. Scotland's independent effort to attract inward investment from overseas also came under pressure from London departments, but eventually a compromise was found in the creation of Locate in Scotland, a joint agency of the SDA and the Scottish Office, the latter being the guarantee that the Scottish effort would be part of a UK programme. By the mid-1990s, the Conservative government had abandoned much of its earlier disdain for manufacturing industry and was actively promoting a reindustrialisation of the old manufacturing regions through foreign capital. Winning inward investment in competition with other parts of the UK and of Europe thus became a major focus of the Scottish development effort and a source of some tension with rival territories.

Much of this reflected common trends in Europe, where governments had moved away from diversionary regional policy after the economic shocks of the 1970s. With all regions suffering from closures, there was no surplus of industry to be guided into the development areas and the old consensus that the policy benefited everybody was unsustainable. In a globalising world and a single European market, industries not allowed to invest in booming regions could leave the country altogether. At the same time, academic research has started to emphasise the importance of local institutions, social networks, values and behaviour as the key factor in explaining regional success and failure. Policy has moved away from subsidising investment, towards human capital, training, research and business advice. While regions are still glad to get inward investment, they realise that these projects can leave as easily as they come, and may not spill over into the wider economy. Hence there is a focus on local firms, endogenous development and fostering entrepreneurship, rather than dependence on government or outside capital. Regions, rather than being complementary elements in a national economy, to be integrated through central government programmes, are seen as competitors in national and international markets, more reliant on their own skills and resources. Yet, despite the emphasis on local entrepreneurship, there is much less emphasis on domestic ownership and an acceptance that regions, rather than being protected, must be fully integrated into international markets. Hence development policy, previously managed by the centre in the interests of balance, has been decentralised to the local and regional levels. This 'new regionalist' paradigm has been criticised in some quarters as exaggerated, or as the product of ideology (Lovering 1999), but it has become the dominant way of thinking about spatial development in Europe.

It was into this new climate that the Scottish Parliament was born in 1999. Whereas the 1979 devolution proposals had left all the instruments for economic development in the hands of the central government, in the form of the Secretary of State for Scotland, this time they could be devolved. On the other hand, the macroeconomic policy, including taxation and monetary policy, remains the prerogative of Westminster. Central government also retains the main regulatory powers, including competition and mergers policy, on a UK basis to avoid market distortions. The European Union also has significant regulatory powers to sustain the single European market, and these affect the exercise of the powers both of the UK Government and of the Scottish Executive.[2] Broadly, policies affecting aggregate demand and sustaining market competition are reserved, while the 'supply side' items, which might be used to enhance the competitiveness of Scotland, are devolved. These include education and training, regional development grants, the universities with their research base, promotion of trade and inward investment, business advice and support for new firms, and renewable energy. Given the current emphasis on these very supply-side factors as the key elements in growth, there was an expectation that the Parliament and Executive could forge their own economic development strategy and make a real impact on the Scottish economy.

In practice, many of the economic powers are shared among the European, UK and Scottish levels. So the Scottish Executive can give regional development grants to firms investing in Scotland, but the designation of the parts of Scotland that qualify is a matter for the UK government and the European Union. Terms and conditions are subject to a concordat between the Executive and the Department of Trade and Industry (DTI) to ensure a level playing field. Tax credits to encourage research and development are controlled from London, while the Scottish Executive has a limited ability to give relief on business rates. Industrial policy in the old sense of planning the growth and development of specific sectors was largely abandoned in the 1980s, but made a slight comeback under the Labour government from 1997. It is the responsibility of the Department of Trade and Industry in London, but with an involvement from the Scottish Executive when it concerns Scotland. Policies on sectors identified as important for Scotland are the responsibility of the Scottish Executive, but UK policies make a larger impact. Energy policy in the sense of regulation and taxation is the responsibility of the DTI, which is also the sponsoring department for the oil industry, but the devolved bodies have an explicit remit in renewable energy. Generally, the economic responsibilities of the Scottish institutions represent administrative devolution, with the power to use and reshape the instruments of policy, while the broad legislative responsibility lies with Westminster.

The main responsibility for economic development policy within the Scottish Executive lies with the Enterprise, Transport and Lifelong Learning Department. Combining economic development (Enterprise) with further education and universities (Lifelong Learning) is intended to further linkages between higher education and research, and economic innovation. Much of the actual policy delivery is in the hands of Scottish Enterprise and its associated Local Enterprise Companies (LECs). After the change of government in 1997, these were brought back more closely under the central agency and relabelled as 'Scottish Enterprise (name of area)'. About 30 per cent of SE's budget goes to training, another third to business services, with the rest spent on research and administration. In the Highlands and Islands, the SDA is replaced by Highlands and Islands Enterprise, which has a similar remit. Alongside the LECs there is an array of local development agencies and forums of

Figure 7.1   Division of economic responsibilities

	Europe	UK	Scotland
Macroeconomic		Monetary Policy (Bank of England) Taxation	Business rates
Regulatory	Competition policy Designation of assisted areas Interstate transport Movement of labour	Competition policy Designation of assisted areas Air, rail transport Immigration	
Assistance	Structural Funds	Tax incentives	Regional Development Grants Management of Structural Funds
Sectoral, promotional and microeconomic	Agriculture and fisheries External trade		Agriculture and fisheries Trade promotion and inward investment
		Sectoral industrial policy Energy	Regional industrial policy Renewable energy
	Trans-European transport networks	Rail, sea and air transport	Road transport Promotion of rail and air transport Business advice Tourism
	Research framework programmes	Research councils	University research Education

various sorts, referred to as the enterprise support network. Critics have charged that this makes for duplication and confusion, and that many of the agencies lack a clear purpose and make a questionable impact, but local politics has made it difficult to rationalise them. An inquiry by the Scottish Parliament Enterprise and Lifelong Learning Committee in 2000 criticised the proliferation of bodies and suggested the creation of local economic forums, including business, local government and educational institutions, with the task of producing a local strategy. These were duly set up, and SE has sought to provide a stronger lead, but Scotland still has perhaps the largest number of agencies per capita in Europe.

Economic development is thus a field in which Scotland has long experience and well-established institutions. While the overall thrust of policy has been similar to that in England since the 1960s, the mode of delivery, with the emphasis first on strategic planning and then on the agency model, has marked Scotland out within the UK and Europe. It has been argued that, since these features were already in existence before 1999, devolution has made little difference and indeed that, since economic development strategies are tending to converge across the UK (often learning from the Scottish model), they are less distinct now than in the past (Newlands 2003). There is an element of truth in this, as policy makers across Europe have adopted the endogenous-growth model and the idea of inter-regional competition. On the other hand, there have been changes since devolution and, while some of these reflect the advent of the Labour government in 1997, others are linked to devolution itself.

Devolution has broadened the policy community around economic development and focused attention on what can be done within the powers of the Scottish Parliament. Groups can no longer opt out of the Scottish arena, claiming that their concerns are reserved to London or that they operate in global markets, since just about everybody has some matter requiring attention from the Scottish level. By strengthening the Scottish political arena, devolution has also encouraged sectoral groups to pay attention to what each other is saying. It has raised the political profile of economic development, as this is seen as one of the challenges by which the governing parties will be judged. The bundle of responsibilities under the Scottish Executive has permitted linkages across policy fields which, while theoretically possible under the Scottish Office, were less likely when the various groups could look to UK policy communities as an alternative to the Scottish one. Universities, for example, have been incorporated into the economic development programme to a greater extent than in the English regions, while retaining their academic autonomy. Social and environmental concerns feature in economic development documents, at least at a rhetorical level.

Scotland has attracted a great deal more international attention since devolution, and has been drawn into European networks of collaboration, exchange and learning, which offer an alternative to taking models from London. It may even be that there is a psychological effect, as Scottish political and economic leaders escape from what has been seen as a dependency culture or a lack of self-confidence (Craig 2003). While it would be a mistake to fall into stereotypical notions of Scots being inherently unwilling to take risks or stand out from the crowd, the institutional arrangements since at least the nineteenth century may have encouraged a tendency to look to the centre for solutions or to blame London, rather than seeking innovative ways of working at home. Devolution does seem to have had some of these positive effects, but the process of change has been slower than expected and is far from complete.

In the early years of the Scottish Parliament and Executive, economic development was not a high priority. Business groups were rather detached from devolution, having been indifferent or even hostile to it, viewing the UK as their main policy arena, and were concerned mainly to limit the potential of the devolved institutions to increase regulation or business costs. The Scottish Executive's first policy document, the *Framework for Economic Development* (Scottish Executive 2000a), reaffirmed the main lines of Labour strategy. There was an emphasis on the market as opposed to intervention or planning, and an insistence that declining sectors would not be supported if they had no long-term promise. Growth was to be fostered through 'clusters', a fashionable term in the regional development literature referring to an old idea that linked and complementary industries could provide mutual support and create a self-sustaining dynamic of growth. The importance of skills and technology was stressed, and there was an acknowledgement that Scotland may be falling behind its competitors in these areas. Social inclusion was part of the strategy but subordinated to growth as the Executive was 'committed to an economy-led social justice agenda'. Environmental issues were recognised, and seen as a potential contributor to growth rather than a cost. It was acknowledged that these issues might be in conflict and that trade-offs and hard choices might be necessary, but there was little indication of a distinct Scottish approach to this. Nor was there a recognition of Scotland's place in Europe, other than as a recipient of Structural Funds. There was a hint that cultural factors might play a role in economic development, but this was left as a question to be explored (Keating et al. 2003). All this amounted largely to a restatement of conventional ideas about development and a summary of recent experience; there was no strong narrative and little effort to harness national identity and collective capacity to the development effort or to exploit the new opportunities of devolution.

Matters did change in the following years. One factor was the drying-up of inward investment flows, which forced a renewed emphasis on endogenous growth. A series of critical issues were identified, some new and some old, including the weakness of entrepreneurship, the low rate of firm formation and the lack of innovation. While Scotland's public research effort compares well with that of other parts of the UK, there is a lack of private-sector research, and a failure to connect research to innovation in production systems. A psychological shock was given by a series of gloomy economic figures from 2001 to 2004, which seemed to show that devolution had failed to reverse a long-term downturn in Scotland's economic fortunes. Much of this was fed by the media, who painted a picture of decline going back almost a century, failing to acknowledge Scotland's better performance in many decades, including the 1970s and 1990s. It later turned out that the doom-laden statistics for the late 1990s and early 2000s were inaccurate and that Scotland had been doing rather well compared with the rest of the UK. Nonetheless, the bad-news stories did stimulate a debate on the Scottish economy, such as would not have happened without devolution, and a search for new solutions. At the same time, the business community abandoned its rather hostile attitude, accepted that devolution had not in itself damaged its interests, and began to come back into the policy process in a more active way, encouraged by the Scottish Executive and gestures (albeit rather symbolic) such as freezing the Unified Business Rate. Another catalyst was the publication in 2001 of the document *A Smart, Successful Scotland* (Scottish Executive 2001b), setting out goals for the enterprise networks. This was a glossy publication presented in a vigorous tone, stressing the need for innovation, training and entrepreneurship and placing Scotland in a European and global context, and it seems to have caught the imagination of people within the economic development community. It thus became the reference point for much of the debate, building a new consensus around another fashionable theme, the 'knowledge economy'.

The policy has been given concrete form in new partnerships between universities and industry. A Proof of Concept Fund supports innovation and application of research, and in 2003 plans were announced for Intermediate Technology Institutes. At the same time, the contribution of existing areas of strength was more fully recognised, including the financial sector, which has boomed in recent years, and medicine, in which Scotland has a historic investment. Following a review in 2001–2, regional selective assistance (grants for investors) was recast to place more emphasis on jobs rather than capital investment and on Scottish rather than international firms. Partly as a result of this but also because of the shortage of inward investment, the proportion of grants going to foreign firms declined from around 60 per cent to between a third and a half. A *Science Strategy for Scotland* (Scottish Executive 2001c) promised to focus on key economic priorities, including bioscience and genomics, medical research and e-science, to appoint a Scientific Advisory Committee and to link science policy to training and to application. A *Report on the Knowledge Economy Cross-Cutting Initiative* (Scottish Executive 2001d) went in the same direction. The higher-education review conducted in stages (see above) also allowed a dialogue between government and universities over science, innovation and application. The renewed stress on development also produced more conventional responses, such as increased spending on infrastructure, including roads. The Scottish Executive even opened up a debate on immigration, focusing on the need for more workers and skills, a subject largely closed at UK level because of the anti-immigrant hysteria fomented by the popular press. A Fresh Talent working group was set up, working with the Home Office, to look at ways to attract newcomers to Scotland and keep overseas students after their graduation.

Of course, many of these initiatives had been started earlier and built on ideas developed before devolution. What has changed is the willingness of the actors to engage in the process and a growing consensus around the theme of endogenous growth, entrepreneurship, training and education, and the need for innovation and application of research. A more cohesive policy community has emerged and the emphasis has shifted from lobbying within the UK towards policy development within Scotland. Social inclusion features more strongly in the Scottish debates and documents than is generally the case in Whitehall. This does not imply an overarching political consensus or shared interest. Business still complains about over-regulation and the Unified Business Rate; educators are still wary about subordinating education to economic goals; there are disputes between environmentalists and growth advocates; and the proliferation of organisations and strategies still causes confusion, despite efforts to rationalise the enterprise support network. Other critics have complained about the weakness of spatial strategy in Scotland, particularly the need to link the cities of the central belt in order to spread the benefits of Edinburgh's prosperity (Turok 2003; Turok et al. 2003). There is still a certain failure of imagination compared with other European regions and nations, which have been able to harness their distinct culture, identity and civil society to a vision for change within the new Europe (Keating et al. 2003).

There has also been an attack from the neo-liberal right on the new consensus. *The Scotsman*, under the editorship of Andrew Neil, has campaigned stridently against economic interventionism of any sort and against Scottish Enterprise in particular, one factor leading to the resignation of its Chief Executive, Robert Crawford, in 2003. The Policy Institute, run from the *Scotsman* offices, has provided an alternative set of ideas, based on low taxation, deregulation and the minimal state (Kerevan and Don 2003; Bruce and Miers 2003). In the early 2000s, the SNP retreated from its former social democratic stance to support a strategy of tax-cutting to make Scotland a low-cost haven for inward investors. There is a debate on fiscal autonomy and the impact which various models might have on the economy. Other voices have suggested that Scotland's situation is so dire that service development might need to be subordinated to the imperative of growth (Alexander 2003).

Yet the very existence of these dissenting views outwith the new mainstream indicates the extent to which there is an economic debate focused on Scotland, with its own actors and interests. Certainly, the main macroeconomic questions are determined at the UK or European levels and many Scottish policies involve influencing these levels or working with them. The over-valuation of the pound under successive Conservative and Labour governments has hit the Scottish manufacturing sector hard and Scotland is vulnerable to UK or international recessions. Yet the autonomous Scottish sphere has grown. As in other fields, actors have become aware that they no longer have the same scope for lobbying Whitehall departments, directly or through the Secretary of State, and must manage their own resources. The Treasury, which has become rather active as a promoter of regional development strategies in the English regions, does not play this role in Scotland and the Department of Trade and Industry's regional responsibilities are now confined to England, as its rather muddled attempt to formulate a UK response to the European Commission's proposals on reformed regional policy show (DTI 2003). This does not necessarily mean that Scottish policy will diverge from that in England. This is a field in which there is a lot of policy competition, learning and diffusion of practice, so that ideas pioneered successfully in one jurisdiction are likely to spread to others (Gillespie and Benneworth 2002). It is a clear example of Dente's (1997) third category, in which policy makers are unsure both of the problem and the solution. This learning is not confined to the nations and regions of the United Kingdom, but is part of a broader European trend in thinking on regional policy (Bachtler and Yuill 2001). While some pundits are given to drawing instant conclusions (invariably unfavourable to Scotland) from fleeting visits to foreign parts, Scotland is in fact now part of an international mainstream in which ideas are developed, adapted and shared in a process of continual learning.

Social Inclusion

Governments have long been concerned with the question of poverty and how to address it. From the early twentieth century, a set of income-support measures was put in place to deal with the insecurities of old age, unemployment and family hardship, providing a basic social safety net for all. After the Second World War and during the 1960s and 1970s, this system was considerably extended. Yet, in the 1960s, social observers made a startling 'rediscovery of poverty', revealing substantial numbers of people who seemed to have fallen through the safety net for one reason or another. These people, it was argued, suffered from a syndrome of problems, a 'multiple deprivation' of unemployment, ill health, poor housing and low educational achievement, each of which reinforced the others in a cycle of poverty to prevent them taking advantages of the new prosperity of postwar Britain. In the United States, and sometimes in Britain, there was much talk of an 'underclass' of families, trapped in a spiral of decline and threatening social cohesion and prone to crime. From this stemmed a series of active policies of social intervention, aimed at helping to break the cycle, or to address the range of problems simultaneously, enabling people to escape the trap and become fully functional members of society. There were conflicting interpretations of the cause of the problem. Some observers diagnosed the problem as an individual or family-level one, stemming from the unpreparedness of people to compete. The answer was to focus on individuals and families, improving their skills and conditions. More radical analysts condemned this as 'blaming the victim', insisting that the fault lay with society in general, or at least the physical, economic and social structure of cities, which systematically generated a pattern of winners and losers. If one family were helped out of poverty, in this view, they would just be replaced by another. Some blamed the organisation of government services and the welfare state, for providing uncoordinated and often conflicting programmes, rather than addressing social problems in the round.

The result was a series of social programmes, starting in the 1960s with the Urban Programme, trying to address the problem on a neighbourhood basis, while seeking at the same time to learn more about its causes and persistence. In Scotland, the Glasgow Eastern Area Renewal Project (GEAR) was the most ambitious effort at simultaneous physical, economic and social regeneration, replicated on a smaller scale in the Scottish Development Agency's (SDA) Area Projects (Keating and Boyle, 1986). Strathclyde Regional Council had its own Social Strategy, aimed at tackling multiple deprivation in defined areas. These had their parallels in England, but the Scottish model was distinct in the existence of regional councils, with substantial resource bases, allowing them to give some priority to needy areas, in the existence of the SDA with its broad remit, and in the ability of the Scottish Office to bring together the various strands of policy within a single department. The policy field, being defined by problems and not by functions, cut across levels of government and agencies, requiring a great deal of joint working and collaboration. Yet there was still something of a divide between national welfare policies, delivered through Social Security benefits, and local-level social policy initiatives, and between economic and labour market policies and social policy.

Under the Conservative government after 1979, the social dimension of urban and local development policy was de-emphasised in favour of a stronger economic focus. Ministers argued that social welfare programmes, far from being the solution to multiple deprivation, were the cause of it, fostering a 'dependency culture' in which individuals had no incentive to seek work or to take risks. So at a national level there was a move, paralleling those in the United States, from welfare to 'workfare', in which individuals would be obliged to take work as a condition of receiving support, although much of this was in the form of make-work schemes sponsored by government agencies. Workfare is an idea associated with the political right and a punitive attitude towards the poor. The idea of connecting policies on work with welfare, however, is much broader and, in the form of active labour-market policy, can be traced to Scandinavian social democracy. Here the aim is to get unemployed people back into the labour market as quickly as possible, before deep-seated social problems develop. By the late 1990s, active labour-market policy, promoted by the Organisation for Economic Cooperation and Development (OECD), had become the new orthodoxy across the developed world. Its details, however, vary from one jurisdiction to another, as does the degree of coercion involved, so that there is still a distinction among the social democratic and the conservative versions.

In 1997, Labour inherited this policy mix and developed the workfare idea in the form of the New Deal, sponsored by the Treasury, requiring young people to be in work or training as a condition of receiving benefits. At the same time, however, they brought a new focus on the social dimension, in the concept of 'social exclusion'. This term, which originated in France, represented a new way of framing the issue of poverty, its causes and cures. It had the advantage of drawing attention away from older ideas of class, no longer sociologically meaningful or politically appealing, and away from social policy as a transfer from the better off to the poor. Instead, the emphasis is on reintegrating failing individuals into society and allowing them to make their contribution to economic and social life, to the ultimate benefit of all. It is consistent with workfare, but implies a stronger role for the public authorities in identifying the causes of exclusion and the obstacles to participation, and in helping people overcome disadvantages that might not be their own fault. It is clearly related to earlier notions of multiple deprivation and shares some of its vocabulary of linked problems and transmission of disadvantage. The concept came to Scotland in 1997, but with a subtle change. Following a consultation on the early document, *Social Exclusion in Scotland*, the theme was changed from combating social exclusion to promoting social inclusion. As well as giving the policy a more positive gloss, this avoided the connotations of social exclusion, with its resemblance to earlier theories of the underclass or 'blaming the victim' or 'pathologising' certain groups (Fawcett 2003). There was also a broader conception of the issue in Scotland, extending to issues of gender, race, disability and sexuality, which in England tend to be treated separately (Fawcett 2004). Social exclusion/inclusion was promoted as a flagship item in New Labour's programme of 'joined-up government', a coordinated approach to social problems. In London, the lead was given to a special Social Exclusion Unit located in the Cabinet Office.

In Scotland, the lead was taken by the Scottish Office, which defined the objectives of the Social Inclusion strategy as:

- to increase participation in the labour market
- to tackle poverty through both national and local action
- to ensure that every child entering primary school is ready to learn and to make best use of their school years
- to reduce, if possible to zero, the number of children who leave school unqualified or ill-equipped to cope with life
- to widen participation in and demand for lifelong learning
- to tackle specific barriers to participation individuals face, including ill health, low self-esteem, homelessness and drug misuse
- to eliminate discrimination and inequality on the grounds of gender, race or disability
- to ensure that decent and affordable housing is available to everyone
- to tackle inequalities between communities by empowering and regenerating deprived communities
- to support and encourage the contribution of business to the wellbeing of communities
- to promote a culture of active citizenship, in which self-development, participation in community and civic life and caring for our disadvantaged neighbours are key features (Scottish Office 1999)

At this stage, the Scottish Office formed part of the UK Government and remained closely in touch with the work being done in London.

Devolution of responsibility for social cohesion is not unique to Scotland, but follows a pattern widely seen across the world. As in other policy fields, changing the spatial level does have effects on the policy environment and on the sorts of policies likely to be pursued, but there are conflicting ideas on what these effects are. Three distinct hypotheses are put forward. The first, derived from the literature on competitive regionalism (see above), states that, faced with competition for investment and business growth, territorial governments will cut their social expenditures, spend heavily on development policies, and reduce business regulation to the minimum. Kenichi Ohmae (1995), in a much-cited but contentious work, both advocates and celebrates this trend, which he claims to be sweeping the globe. This is the 'race to the bottom' hypothesis. In an era of global capital flows and the single European market, the race among regions becomes more acute and, so some anti-globalisation campaigners fear, the threat to social solidarity increases as those with the skills and opportunities come out on top. A second hypothesis is that territorial communities that are naturally solidaristic will emphasise social cohesion in the face of market forces. This has been argued in the case of Quebec (Noël 1999) and might be considered in the case of Scotland (McEwen 1999). The third hypothesis is that, at the right spatial level, it is possible to find a new synthesis of economic competitiveness and social cohesion (Cooke and Morgan 1998). Indeed, it may be that social cohesion itself can promote competitiveness and that nations and regions carrying the burden of social distress are thereby less competitive. Neo-liberal commentators in Scotland have favoured the first hypothesis and advocated a strategy of tax reduction with more fiscal autonomy to make this possible (Bruce and Miers 2003). The SNP, as noted above, also promoted the idea of tax cutting as a recipe for international competitiveness. Few of the advocates of tax reduction, however, have drawn the consequences for social policy explicitly, tending to take refuge in various forms of wishful thinking, such as the idea that this will so increase economic growth that tax yields will actually increase.[3] The second hypothesis is favoured by some nationalists and sections of the political left. Social democratic parties in Europe have tended to the third, exploring the scope for policies that are both socially inclusive and economically efficient, although here too there has sometimes been wishful thinking, and some avoidance of the need to make choices. Policy in Scotland since devolution has tended to follow this third track, which includes an effort to bring together economic and social considerations, notably through active labour market policies.

Following devolution, the Executive, as in other policy fields, has taken the view that what matters is delivery, not the precise distribution of responsibilities across agencies and levels of government, so that the delineation of roles has not as yet been clearly established (Parry 2003). Responsibility for the social inclusion agenda is spread across several departments in London and Edinburgh, as well as Scottish local authorities. Taxation comes under the Treasury, which has also taken the lead in a number of sectoral policy initiatives, notably the New Deal. The UK Department of Work and Pensions, renamed to remove the expression 'social security' and to link welfare to work, is responsible for pensions, benefits, the minimum wage introduced by Labour after 1997, and labour market regulation. Under the Scottish Executive come social work, housing, health, education, training, urban and rural policies and economic development. Local authorities and agencies in Scotland have an important role in the delivery of these services. Indeed, the policy network spreads beyond the United Kingdom, as social inclusion was adopted as one of the themes to be developed through the British–Irish Council in 2002, with the Scottish Executive and the Welsh Assembly Government taking the lead. There is also a European dimension, as the member states of the European Union have to submit a three-yearly National Action Plan on Social Inclusion as part of the effort to promote the European social model of development alongside the single market. Both the British–Irish and the European programmes are intended to further policy learning, innovation, and the spread of good practice. The wider policy community includes voluntary sector groups, charities, churches, community bodies and, as the reach of the policy is extended, the business community. The small size of Scotland's policy communities and the fact that most of those in the voluntary sector are Scottish-based rather than branches of UK bodies, perhaps makes this more feasible than in England, and the idea of social inclusion has certainly permeated the discourse very widely. On the other hand, the diversity of the issues involved and their ramifications into other fields makes it difficult to identify a cohesive community with strongly shared values. There is also some tension between public sector service providers, often in local government, and the voluntary sector. A Social Inclusion Network established before devolution brought together the main groups and agencies concerned, and identified priorities in a field where the Scottish Executive itself had limited policy capacity (Fawcett 2004), but this was abandoned in 2003 as having served its purpose.

There has been a strong element of continuity between Scottish Office strategies under New Labour (1997–9) and those of the Scottish Executive, and a lot of joint working with other levels of government. The 1999 strategy was reaffirmed by the Scottish Executive (2000c) under the new heading of Social Justice, setting out a series of targets for achievement. Since then, the Executive has issued an annual report on Social Justice, with progress towards targets and articles on selected issues. By 2004, this had twenty-nine 'milestones' complete with progress reports. Another strand has been work on defining, measuring and modelling social deprivation so as to develop a series of Scottish indicators valid for urban and rural areas using the latest census data. There has also been an emphasis on 'mainstreaming', so that social inclusion should not be a separate programme but should become a criterion for judging programmes across the board. Consequently, we find references to inclusion across the whole range of policy fields, including higher education, economic development and rural policy, as well as the more obvious areas like housing, urban regeneration and health. The Executive's budget for 2003–6 took the cross-cutting theme of 'Closing the Opportunity Gap', and this is used in order to remind other departments of their responsibility. It is difficult to know how effective this is, but a survey of Scottish and Westminster legislation found that references to social inclusion were more common in the former (Keating et al. 2003).

At the local level, the social inclusion policy has built on and developed previous strategies of area-based regeneration going back to the 1970s. Just before devolution in 1999 the old Urban Programme, a fund that operated across Great Britain but was administered in Scotland by the Scottish Office, was replaced by the Social Inclusion Partnership Fund. Regeneration Programmes and Priority Partnership Areas set up by the previous government in 1996 were converted to Social Inclusion Partnerships (SIPs) and localities were invited to bid for additional ones. By 2003 there were forty-eight SIPs, some of which were area-based, focused on small urban or rural areas, while others were thematic, covering whole cities but limited to specific topics such as young people, ethnic communities or prostitution. Sponsorship of these was assumed by Communities Scotland, an Executive agency that had grown out of Scottish Homes. By 2004 the leadership had passed to local authorities under the new instrument of Community Planning. This is a procedure by which local government, public agencies and the voluntary sector agree on projects and priorities cutting across their responsibilities. Community Planning Partnerships (CPPs) have no dedicated resources of their own, but are to make better use of existing funding by cooperation. In practice, they have not developed into a universal system of planning, but have focused on particular issues, according to the area, and the link to other instruments like land-use planning or local economic development strategies from the local economic development forums is not always straightforward. They did, however, take over as the main channel for SIP funding, with the choice as to whether to incorporate them or leave them as they are. One effect of this has been to put local government in a stronger role at the expense of Communities Scotland, causing some apprehension in the voluntary sector, which had seen CPPs as a way of expanding its role.

There have been some efforts to explore the distinct urban and rural facets of social inclusion. In 2000, the Executive commissioned a cities review focused on Scotland's six cities (Glasgow, Edinburgh, Aberdeen, Dundee, Inverness and Stirling). The choice of the cities as units of analysis was a little strange, since they are defined by a rather formal civic status and exclude other important urban areas with serious social problems. There was a great deal of useful analysis of problems, but this has not led to a major policy initiative (Scottish Executive 2003d). Indeed, there has been quite a lot of criticism of the Executive for failing to develop integrated urban policies, bringing together the physical, social and economic aspects, and linking the urban concentrations in the central belt in a strategic framework (Turok 2003). Historically, urban policy in Scotland for a long time meant policy for the Glasgow conurbation, an idea that only started to change in the 1980s (Keating and Boyle 1986) with the SDA's area projects. After 1999, evidence again began to accumulate that the Glasgow area still faced the most intractable problems and was failing to benefit from the overall economic growth and the boom conditions around Edinburgh (Webster 2000). Yet, politically, it is now more difficult to focus resources on the west-central region than it was under previous Labour governments, with their Scottish power base there. Power in the Scottish Parliament is more dispersed, Labour is in coalition with the Liberal Democrats, and the Labour Party itself has parliamentary representation in all parts of Scotland. The rural initiatives, reflecting this new balance of influence, are discussed in the next section.

Faced with the need to reconcile conflicting pressures, to competition and to social solidarity, the Scottish Executive (2000a) has emphasised that its economic and social goals are in practice compatible in an 'economy-led social justice agenda'. This implies a continuation of the economic emphasis in spatial development policies as laid down in the 1990s. There have been efforts to inject social considerations into broader economic policy debates, encompassing the private sector, but these have had limited effects. Private firms have been persuaded to sponsor some 'social economy' initiatives through Business in the Community, Scotland, to promote job opportunities. The banks have also been involved through measures to extend bank accounts to low-income people or those with no fixed address, but generally, while not opposed to social inclusion policies, business tends to regard them as a matter for government.

Generally, social inclusion has been a low-key policy, a series of small initiatives or an effort to bend mainstream programmes to give them a better social orientation. It is not the stuff of party politics and is almost entirely neglected by the media. One report (Payne 2004) complained that the 2003 Social Justice report had produced very little reaction either from interest groups or from media commentators. It is not, therefore, an attractive area for politicians wanting to make their mark or to rouse public support.

Following the 2003 election, there was a sharp shift in policy within the Scottish Executive towards a tough law and order stance focused on 'antisocial behaviour' especially among youth. Labour took control of the Justice portfolio from the Liberal Democrats, who had pursued a rather progressive line, and introduced a series of measures including the Antisocial Behaviour Bill. This was widely criticised as a move from social intervention towards repression and for stereotyping young people as potential criminals, but it caught a public mood in which crime was perceived to be rising even as it was falling. While the various social inclusion initiatives were not strictly affected by this, it did represent an important reframing of the issue, seeing antisocial behaviour as the product of individual misconduct rather than social conditions, and as such amenable to solutions drawn from the police and law and order toolbox. In fact, the police themselves were critical of some of the provisions of the bill, which they saw as addressing superficial symptoms and potentially making matters worse. This allowed the First Minister in turn to bracket them with the lawyers and other professionals as part of an elite consensus remote from the concerns of ordinary people, in a rare break from the Scottish tradition of working with public sector professionals.

Social inclusion is another field in which the problem itself is continually being redefined even as policy is developed. There is intense interest in what is happening in other jurisdictions, although policy makers have tended to look to America rather than Europe. Innovations in one place are quickly taken up elsewhere, so that Scottish policy, while autonomous, is part of a wider process of learning and adaptation.

Rural Policy

Rural policy has come onto the agenda across Europe, largely as a result of the reform of the Common Agricultural Policy (CAP), together with the declining influence of the farming lobbies. The idea, encouraged by the European Commission, is to move from a sectoral policy based upon one industry to a spatial policy focused on the broad economic, social and environmental needs of people living in rural areas (Bryden 2000; Keating 2000). In the United Kingdom the move was given further impetus by the BSE and foot-and-mouth crises of recent years. Yet the concept of rural policy is still rather open, since it is defined by territory and not by function, providing another example of problem definition alongside policy development. It is a cross-cutting or transversal policy, linking a number of sectoral concerns and interests. The main instruments of rural policy are devolved to Scotland, but agricultural and environmental matters are highly Europeanised, bringing in not only the European Union but also the UK Government, given Whitehall leadership in EU negotiations.

Rural conditions in Scotland are different from those in the rest of the United Kingdom.[4] Farming is a small economic sector everywhere but larger in Scotland, where it accounts for 1.4 per cent of GDP and 1.6 per cent of employment, against 0.9 per cent of both GDP and of employment in England. Twenty per cent of farming land in England is designated Less Favoured Area, compared with 84 per cent in Scotland (of which 98 per cent is Seriously Disadvantaged) (MAFF 2001; Scottish Executive 2001a). Scotland is thus more dependent on CAP support for agriculture and has fewer possibilities for higher value-added speciality farming. The population of England has steadily grown, expanding by 6 per cent between 1971 and 1996, while the rural population went up by 24 per cent (MAFF 2001). Scotland has stagnated demographically since the mid-twentieth century and the move to rural areas has been less dramatic. Between 1981 and 1991 its population fell by 1.4 per cent, while its rural population increased by 3.5 per cent (Shucksmith 2000). Rural England has thus faced pressures for urban expansion and housing, especially in the south, so that conservation and development control are important issues. In most of rural Scotland, by contrast, the emphasis has been on promoting economic development and retaining the population, especially in the Highlands, where a distinct culture and way of life are at stake. As important as the objective differences are the social constructions of rurality (Woodward and Halfacree 2002; Macaulay Land Research Institute 2001). England has its 'rural idyll' focused on traditional agriculture and social relations, while Scottish identity incorporates a different rural myth, less clearly linked to agriculture and often focused on the Highlands.

Scotland has the most concentrated land ownership in Europe, with 50 per cent of the land owned by just 608 people and 10 per cent by eighteen (Callender 1997). The social and economic power of landowners has been a political issue since the early nineteenth century, and land reform has been a periodic preoccupation of the political left. Land reform is also historically linked into the issue of home rule, although in the 1960s, when Labour was hostile to devolution, it used the device of the Highlands and Islands Development Agency to circumvent landlord obstruction (Keating and Bleiman 1979). Over recent years, many estates have come into foreign ownership and are run on capitalist lines, often as sporting ventures, raising concerns about foreigners buying up Scotland and their real contribution to the economy (Wightman and Higgins 2000). Many Scottish farms are small and there are few of the big agribusiness concerns found in southern England. Conditions in the Highlands differ from those in the Lowlands, as do systems of tenure. The Highlands have been subject to other special measures of intervention, notably the Highlands and Islands Development Board (now Highlands and Islands Enterprise).

Political pressures are also rather distinct in Scotland, where the main impetus for rural policy comes from the presence in the governing coalition of the Liberal Democrats, who have their power base in the rural areas. In England, political pressure comes from the large number of Labour MPs representing rural areas since 1997 and from the vocal lobbying of groups like the Countryside Alliance, which exists in a much weaker form in Scotland.

Immediately after devolution, Scotland gained the first Rural Affairs Minister and department in the United Kingdom. The Scottish Executive Environment and Rural Affairs Department (SEERAD) groups its responsibilities under three headings: for agriculture, food and fisheries together with rural development; for the environment; and to promote rural interests across the Executive. These three strands of policy are still rather separate, especially environmental policy, which also covers urban areas. There is also no 'rural affairs' budget, so this general remit must be pursued through the other regulatory and spending departments. A Cabinet sub-committee on Rural Development consists of ministers and deputy ministers with responsibilities for key rural priorities, supported by the Rural Core Network of civil servants. The Scottish Parliament's Rural Development Committee has a remit similarly covering agriculture, forestry and fisheries, employment, housing, transport and poverty.

The wider policy community is almost entirely contained within Scotland. The National Farmers Union of Scotland (NFUS) is separate from the NFU in England, as is the Crofters' Foundation in the Highlands and Islands. NFUS insists on its role as a sectoral body representing the interests of farmers, and has been reluctant to be drawn into wider questions of rural policy. The Scottish Rural Property and Business Association (formerly the Scottish Landowners' Federation) is separate from its English counterpart and represents the large estates. Since these are diversifying out of agriculture, they have more input into the broader rural agenda, although their main preoccupation in the early years of devolution was with the Scottish Parliament's Land Reform Bill.

It was to be expected that the move to rural policy should bring into the process a wider range of groups and to some extent this has happened (Woodward and Halfacree 2002), drawing in groups concerned with environmental issues, social issues and economic development. They come together with the Scottish Executive in the Scottish National Rural Partnership (SNRP) to flag up rural concerns, to assist civil servants in setting their research agenda, and to provide feedback to ministers and service providers. There has been a politicisation of the policy field (Lowe and Ward 2002), which has produced some conflict around SNRP, its role and the position of civil servants in it. This provoked the setting up of a rival, the Rural Dialogue Group, that brings together a wider range of groups, organisations and agencies, and which sets its own agenda.

There has been a limited integration of the various groups into a common agenda of rural policy. Many are also reluctant to stray beyond their sectoral remit, citing lack of time and resources and the risk of diluting their policy priorities. Groups concerned with social issues had highest expectations but complain that the rural agenda is still too dominated by farming. Environmental groups have generally seen an improvement in matters and their interests are taken more seriously, although it is not always possible to separate the influence of devolution in 1999 from that of the change of government in 1997. Actors concerned with economic development have tended to look to the established enterprise support network before devolution, under Scottish Enterprise and Highlands and Islands Enterprise. Agriculture has long been outside the enterprise support network, dealing with the agricultural department in Edinburgh, although there are now efforts to bring it closer. With reform of the CAP, diversification out of farming and the new rural development approach, however, agriculture is gradually being brought within the remit of the Enterprise agencies. In 2002, the Convention of Scottish Local Authorities (CoSLA) established a Rural Affairs Executive Group, prompted by the new legislation on Community Planning.

Rural policy is very broad in its scope and could include a vast range of measures, but three issues illustrate the scope for Scottish initiative: general statements of rural policy reflecting the new orientation; agriculture; and land reform.

Early efforts at defining rural policy predate devolution, with White Papers in 1995–6 for England, Scotland and Wales. These were very similar, even to sharing identical paragraphs, although there were some differences of emphasis (Lowe 1996). Another Scottish White Paper was issued in 1998 (Scottish Office 1998) after the change of government, raising a broad range of economic and social issues for discussion. Two further discussion papers were issued in 2000 in England and Scotland, looking at rural policy across the board: *Rural Scotland. A New Approach* (Scottish Executive 2000b) and *Our Countryside: The Future. A Fair Deal for Rural England* (DETR/MAFF 2000). Then, following the foot-and-mouth outbreak, three reports were commissioned: The *Foot and Mouth Disease 2001: Lessons to be Learned Inquiry* (Anderson 2002), covering England, Scotland and Wales; the Policy Commission on the Future of Farming and Food (Curry 2002), covering England; and *Infectious Diseases in Livestock* (Royal Society 2002), covering the United Kingdom. There was also a response to consultation on the rural White Paper for England and the task force of Lord Haskins to look at the handling of foot-and-mouth (DEFRA 2001).

Comparison of the two rural policy papers issued in 2000 shows a completely autonomous policy process. Some proposals occur in both, or in related papers, such as the emphasis on diversification and derating, or restrictions on the right to buy council houses in rural areas. The general approach, however, was quite different.

The English paper was lengthy, tried to address myriad problems at the same time, and is replete with targets for public services. Strategically, it focused on the need to control and shape development and emphasised the role of villages and market towns. A rural advocate was proposed for bringing rural issues to the attention of departments, and all English policies were to be 'rural-proofed' to ensure that they do not damage rural areas. There was an emphasis on planning and development control, and a focus on towns and villages. Most of the rest of the paper was about delivery of public services in areas that happen to be rural, rather than an analysis of the nature of rurality.

The Scottish paper was shorter, more reflective and less conclusive. It was an effort to start a process of thinking about rurality and how to model rural social and economic problems. There was a stronger emphasis on social inclusion than in the English paper, as well as an insistence on the importance of rural areas for Scottish national identity. There was an emphasis on economic development and less concern about housing pressures on the urban fringe. There were no service delivery targets or 'rural-proofing'. Following the paper, the process was taken forward in a series of groups and initiatives with departments. Initially, working groups were set up on rural poverty and social inclusion, the SNRP was asked to look at questions of service delivery, and further work was done on modelling rural issues (Scottish Executive 2003c). Scottish policy makers have also looked for inspiration to European, particularly Nordic, examples, and ideas have also been imported through the European Rural Exchange Network, for which Dumfries and Galloway Council provides the secretariat. All this is consistent with Scottish policy style in other fields, working with stakeholders rather than taking a strong lead from the centre or imposing targets from above.

Agriculture, however, does seem to remain somewhat apart from the debate on broader rural policy. *Rural Scotland. A New Approach* emphasises that agriculture is at the core of the rural economy, and the agricultural strategy published as *A Forward Strategy for Scottish Agriculture* (Scottish Executive 2002) emphasises the need to look at rural development as a whole. Yet the farming lobby stayed out of the process of producing the rural policy paper and was not represented on the subsequent working groups. Scottish policy has generally been more sympathetic to farmers, emphasising the need to sustain the small hill farmers, while English policy has placed more emphasis on diversification and the non-agricultural uses of the countryside.

The big decisions on agricultural policy are taken at European level, and the United Kingdom has been a strong supporter of CAP reform. It favoured the modulation arrangements under the Agenda 2000 reform, under which a proportion of direct subsidies to farmers can be diverted into rural development measures under the Rural Development Plan. Alone of EU member states, the United Kingdom does not have a state-wide Rural Development Plan (RDP). Instead, England, Scotland, Wales and Northern Ireland have their own

RDPs, with the Scottish and Welsh ones drawn up by the devolved administrations.[5] Given the prevalence of marginal farming in Scotland, modulation was seen as a threat and Scottish ministers were reluctant to apply it, but the UK Government's interpretation was that any spatial differentiation within a member state was permissible only on the basis of objective criteria, not between jurisdictions. Scottish Rural Affairs Minister, Ross Finnie (2002) merely told the House of Lords inquiry that his legal advice was that this was 'very difficult'. There were also financial implications, since modulation funds must be matched 50–50 by contributions from member states. If the English contribution were run through the Barnett formula, Scotland would end up with a much smaller share than its normal share of agriculture spending. Eventually, the devolved administrations agreed to modulation on the condition that the Treasury would provide the national matching funds. Accordingly 2.5 per cent, rising to 4.5 per cent, of payments were modulated.

Unable to opt out of modulation, the Scottish minister promised farmers that the modulated funds applied in the Rural Development Plan (Scottish Executive 2001a) would be cycled back to them and this was done. In England, the two key objectives of the RDP were 'creating a productive and sustainable rural economy' and 'conserving and enhancing the rural environment'. In Scotland, they were 'to assist the viability and sustainability of Scottish farming' and 'to encourage farming practices which contribute to the economic, social and environmental sustainability of rural areas'. Financial allocations for the RDP in general and from modulation in particular, also favoured Scottish farmers, with some 90 per cent of funding going to the first objective. Indeed, most of the Scottish, but not the English, funding goes to direct support for farmers in Less Favoured Areas. Tensions between the Scottish and English perspective persisted after this compromise. The Policy Commission on the Future of Farming and Food (Curry 2002), set up by DEFRA for England alone, caused an outcry in Scotland when it exceeded its brief in 2001 and called for modulation of up to 20 per cent for the whole of the United Kingdom.

The next stage of CAP reform, in 2003–4, involved two key elements: a rise in modulation; and a decoupling of agricultural payments from production, with farmers receiving a fixed sum based on acreage or on historic support levels, at the discretion of member states. This time the Scottish Executive pressed for a clear right to differentiate policy and was able to achieve this, while keeping its existing proportion of agricultural spending. It subsequently undertook a consultation within Scotland as to how it should proceed, receiving just under 300 responses (proportionately much higher than in England). Farmers in Scotland generally continued to oppose modulation, but the Scottish Executive nonetheless followed DEFRA in going for 10 per cent, so attracting the corresponding Treasury support and leaving decisions on whether to raise the total further until the additional Treasury funding was secured. Both Scotland and England went for full decoupling. In Scotland this was based on historic payments, as favoured by farmers and opposed by environmentalists. England, by contrast, opted to move to a flat-rate system by 2012, but with different rates for three regions. Scotland, but not England, also opted to 'top-slice' the single payments to allow continued support for the beef sector. So the overall picture is of a policy driven by EU decisions, with a strong role for DEFRA and the Treasury in determining the finance available, but with the Scottish Executive exercising an important discretion in maintaining the small farmers and the remote areas.

Another agricultural issue with European implications concerns trials of genetically modified (GM) crops. Scottish ministers took the view that European law does not allow it to prohibit trial crops, despite opposition in Scotland. Trials did therefore go ahead. Another confrontation loomed in 2004 when the UK Government determined to press ahead with the commercial growing of GM crops, starting with maize. By this time, the Scottish Executive had firmed up its position and under the Partnership Agreement was committed not to permit planting. This, it turned out, would require a joint decision by London and the devolved administrations to allow the relevant crops onto the national seed list, apparently giving the Scottish Executive a veto over commercial growing throughout the United Kingdom, but not a separate veto for Scotland. It was also suggested that EU law would not allow Scotland to ban the crops without scientific backing and, given the results of the DEFRA tests, this was not forthcoming. Unable politically to force DEFRA to abandon its policy of giving permission in England, the Scottish Executive arrived at a compromise. It agreed to allow the growing of GM maize, a crop hardly suited to Scotland in any case, while pressing Scottish farmers to observe a voluntary ban. The measure was approved in the Scottish Parliament by just one vote, with the Liberal Democrats sustaining the Executive, although their English and Welsh counterparts had voted against.

This confused outcome tested the Scottish style of intergovernmental policy making by consensus to its limits, and contrasted with the more robust Welsh position, which was to try to ban GM crops but to accept defeat if a legal challenge went against them. It also left open the question of a future expansion of GM crops, although the lack of consumer demand might resolve the issue, getting the Scottish authorities off the hook.

Land reform is historically an important issue in Scotland and it was inevitable that a Scottish Parliament would make it a priority. Under the Land Reform Bill, tenants can buy estates as they come on the market. Crofters (a category defined strictly in legislation since the nineteenth century) have a stronger right, being able to acquire estates compulsorily, adding a collective right to buy to the individual rights they have long enjoyed. The legislation was not surprisingly opposed by the Scottish Landowners' Federation and supported by the crofting organisations. This is a matter that was decided entirely within the Scottish political system, with no involvement by the UK Government or interest groups. In the same legislation there is provision of rights of access to land for recreation, parallel to legislation in England.

National Parks were first created in England and Wales after the Second World War. Scotland at that time was excluded, largely because of the power of the big landowners. The low priority of the issue and lack of legislative time meant that it was never taken up subsequently, but this was an issue on which the Scottish Parliament could legislate without reference to broader UK considerations. This might be seen as a case of convergence, with Scotland catching up to England and Wales, yet the legislation contains significant differences from its counterparts south of the border and is the product of a purely Scottish debate.

Abolition of fox hunting has long been a favoured cause within the urban Labour Party across Great Britain, but has raised strong emotions since it is a proxy for bigger social cleavages. Many see the issue as a class one, fox hunters being portrayed as a mixture of old gentry and nouveaux riches seeking upward social mobility in the arcane British class system. Hunters themselves dispute this, pointing to the existence of popular farmers' hunts, yet the image of the hunt does seem linked to the rural hierarchy. It is also an urban–rural issue, with urban liberals seeing hunting as a survival of rural barbarity and hunters themselves insisting that it is part of their essential culture. Beside these emotive concerns, technical considerations carry little weight. As an issue of conscience this is something regulated by private members' bills on a non-party basis, with a free vote in the legislature. After 1999 it became obvious that there were majorities for abolition in both Westminster and the Scottish Parliament, but the Labour government, and Tony Blair personally, seemed reluctant to upset the rural lobby and provoke the Countryside Alliance by pushing legislation for England through. Accordingly, they allowed the bill to be sabotaged by parliamentary obstruction and the House of Lords. The Scottish legislation had a difficult time in the Rural Affairs Committee, where it was criticised for being badly drafted and ill-thought out, but eventually it passed. Hence, from 1 August 2002 hunting with hounds is illegal in Scotland but legal in England and Wales.

Rural policy, as a rather new field, provides scope for developing policy differently in Scotland, but it is constrained, especially in agriculture, by UK and European considerations. There is also the burden of existing policies and of interests embedded in the old policy networks. Yet devolution has produced divergence in response to differing conditions and a distinct policy community, to an extent that certainly did not exist before 1999.

Notes

1. This was calculated by taking into account performance in the previous RAE as well as the current one. The RAE had, not surprisingly, produced grade inflation, with a huge number of departments getting the top rating of 5.
2. Were the United Kingdom to adopt the Euro, it would also be subject to European monetary policy and its fiscal policies would be subordinated to the Stability Pact limiting permitted government deficits.
3. The theory is known as the Laffer curve and was the justification for deficit spending under the Reagan administration in the United States, where it led to ballooning budget deficits.
4. Although there is a lot of difference within England.
5. For some reason, many people I speak to have refused to believe this. Yet in other countries with devolved government there have been both national and regional RDPs.

CHAPTER EIGHT

New Politics, New Policies?

This book started out asking what a devolved Scotland could do more than the old system of administrative devolution. It traced two dimensions of change in power and influence, between London and Edinburgh, and within Scotland. Devolution is not independence, and there are many tangled responsibilities and interdependencies between the two levels, limiting the scope for independent action. Even were Scotland independent, there would still be contextual pressures for similarities in policy across the border and indeed more broadly within Europe. The chapters have indeed found a broad similarity in economic and social policy, but with important emerging differences in policy style and in ways of doing things. Of course, during the first two sessions of the Scottish Parliament, between 1999 and 2007, the governing coalitions at both levels have been rather similar, so that there has been a limited demand for policy divergence. There has, on the other hand, been less enthusiasm emerging from the Scottish political system for the forms of public service reform pioneered under the Conservative governments of the 1980s and 1990s and carried on in modified form by New Labour, while the presence of the Liberal Democrats in the Scottish coalition has been responsible for distinct policies in a number of fields. Nor, in contrast to countries like Spain or Canada, has the division of powers been tested in the courts to produce a body of case law. In fact, there has not to date been a single challenge by central government to the competences of the devolved bodies. It is difficult to be categorical, then, on what Scotland can and cannot do, but we can draw some provisional conclusions.

Five types of policy might be distinguished.

First, there are non-comparable policies, where an issue exists only in certain parts of the United Kingdom. Here, we have seen that Scotland has been able to go its own way, the most prominent example being on land reform, although some reforms of civil law would also fall into this category. Such was not generally the case before devolution.

Second, there is policy autonomy, where the issues are the same but Whitehall and Scotland make their own distinct policy according to local needs and preferences. This has happened in wide areas of education, where Scotland has not gone down the English road and has retained the comprehensive model. In previous eras, while it developed its own educational system, it had to follow the British school line on comprehensivisation, opting out, or such ideological initiatives as the Technical and Vocational Education Initiative sponsored in the 1980s by the Manpower Services Commission. Scotland has also demonstrated a high degree of autonomy in the way it organises health and higher education, going well beyond the forms of administrative differentiation that existed before devolution. In the first session, there was a distinct line on criminal justice, where the presence of the Liberal Democrats tempered the kind of authoritarianism shown in the Home Office under Jack Straw and David Blunkett. The subsequent adoption in Scotland of a hard-line attitude on youth crime was a response to Scottish domestic political factors and choices, not something imposed from outside. Although local government structures were distinct before 1999, it is difficult to imagine the old Scottish Office introducing proportional representation in local government independently of a similar decision for England. Scotland has also been able to combine policy instruments in distinct ways, in the link between education and economic development or education and health. The different structure of departments and ministerial portfolios and the difficulty in reading across functional expenditure patterns from England to Scotland has encouraged this form of innovation, although the Executive has so far not engaged in the type of radical redefinition of problems that could be possible.

Third, there are concurrent policies, where the territorial administrations pursue the same broad policies because of pressure from UK groups, similarity of conditions, or European regulation. Regional economic development policies are following similar lines, which is also true broadly across Europe. A great deal of transport policy in Scotland and England follows similar lines and, free personal care for the elderly apart, the Community Care and Health (Scotland) Act 2002 bears much similarity to the Westminster Health and Social Care Act 2001. Reforms of the Common Agricultural Policy apply on both sides of the border, with the Scottish Executive constantly seeking room for manoeuvre in the detailed transmission.

Fourth, there is policy uniformity, where practical considerations or international obligations and external pressures make for a single line, as with the legislation on the International Criminal Court, which the Scottish Parliament took itself rather than trusting to a Sewel motion, but which had to be the same in both jurisdictions.

Fifth, there is policy competition, a form of policy autonomy, but which is worth highlighting separately. In this case, England and the devolved countries make policy for themselves in a way to demonstrate their credentials in innovation and imagination. Such initiatives make the news and are taken up by interest groups in the other jurisdictions, and the effect is a diffusion of innovation and perhaps a reconvergence around the new practice. This type of convergence might be considered one of the greatest contributions of devolution, in encouraging experimentation and learning from best practice. One example of this is the introduction of a Children's Commissioner, an idea that originated in the National Assembly for Wales and was taken up next in Scotland. Ideas have also been pioneered and transmitted in economic development, in this case across Europe.

While this suggests considerable scope for diversity, the main domestic policy actor within the United Kingdom is the government in London, which has usually set the agenda, with the devolved administrations obliged to react. The financing system of the Barnett formula has reinforced this, as it determines the resources that will be available to the devolved governments. Although the block transfers are freely disposable among the various devolved services, Westminster's decisions on how much will be available and on the balance between taxation and fees constrain the decisions in important ways. As we have seen, the move to fees for university education has placed immense pressure on Scotland and, while the Scottish Parliament did abolish up-front fees, it had to compromise in requiring a payment afterwards. The funding formula also deprives the Scottish Parliament of the ability to make a fundamental choice in a modern democratic welfare state, about the overall size of public spending and the balance between public and private consumption. In so doing, it empties Scottish politics of part of its meaning, reduces the interest in Scottish elections and contributes to the public view that the Scottish Parliament is the lesser influence on public policy even within devolved matters.

Within Scotland, there has been a slow but steady adaptation. Groups that thought they could ignore devolution and continue to deal with Whitehall have gradually been brought into the Scottish policy communities. Groups that believed that, after devolution, new vistas would be opened have learned more realism. There is undoubtedly much more political competition, more pluralism in interest politics, more transparency and more consultation. The area of law, previously a largely self-governing enclave, has been given much-needed attention (Black 2003). There is also a distinct Scottish policy style. Like other devolved governments in Europe, the Scottish Parliament and Executive are weak compared with nation-states, limited in their powers, resources and policy capacities. This is not merely the result of the limited devolution settlement, but is also a question of size, since small independent states are also limited in their policy capacity. As a result, Scottish government is obliged to cooperate with outside groups and policy making tends to be negotiated, gradual and, to a large extent, consensual. This certainly represents a broadening of participation in the policy process and helps avoid social confrontations, and to that degree represents a new politics. There is broad support for government action and a degree of respect for the public sector, which is part of a broader Scottish ethos. It may also have something to do with the education and background of civil service and political elites, who are less likely than their counterparts in London to have been educated privately, while the politicians often have backgrounds in the public sector or professions tied to social intervention. Supporters of this type of policy making talk of partnership, stakeholder empowerment, of consensus, and learning by doing. They seek to gain the cooperation of public sector workers and professionals and to make use of their knowledge and skills. Critics lambast it as pandering to 'producer interests' (Hassan and Warhurst 2002), a phrase formerly used of private business but which now seems to refer to workers in the public services.[1] Policy making by consensus, part of the design of the new Scottish Parliament, can be relabelled as 'a futile search for consensus' (Ross Martin 2004).

It is important to emphasise that we are talking of the same policy style here, given a positive or negative spin. Scotland, by both accounts, is different. The Scottish policy style, which is low key and less politicised, makes for fewer headlines and is an easy target for those looking for the breathless style that government in London has sometimes shown in recent years. It could well produce more considered and better policy in the longer run, but it does run the risk of stifling innovation and postponing difficult decisions. Scotland has yet to learn the forms of social concertation that, in small states in Scandinavia, the Netherlands or, more recently, Ireland, deliver rapid and effective responses to external shocks without resort to Thatcherite shock therapy. It does, however, have the institutions for this, and the social partners may be engaged in a slow process of learning, including the re-evaluation of its national myths and linking this to a project for development (Bond et al. 2003).

For some critics, the obstacles to change are cultural. A long tradition of Scottish writing attributes to Scots a lack of self-confidence (Craig 2003), a parochialism or even a cultural cringe typical of colonised peoples (Beveridge and Turnbull 1989). This in turn is used to explain large social processes, albeit, as McCrone (2004) notes, usually without any evidence at all. In fact, stereotypes like this abound across Europe, and not just in small nations. So do positive stereotypes, of confidence, entrepreneurialism and internationalism. What is extraordinary is that the components of the positive and negative stereotypes are usually identical; all that differs is the way they are interpreted (Keating et al. 2003). So individualism may be portrayed as a lack of social capital and an obstacle to cooperation; or as the quintessential capitalist virtue. Collectivism can be portrayed as an obstacle to entrepreneurship; or as 'social capital', the key to success in the modern economy. Local identity can be seen as parochialism or, again, as the basis for social capital. Tradition may be an obstacle to modernisation or the foundation of social cohesion. The transformation of Ireland, in which the very factors cited to explain its secular stagnation are now given as the explanation of its success, shows how images and stereotypes are epiphenomena rather than the basic building blocks of society. This reminds us once again that Scotland is not some cultural exception, but a small European nation that needs to be understood in its own right (McCrone 2001). In understanding how images of the nation are used, it is politics that is primary.

There was a great deal of talk in 1999 about a new politics although, as noted earlier, much of this was naïve and ignored the need, in a healthy democracy, for argument as well as consensus.

The taste for argument was perhaps blunted in the early years by the two most prominent public debates, over the abolition of Section 28 2A (on 'promoting' homosexuality) and over sectarianism, which seemed to show Scotland mired in the past and, contrary to the politically correct myths, rather socially conservative in its attitudes. Yet it could be argued that these debates were a necessary catharsis, to show that the country could confront its past and look to the future. The Parliament showed considerable political courage in proceeding with the repeal of Section 28 in the face of a type of 'new politics' that few had anticipated, a well-financed campaign backed by a local millionaire and the Catholic Church. Scottish politics is transparent as never before, politicians are accountable and they face much more intense political competition than those in Westminster. In the words of Mrs Howden, they can again be *peebled wi stanes*. This no doubt enhances the quality of democracy and is another advance on what went before, but it also encourages political timidity and a tendency to shy away from risky innovations. The new institutions have faced a campaign of unremitting and ill-informed hostility by a Scottish press that generally welcomed devolution as something that would expand their market, but showed an extraordinary lack of maturity in adapting to its role. Criticism of Executive policies is confused with criticism of devolution as a project, and the lazy headline of 'devolution fails' becomes a substitute for serious policy analysis.[2]

Devolution has occurred at a time when politicians and politics generally are in discredit, but there is no evidence that the Scottish Parliament suffers from more of this than do other institutions – indeed, Scots seem to have more faith in it than they do in Westminster, to judge by the majorities in favour of giving it more powers. Party politics is particularly discredited, with people regarding the parties as more or less the same and merely in it for power. Parties are in fact an essential part of any democratic process and one that was rather neglected in the design of the devolution settlement. Yet the professionalisation of politics and the tight grip of the parties have reduced the liberating potential of devolution. Loyalty to the leadership has often counted more than ability in determining who is on the party list and who gets promoted, and Holyrood seems to be following the Westminster pattern of recruiting career politicians with little experience elsewhere. A bold move would be to open up their lists to outsiders to renew the political class, as happens regularly in federal and provincial politics in Canada, including Quebec. If they do not, they risk losing ever more seats to minor parties, which would force them to adapt.

There has also been a certain lack of vision since the glory days of 1999. The Scottish Executive has been content to follow mostly sensible policies, but without firing the imagination or constructing its own narrative to make sense of what it is doing. This contrasts with other stateless nations and regions, where dynamic leadership is able to mobilise social forces around the need for change and to engage in a process of nation- or region-building, constantly exploring the room for manoeuvre. Scottish ministers have failed to boast about their policy divergences in the way that Rhodri Morgan, First Minister of Wales, has done. There has been little intellectual response to New Labour critics, possessed of total intellectual certainty, who too often believe that the only way for Scotland to innovate is to follow the latest wisdom coming from the south.[3] Outsiders invited to comment on Scottish issues too often repeat what they have said elsewhere, merely pasting in the name of Scotland. Pundits still pay flying visits to foreign locations (usually in the United States) or to England and come back superficially informed but brimming with enthusiasm and utterly convinced that the grass is greener in other jurisdictions. There is, of course, a place for policy learning and policy transfer, but this is a difficult process, which needs to be undertaken with due sensitivity to differences of context (Rose 1991).

Nor has the Executive been willing to speak for Scotland on broader issues, or to take public issue with Westminster where it disagrees. In the summer of 2003, there was a public debate about the treatment of asylum seekers in the detention centre at Dungavel, impinging on the Scottish conscience and to some extent affecting devolved issues, but the Executive stuck firmly to the line that this was a reserved issue, beyond its competence. One exception to this illustrates what can be done: the First Minister's Fresh Talent initiative aimed at attracting more people to Scotland to deal with population decline. Directly tackling the xenophobia that has made it so difficult to deal with this matter at UK level, the initiative aimed to start a rational debate about immigration and its economic benefits, drawing in the social and economic partners.[4]

The new style of Scottish politics will be tested when, as is almost inevitable (and desirable) in a democracy, different parties are in office in London and Edinburgh. This will not necessarily, as some have predicted, mean the end of the United Kingdom. There is plenty of scope for Scotland to make its own policy and, while intergovernmental policy making may be more conflictual, evidence from other countries shows that this will still be possible. Indeed, nationalist parties have governed for long periods in Quebec, Catalonia and the Basque Country without the world coming to an end. In 2003, the Catalan Socialists (equivalent to Scottish Labour) even formed a coalition with the more radical of the two nationalist parties. It will, however, require a new set of conventions recognising that power is indeed divided, and a clearer understanding of Scottish and UK competences, a subject that has been avoided since 1999.

Then there is the future of the United Kingdom itself. Scottish government still exists in the shadow of Westminster and Whitehall, which exert a heavy influence even in devolved matters. Yet as the three devolved territories grow in maturity and confidence, and especially if regional devolution spreads in England, the counterweights to metropolitan domination will grow. Another factor for change, whatever party is in power, is Europe. After paying relatively little attention to this after 1999, the Scottish Executive and Parliament have been drawn into European networks of many types, some of them about particular policy areas and others of a more general political type. Other nations and regions are looking to Scotland and there is a growing exchange of ideas and experience, reaching beyond the old UK networks. Utopian visions of a Europe of the Regions or the Peoples, with the states fading away, have long been abandoned, but a new tier of politics is developing around the networks of devolved and federated governments, and Scotland's pro-European disposition makes it open to these in a way that is less true in London. The trend right across Europe is for states to decentralise and Europeanise at the same time, with central governments shedding responsibilities and 'meso-governments' growing in importance as key actors in shaping economic and social change. Scotland cannot, any more than other small nations, determine its future on its own, but it can shape its own adaptation to these powerful forces.

Notes

1. By a curious inversion, the involvement of private business in public service provision is praised as though it was acting from altruistic motives.
2. As I write this, my eye falls on a headline in today's *Sunday Herald*, 'Island Councils: Devolution has failed us' (Crawford 2004). A reading

of the article fails to find any of the island critics using this expression. Instead, they were making the usual complaints about government policy and organising a lobby to get their concerns better heard. Today's *Observer* has an article in which a proposal to use the Land Reform Act to purchase an estate is referred to as 'Britain's first Mugabe-style land grab' (Lorna Martin 2004).

3. For examples, see Adams (2004) and Ross Martin (2004). While both authors are critical of Scottish Labour for sticking to 'Old Labour' principles, neither suggests a single policy change that does not involve following London.

4. Again, the press did not always live up to the challenge. An article in the *Scotsman* of 1 June 2004 reports a finding that more than half of all Scots supported the idea with the headline 'Scots' welcoming image suffers a blow' (Denholm 2004).

Bibliography

Adams, John (2004), 'Out with the old', *Holyrood*, 104, 23 February.

Adams, John and Peter Robinson (2002), 'Divergence and the Centre', in John Adams and Peter Robinson (eds), *Devolution in Practice. Public Policy Differences within the UK*, London: Institute for Public Policy Research.

Alexander, Wendy (2003), *Chasing the Tartan Tiger: lessons from a Celtic cousin?*, London: The Smith Institute.

Anderson, Ian (2002), *Foot and Mouth Disease 2001: Lessons to be Learned Inquiry*, chairman Dr Ian Anderson.

Arter, David (2002), 'On Assessing Strength and Weakness in Parliamentary Committee Systems: Some Preliminary Observations on the New Scottish Parliament', *The Journal of Legislative Studies*, 8.2, pp. 93–117.

Arter, David (2004a), *The Scottish Parliament. A Scandinavian-Style Assembly*, London: Frank Cass.

Arter, David (2004b), 'The Scottish Committees and the Goal of a "New Politics": a Verdict on the First Four Years of the Devolved Scottish Parliament', *Journal of Contemporary European Studies*, 12.1, pp. 71–9.

Ashcroft, Brian and James Love (1993), *Takeovers, Mergers and the Regional Economy*, Edinburgh: Edinburgh University Press.

Bache, Ian and Gillian Bristow (2003), 'Devolution and the gatekeeping role of the core executive: the struggle for European funds', *The British Journal of Politics and International Relations*, 5.3, pp. 405–27.

Bachtler, John and Douglas Yuill (2001), 'Policies and Strategies for Regional Development. A Shifting Paradigm?', *Regional and Industrial Policy Research Paper*, 46, Glasgow: European Policies Research Centre, University of Strathclyde.

Balme, Richard (1996), 'Introduction. Pourquoi le gouvernement change-t-il d'échelle?', in Richard Balme (ed.), *Les politiques du néo-régionalisme*, Paris: Economica.

Bell, David and Alex Christie (2001), 'Finance – The Barnett Formula: Nobody's Child', in Alan Trench (ed.), *The State of the Nations 2001. The Second Year of Devolution in the United Kingdom*, Thorverton: Academic Imprint.

Beveridge, Craig and R. Turnbull (1989), *The Eclipse of Scottish Culture*, Edinburgh: Polygon.

Black, Robert (2003), 'Law', in Kenneth Roy (ed.), *States of Scotland, 2004*, Glasgow: ICS Books.

Blondel, Jean (1974), *Voters, Parties and Leaders*, Harmondsworth: Penguin.

Bond, Ross, David McCrone and Alice Brown (2003), 'National identity and economic development: reiteration, recapture, reinterpretation and repudiation', *Nations and Nationalism*, 9.3, pp. 371–91.

Brand, Jack (1978), *The National Movement in Scotland*, London: Routledge and Kegan Paul.

Brook, Keith (2002), 'Trade union membership: an analysis of data from the autumn 2001 LFS', *Labour Market Trends*, July 2002, pp. 343–54.

Brown, Alice (2000), 'Designing the New Scottish Parliament', *Parliamentary Affairs*, 53.3, pp. 542–56.

Brown, Alice, David McCrone and Lindsay Paterson (1996), *Politics and Society in Scotland*, London: Macmillan.

Bruce, Adam and Tom Miers (2003), 'Scotland's Hidden Tax Cutting Powers', Series: Economy No. 3, Edinburgh: The Policy Institute.

Bryden, J. M. (2000) 'Is there a "New Rural Policy"?' International Conference: European Rural Policy at the Crossroads, June 2000, University of Aberdeen, Arkleton Centre.

Bulmer, Simon, Martin Burch, Catríona Carter, Patricia Hogwood and Andrew Scott (2002), *British Devolution and European Policy-Making*, London: Palgrave.

Bulpitt, James (1983), *Territory and Power in the United Kingdom. An Interpretation*, Manchester: Manchester University Press.

Cairney, Paul and Michael Keating (2004), 'Sewel Motions in the Scottish Parliament', *Scottish Affairs*, Spring, pp. 115–34.

Callender, R. (1997), *How Scotland is Owned*, Edinburgh: Canongate.

Christie, Alex (2004), 'The Scottish Budget Process. Options for Change', *Scottish Affairs*, 47, pp. 99–114.

Consultative Steering Group (1999), *Shaping Scotland's Parliament*, Edinburgh: Scottish Office.

Cooke, Philip and Kevin Morgan (1998), *The Associational Economy. Firms, Regions, and Innovation*, Oxford: Oxford University Press.

Craig, Carol (2003), *The Scots' Crisis of Self-Confidence*, Glasgow: Big Thinking.

Crawford, Alan (2004), 'Island Councils: Devolution has failed us', *Sunday Herald*, 18 April.

Crossman, Richard (1977), *The Diaries of a Cabinet Minister, Volume Three. Secretary of State for Social Services (1968–70)*, London: Hamish Hamilton.

Curry, Donald (2002), Report of Policy Commission on the Future of Farming and Food, *Farming and Food: A Sustainable Future*, London: Cabinet Office.

Cuthbert, John and Margaret Cuthbert (2001), 'The Barnett Squeeze in spending review 2000', *Fraser of Allander Quarterly Economic Commentary*, May 2001, pp. 27–33.

Davidson, Duncan (2003), 'Medicine', in Kenneth Roy (ed.), *States of Scotland, 2004*, Glasgow: ICS Books.

Davie, George Elder (1981), *The Democratic Intellect. Scotland and her universities in the nineteenth century*, paperback edition, Edinburgh: Edinburgh University Press.

DEFRA (2001), Department of the Environment, Food and Rural Affairs, *England's Rural Future: Government Response to the Reports by the Rural Task Force and Christopher Haskins. Progress on Implementing the Rural White Paper*, London: DEFRA.

Denholm, Andrew (2004), 'Scots' welcoming image suffers a blow', *Scotsman*, 1 June.

Dente, Bruno (1997), 'Federalismo e politiche pubbliche', in Alberto Martelli (ed.), *Quale federalismo per l'Italia? Terzo rapporto sulle priorità nazionali*. Milan: Fondazione Rosselli/Mondadori.

DETR/MAFF (2000), Department of Environment, Transport and the Regions and Ministry of Agriculture, Fisheries and Food, *Our Countryside: The Future. A Fair Deal for Rural England*, London: DETR/MAFF.

Dicey, Albert Venn (1912), *A Leap in the Dark. A Criticism of The Principles of Home Rule as Illustrated by the bill of 1893*, 3rd edition, London: John Murray.

Dicey, Albert Venn and Robert Rait (1920), *Thoughts on the Union between England and Scotland*, London: Macmillan.

Donnachie, Ian, Christopher Harvie and Ian S. Wood (eds) (1989), *Forward! Labour Politics in Scotland 1888–1988*, Edinburgh: Polygon.

DTI (2003), *A Modern Regional Policy for the United Kingdom*, London: Department of Trade and Industry.

Dyer, Michael (2001), 'The Evolution of the Centre-Right and the State of Scottish Conservatism', *Political Studies*, 49.1, pp. 30–50.

Fawcett, Helen (2003), 'Social Inclusion Policy-Making in Scotland: Assessing the "Capability Expectations"', *The Political Quarterly*, 74.4, pp. 439–49.

Fawcett, Helen (2004), 'The Making of Social Justice Policy in Scotland.

Devolution and Social Exclusion', in Alan Trench (ed.), *Has Devolution Made a Difference? The State of the Nations, 2004*, Exeter: Imprint Academic.

Finer, Samuel (1974), *Comparative Politics*, Harmondsworth: Penguin.

Finnie, Ross (2002), Oral evidence to the House of Lords Select Committee on the Constitution, 15 May 2002, *Devolution: Inter-Institutional Relations in the United Kingdom, Evidence Complete to 10 July 2002*, HL147.

Fry, Michael (1987), *Patronage and Principle. A Political History of Modern Scotland*, Aberdeen: Aberdeen University Press.

Gillespie, Andrew and Paul Benneworth (2002), 'Industrial and regional policy in a devolved United Kingdom', in John Adams and Peter Robinson (eds), *Devolution in Practice. Public Policy Differences within the UK*, London: Institute for Public Policy Research.

Greer, Scott (2004), *Four Way Bet: How devolution has led to four different models for the NHS*, London: The Constitution Unit.

Haddow, Douglas (1969), Oral Evidence of Sir Douglas Haddow to Select Committee on Scottish Affairs, 19 May 1969.

Hanham, H. J. (1969), *Scottish Nationalism*, London: Faber.

Harper, J. Ross and Iain Stewart (2003), 'Paying Our Way. Should Scotland Raise Its Own Taxes?', Series: Governance No. 4, Edinburgh: The Policy Institute.

Hassan, Gerry (2002) 'Scotland's Copycat Parliament', *The Herald*, 4 September.

Hassan, Gerry (2004), 'The People's Party, Still? The Sociology of Scotland's Leading Party', in Gerry Hassan (ed.), *The Scottish Labour Party*, Edinburgh: Edinburgh University Press.

Hassan, Gerry and Chris Warhurst (2002) 'Future Scotland', in Gerry Hassan and Chris Warhurst (eds), *Tomorrow's Scotland*, London: Lawrence and Wishart.

Hazell, Robert (2003), 'Conclusion', in Robert Hazell (ed.), *The State of the Nations, 2003*, Exeter: Imprint Academic.

Heald, David (1983), *Public Expenditure: Its Defence and Reform*, Oxford: Martin Robertson.

Heald, David (1992), 'Formula-Based Territorial Public Expenditure in the United Kingdom', *Aberdeen Papers in Accountancy*, W7, Aberdeen: University of Aberdeen.

Heald, David and Alastair McLeod (2002a), 'Beyond Barnett? Financing devolution', in John Adams and Peter Robinson (eds), *Devolution in Practice. Public Policy Differences within the UK*, London: IPPR.

Heald, David and Alastair McLeod (2002b), 'Public Expenditure', in Law Society of Scotland, *The Laws of Scotland. Stair Memorial Encyclopaedia*, Edinburgh: Butterworths.

Heald, David and Alastair McLeod (2003), 'Revenue-raising by UK

Devolved Administrations in the Context of an Expenditure-based Financing System', *Regional and Federal Studies*, 13.4, pp. 67–90.

Hearn, Jonathan (2000), *Claiming Scotland. National Identity and Liberal Culture*, Edinburgh: Polygon.

House of Lords Select Committee on the Constitution (2002), *Session 2002–3, Second Report. Devolution: Inter-Institutional Relations in the United Kingdom*, HL28.

Hutchison, I. G. C. (2001), *Scottish Politics in the Twentieth Century*, London: Palgrave.

Jones, Rhys (2001), 'Institutional identities and the shifting scales of state governance in the United Kingdom', *European Urban and Regional Studies*, 8.4, pp. 283–96.

Jordan, Grant and Linda Stevenson (2000), 'Redemocraticizing Scotland. Towards the Politics of Disappointment', in Alex Wright (ed.), *Scotland; the Challenge of Devolution*, London: Ashgate.

Kavanagh, Dennis (1987), *Thatcherism and British Politics: the end of consensus*, Oxford: Oxford University Press.

Kavanagh, Dennis and David Richards (2003), 'Prime Ministers, Ministers and Civil Servants in Britain', *Comparative Sociology*, 2.1, pp. 175–95.

Keating, Michael (1975a), *The Role of the Scottish MP*, PhD thesis, Glasgow College of Technology and CNAA.

Keating, Michael (1975b), 'The Scottish Local Government Bill', *Local Government Studies*, 1.

Keating, Michael (1976), 'Administrative Devolution in Practice. The Secretary of State for Scotland and the Scottish Office', *Public Administration*, 54.2, pp. 133–46.

Keating, Michael (1985), 'Bureaucracy Devolved', *Times Higher Educational Supplement*, 5 April.

Keating, Michael (1998), *The New Regionalism in Western Europe. Territorial Restructuring and Political Change*, Aldershot: Edward Elgar.

Keating, Michael (2000), *Rural Governance. The International Experience*, Agricultural Policy Coordination and Rural Development Research Programme Research Findings No. 9, Edinburgh: Scottish Executive Central Research Department.

Keating, Michael (2001), *Plurinational Democracy. Stateless Nations in a Post-Sovereignty Era*, Oxford: Oxford University Press.

Keating, Michael and David Bleiman (1979), *Labour and Scottish Nationalism*, London: Macmillan.

Keating, Michael and Robin Boyle (1986), *Remaking Urban Scotland. Strategies for Local Economic Development*, Edinburgh: Edinburgh University Press.

Keating, Michael and Christopher Carter (1987), 'Policy Making in Scottish Government. The Designation of Cumbernauld New Town', *Public Administration*, 65.4, pp. 391–405.

Keating, Michael and Barry Jones (1985), 'Nations, Regions and Europe: The UK Experience', in Barry Jones and Michael Keating (eds), *The European Union and the Regions*, Oxford: Clarendon.

Keating, Michael and John Loughlin (2002), *Territorial Policy Communities and Devolution in the United Kingdom*, EUI Working Papers, 2002/1, Florence: European University Institute.

Keating, Michael, John Loughlin and Kris Deschouwer (2003), *Culture, Institutions and Economic Development. A Study of Eight European Regions*, Aldershot: Edward Elgar.

Keating, Michael and Arthur Midwinter (1983), *The Government of Scotland*, Edinburgh: Mainstream.

Keating, Michael, Linda Stevenson, Paul Cairney and Katherine Taylor (2003), 'Does Devolution Make a Difference? Legislative Output and Policy Divergence in Scotland', *Journal of Legislative Studies*, 9.3, pp. 1–30.

Kellas, James G. (1973), *The Scottish Political System*, Cambridge: Cambridge University Press.

Kellas, James G. (1975), *The Scottish Political System*, 2nd edition, Cambridge: Cambridge University Press.

Kellas, James G. (1989), *The Scottish Political System*, 4th edition, Cambridge: Cambridge University Press.

Kerevan, George and Gavin Don (2003), 'The Voyages of the Starship "Scottish Enterprise". Lessons and Ideas for Scotland's Economic Agency', Series: Economy No. 5, Edinburgh: The Policy Institute.

Kerr, Andy (2002), Oral evidence to Scottish Parliament Finance Committee, 23 May 2002.

Lang, Ian (2002), *Blue Remembered Years: a political memoir*, London: Politico's.

Lee, C. H. (1995), *Scotland and the United Kingdom. The economy and the union in the twentieth century*, Manchester: Manchester University Press.

Linklater, Magnus (1992), 'The Media', in Magnus Linklater and Robin Denniston (eds), *Anatomy of Scotland*, Edinburgh: Chambers.

Lovering, John (1999), 'Theory Led by Policy: The Inadequacies of the "New regionalism"', *International Journal of Urban and Regional Research*, 23.2, pp. 379–95.

Lowe, Philip (1996), 'The British Rural White Papers', *Working paper 21*, Centre for Rural Economy, University of Newcastle upon Tyne.

Lowe, Philip and Neil Ward (2002), 'Devolution and the Governance of Rural Affairs in the UK', in John Adams and Peter Robinson (eds), *Devolution in Practice. Public Policy Differences within the UK*, London: IPPR.

Lowell, A. L. (1908), *The Government of England, Vol. 1*, London and New York: Macmillan.

Lynch, Peter (1996), *Minority Nationalism and European Integration*, Cardiff: University of Wales Press.

Lynch, Peter (1998), 'Reactive Capital: The Scottish Business Community and Devolution', in Howard Elcock and Michael Keating (eds), *Remaking the Union. Devolution and British Politics in the 1990s*, London: Frank Cass.

Lynch, Peter (2001), *Scottish Government and Politics*, Edinburgh: Edinburgh University Press.

Lynch, Peter (2002), *The History of the Scottish National Party*, Welsh Academic Press.

Lynch, Peter and Steven Birrell (2004), 'The Autonomy and Organisation of Scottish Labour', in Gerry Hassan (ed.), *The Scottish Labour Party*, Edinburgh: Edinburgh University Press.

Macaulay Land Research Institute (2001), *Agriculture's contribution to Scottish society, economy and environment. A literature review for the Scottish Executive Rural Affairs Department and the CRU*, Aberdeen: University of Aberdeen.

McCrone, David (2001), *Understanding Scotland. The sociology of a nation*, 2nd edition, London: Routledge.

McCrone, David (2004), 'Cultural Capital in an Understated Nation: The Case of Scotland', Institute of Governance, University of Edinburgh.

McCrone, Gavin (1999), 'Scotland's Public Finances from Goschen to Barnett', *Fraser of Allander Quarterly Economic Commentary*, 24.2, pp. 30–46.

McEwen, Nicola (1999), 'The Nation-Building Role of the Welfare State in the United Kingdom and Canada', in Trevor Salmon and Michael Keating (eds), *The Dynamics of Decentralization. Canadian Federalism and British Devolution*, Montreal: McGill-Queen's University Press.

McFadden, Jean and Mark Lazarowicz (2000), *The Scottish Parliament. An Introduction*, 2nd edition, Edinburgh: T. & T. Clark.

McGarvey, Neil (2001), 'New Scottish Politics, New Texts Required', *British Journal of Politics and International Relations*, 3.3, pp. 427–44.

Mackintosh, John (1973), Review of Kellas, The Scottish Political System, *Political Quarterly*, 44.3, pp. 368–70.

McLean, Iain and Alistair McMillan (2003), 'The Distribution of Public Expenditure across the UK Regions', *Fiscal Studies*, 24.1, pp. 45–71.

McLeish, Henry (2004), *Scotland First. Truth and Consequences*, Edinburgh: Mainstream.

MacLeod, Catherine (2003), 'Reid's olive branch to NHS is welcomed', *The Herald*, 27 June.

McPherson, Andrew and Charles Raab (1988), *Governing Education. A sociology of policy since 1945*, Edinburgh: Edinburgh University Press.

MAFF (2001), Ministry of Agriculture, Fisheries and Food, *England: Rural Development Programme, 2000–06*.

Marks, Gary, Richard Hasely and Heather A. D. Mbaye (2002), 'What Do Subnational Offices Think They Are Doing in Brussels?', *Regional and Federal Studies*, 12.3, pp. 1–23.

Martin, Lorna (2004), 'Ill winds as crofters plan land grab', *The Observer*, 18 April.

Martin, Ross (2004), 'Slothful Scotland', *Holyrood*, 104, 23 February.

Maxwell, Stephen (1990), 'The Scottish Middle Class and the National Debate', in Tom Gallagher (ed.), *Nationalism in the nineties*, Edinburgh: Polygon.

Midwinter, Arthur (2000), 'Devolution and Public Spending: Arguments and Evidence', *Fraser of Allander Quarterly Economic Commentary*, 25.4, pp. 38–48.

Midwinter, Arthur (2004), 'Spending Review 2004–7 Expenditure trends in Scotland since 1997: Evidence from the GERS report', Scottish Parliament Finance Committee, paper for meeting of 10 February 2004.

Midwinter, Arthur and Ross Burnside (2004), 'Key Trends in the Scottish Budget', *SPICe briefing, 04/16*, Edinburgh: Scottish Parliament.

Midwinter, Arthur, Michael Keating and James Mitchell (1991), *Politics and Public Policy in Scotland*, London: Macmillan.

Midwinter, Arthur and Jim Stevens (2001), 'The Real Scope for Change: Appraising the extent to which the Parliament can suggest changes to programme expenditure', *Scottish Parliament Paper 322*, Edinburgh: Scottish Parliament.

Mitchell, James (1990), *Conservatives and the Union. A Study of Conservative Party Attitudes to Scotland*, Edinburgh: Edinburgh University Press.

Mitchell, James (1996), *Strategies for Self-Government. The Campaigns for a Scottish Parliament*, Edinburgh: Polygon.

Mitchell, James (2000), 'New Parliament, New Politics', *Parliamentary Affairs*, 53.3, pp. 605–21.

Mitchell, James (2001), 'The Study of Scottish Politics Post-Devolution: New Evidence, New Analysis and New Methods?', *West European Politics*, 24.4, pp. 216–33.

Mitchell, James (2003), *Governing Scotland. The Invention of Administrative Devolution*, London: Palgrave.

Moore, Chris and Simon Booth (1989), *Managing Competition. Meso-Corporatism, Pluralism and the Negotiated Order in Scotland*, Oxford: Clarendon.

Newlands, David (2003), 'The economic strategy of the Scottish Parliament: policy convergence resulting from devolution or coinciding with it?', *Conference Proceedings of the Regional Studies Association Annual Conference*, November 2003, London: Regional Studies Association.

Noël, Alain (1999), 'Is Decentralization Conservative?', in Robert Young (ed.), *Stretching the federation. The art of the state in Canada*, Kingston: Institute of Intergovernmental Relations, Queen's University.

NU Health Care (2003), *Doctor's orders. The Health of the Nation Index*, Eastleigh: Norwich Union Health Care.

Ohmae, Kenichi (1995), *The End of the Nation State. The Rise of Regional Economies*, New York: The Free Press.

O'Neill, Aidan (2001), 'Judicial Politics and the Judicial Committee: The Devolution Jurisprudence of the Privy Council', *The Modern Law Review*, 64, pp. 11–26.

Osborne, David and Ted Gaebler (1992), *Reinventing government: how the entrepreneurial spirit is transforming the public sector*, Reading, MA: Addison-Wesley.

Page, Alan (2002), Memorandum and Evidence, House of Lords Select Committee on the Constitution, *Devolution: Inter-Institutional Relations in the United Kingdom, Evidence complete to 10 July 2002*, HL147, pp. 183–6.

Page, Alan and Andrea Batey (2002), 'Scotland's Other Parliament: Westminster Legislation about Devolved Matters in Scotland since Devolution', *Public Law*, Autumn, pp. 501–23.

Park, Alison (2002), 'Scotland's Morals', in John Curtice, David McCrone, Alison Park and Lindsay Paterson (eds), *New Scotland, New Society?*, Edinburgh: Polygon.

Parry, Richard (2001), 'Devolution, Integration and Modernisation in the United Kingdom Civil Service', *Public Policy and Administration*, 16:3, pp. 53–67.

Parry, Richard (2003), 'The Scottish Executive and the Challenges of Complex Policy Making', *The Political Quarterly*, 74.4, pp. 450–8.

Paterson, Lindsay (1994), *The Autonomy of Modern Scotland*, Edinburgh: Edinburgh University Press.

Paterson, Lindsay (2000), 'Scottish Democracy and Scottish Utopias. The First Year of the Scottish Parliament', *Scottish Affairs*, 33, pp. 45–61.

Paterson, Lindsay (2001a), 'Governing from the Centre: Ideology and Public Policy', in Lindsay Paterson, Alice Brown, John Curtice, Kerstin Hinds, David McCrone, Alison Park, Kerry Sproston and Paula Surridge, *New Scotland, New Politics?*, Edinburgh: Polygon.

Paterson, Lindsay (2001b), 'Higher Education and European Regionalism', *Pedagogy, Culture and Society*, 9.2, pp. 133–60.

Paterson, Lindsay (2002a), 'Civic Democracy', in Gerry Hassan and Chris Warhurst (eds), *Anatomy of the New Scotland. Power, Influence and Change*, Edinburgh: Mainstream.

Paterson, Lindsay (2002b), 'Is Britain Disintegrating? Changing Views of "Britain" after Devolution', *Regional and Federal Studies*, 12.1, pp. 21–42.

Paterson, Lindsay (2003), 'The survival of the democratic intellect: academic values in Scotland and England', *Higher Education Quarterly*, 57, pp. 67–93.

Paterson, Lindsay, Alice Brown, John Curtice, Kerstin Hinds, David McCrone, Alison Park, Kerry Sproston and Paula Surridge (2001), *New Scotland, New Politics?*, Edinburgh: Polygon.

Payne, Jude (2004), 'Social Justice Indicators of Progress 2003', *SPICe briefing, 04/25*, Edinburgh: Scottish Parliament.

Procedures Committee (2003), *3rd Report 2003, The Founding Principles of the Scottish Parliament, SP Paper 818*, Edinburgh: Scottish Parliament.

Raco, Mike (2003), 'The Social Relations of Business Representation and Devolved Governance in the UK', *Environment and Planning, a*, 35, pp. 1853–76.

Reid, Harry (2003), 'Journalism', in Kenneth Roy (ed.), *States of Scotland, 2004*, Glasgow: ICS Books.

Ritchie, Murray (2003), *The Herald*, 18 December.

Rokkan, Stein and Derek Urwin (1983), *Economy, Territory, Identity. Politics of West European Peripheries*, London: Sage.

Rose, Richard (1991), 'What is lesson-drawing?', *Journal of Public Policy*, 11.1, pp. 3–30.

Ross, James (1981), 'The Secretary of State for Scotland and the Scottish Office', *Studies in Public Policy, 87*, Glasgow: University of Strathclyde.

Royal Society (2002), *Infectious diseases in livestock. Policy document 19/02*, London: Royal Society.

Sandford, Mark and Lucinda Maer (2003), *Scrutiny under Devolution – committees in Scotland, Wales and Northern Ireland*, London: The Constitution Unit.

Schlesinger, Philip (2004), 'The New Communications Agenda in Scotland', *Scottish Affairs*, 47, Spring 2004, pp. 16–40.

Schlesinger, Philip, David Miller and William Dinan (2001), *Open Scotland? Journalists, Spin Doctors and Lobbyists*, Edinburgh: Polygon.

Scott, James (2003), 'Real Devolution', *Holyrood*, 97, 20 October.

Scottish Council Foundation (1997), *Scotland's Parliament . . . a Business Guide to Devolution*, Edinburgh: Scottish Council Foundation.

Scottish Executive (2000a), *A Framework for Economic Development*, Edinburgh: Scottish Executive.

Scottish Executive (2000b), *Rural Scotland. A New Approach*, Edinburgh: Scottish Executive.

Scottish Executive (2000c), *Social Justice – a Scotland where everyone matters*, Edinburgh: Scottish Executive.

Scottish Executive (2001a), *Rural Development Plan for Scotland*, Edinburgh: Scottish Executive.

Scottish Executive (2001b), *A Smart, Successful Scotland. Ambitions for the Enterprise Network*, Edinburgh: Scottish Executive.

Scottish Executive (2001c), *A Science Strategy for Scotland*, Edinburgh: Scottish Executive.

Scottish Executive (2001d), *Report on the Knowledge Economy Cross-Cutting Initiative*, Edinburgh: Scottish Executive.

Scottish Executive (2002), *A Forward Strategy for Scottish Agriculture*, Edinburgh: Scottish Executive.

Scottish Executive (2003a), *Government Expenditure and Revenue in Scotland (GERS)*, laid before Scottish Parliament by Scottish Ministers, January 2003.

Scottish Executive (2003b), *Comparative Study of Business Tax Revenues*, Edinburgh: Scottish Executive.

Scottish Executive (2003c), *Rural Scotland: Taking Stock*, Edinburgh: Scottish Executive.

Scottish Executive (2003d), *Building Better Cities*, Edinburgh: Scottish Executive.

Scottish Executive (2004), *European Strategy*, Edinburgh: Scottish Executive.

Scottish Office (1998), *Towards a Development Strategy for Rural Scotland*, Edinburgh: Scottish Office.

Scottish Office (1999), *Social Inclusion – Opening the door to a better Scotland*, Edinburgh: Scottish Office.

Scottish Parliament, European Committee (2000), *Report of the Inquiry into European Structural Funds and their implementation in Scotland*, SP Paper 210, Session 1, Edinburgh: Scottish Parliament.

Scottish Parliament Finance Committee (2004), *5th Report 2004*, SP Paper 282, Session 2, Edinburgh: Scottish Parliament.

Sharpe, L. J. (1993), 'The European Meso: an appraisal', in L. J. Sharpe (ed.), *The Rise of Meso Government in Europe*, London: Sage.

Shephard, Mark, Neil McGarvey and Michael Cavanagh (2001), 'New Scottish Parliament, New Scottish Parliamentarians?', *Journal of Legislative Studies*, 78.2, pp. 79–104.

Short, John (1982), 'Public Expenditure in the English Regions', in Brian Hogwood and Michael Keating (eds), *Regional Government in England*, Oxford: Clarendon.

Shucksmith, Mark (2000), *Exclusive Countryside? Social Inclusion and Regeneration in Rural Britain*, London: Joseph Rowntree Trust.

Smith, Maurice (1994), *Paper Lions. The Scottish Press and National Identity*, Edinburgh: Polygon.

Surridge, Paula (2003), 'A Classless Society? Social Attitudes and Social Class', in Catherine Bromley, John Curtice, Kerstin Hinds and Alison Park, *Devolution – Scottish Answers to Scottish Questions?*, Edinburgh: Edinburgh University Press.

Surridge, Paula (2004), 'The Scottish Electorate and Labour', in Gerry Hassan (ed.), *The Scottish Labour Party*, Edinburgh: Edinburgh University Press.

Taylor, Brian (2002), *The Road to the Scottish Parliament*, revised edition, Edinburgh: Edinburgh University Press.

Thatcher, Margaret (1993), *The Downing Street Years*, London: HarperCollins.

Treasury (2000), *Funding the Scottish Parliament, National Assembly for Wales and Northern Ireland Assembly. A Statement of Funding Policy*, London: HM Treasury.

Treasury (2003), *Public Expenditure. Statistical Analyses 2003, Corrigendum. Corrected tables for Chapter 8*, London: HM Treasury.

Trench, Alan (2004), 'The More Things Change, The More They Stay The Same. Intergovernmental Relations Four Years On', in Alan Trench (ed.), *Has Devolution Made a Difference? The State of the Nations, 2004*, Exeter: Imprint Academic.

Turner, A. C. (1952), *Scottish Home Rule*, Oxford: Blackwell.

Turok, Ivan (2003), 'Urban Policy in Scotland After Devolution: Retrospect and Prospect', *Conference Proceedings of the Regional Studies Association Annual Conference*, November 2003, London: Regional Studies Association.

Turok, Ivan and fifteen others (2003), *Twin Track Cities. Linking prosperity and cohesion in Glasgow and Edinburgh*, Glasgow: Department of Urban Studies.

Walker, Jim (2002), Oral evidence to the House of Lords Select Committee on the Constitution, 14 April 2001, *Devolution: Inter-Institutional Relations in the United Kingdom, Evidence Complete to 10 July 2002*, HL147.

Wallis, Gavin (2004), 'The demand for private medical insurance', *Economic Trends*, 606, May.

Ward, Neil and Philip Lowe (2002), 'Devolution and the governance of rural affairs in the UK', in John Adams and Peter Robinson (eds), *Devolution in Practice. Public Policy Differences within the UK*, London: Institute for Public Policy Research.

Webster, David (2000), 'Scottish Social Inclusion Policy: A Critical Assessment', *Scottish Affairs*, 30, Winter.

Whitaker's Scottish Almanack (2003), 4th edition, London: A. & C. Black.

Wightman, Andy and P. Higgins (2000), 'Sporting Estates and the Recreational Economy in the Highlands and Islands of Scotland', *Scottish Affairs*, 31, pp. 1–17.

Williams, Martin (2004), *The Herald*, 20 February.

Winetrobe, Barry (2002), 'The Scottish Parliament', in Law Society of Scotland, *The Laws of Scotland. Stair Memorial Encyclopaedia*, Edinburgh: Butterworths.

Woods, Kevin (2002), 'Health Policy and the NHS in the UK, 1997–2002', in John Adams and Peter Robinson (eds), *Devolution in Practice. Public Policy Differences within the UK*, London: Institute for Public Policy Research.

Woods, Kevin (2003), 'Scotland's Changing Health System', in Kevin Woods and David Carter (eds), *Scotland's Health and Health Services*, London: TSO and Nuffield Trust.

Woodward, Rachel and Keith Halfacree (2002), 'Influences on Leadership and Local Power in Rural Britain', in Keith Halfacree, Imre Kovách and Rachel Woodward (eds), *Leadership and Local Power in European Rural Development*, Aldershot: Ashgate.

Young, Alf (2003a), 'Why companies must stop girning about rates' *The Herald*, 12 October.

Young, Alf (2003b), 'Where the truth lies', *Holyrood*, 98, 3 November, pp. 18–19.

Index